RAND NATIONAL DEFENSE RESEARCH INSTITUTE

T0289474

An Assessment of the Military Survivor Benefit Plan

James Hosek, Beth J. Asch, Michael G. Mattock, Italo A. Gutierrez,
Patricia K. Tong, Felix Knutson

Prepared for the Office of the Secretary of Defense

For more information on this publication, visit www.rand.org/t/RR2236

Library of Congress Cataloging-in-Publication Data is available for this publication.

ISBN: 978-0-8330-9993-8

Published by the RAND Corporation, Santa Monica, Calif.

© Copyright 2018 RAND Corporation

RAND® is a registered trademark.

www.rand.org

Preface

The Survivor Benefit Plan (SBP) provides income security for the survivors of U.S. service members who perform in an authorized-duty status—whether active or inactive—and die in the line of duty, as well as for the survivors of retired members enrolled in SBP. This report responds to Congress's request for an assessment of SBP. The assessment includes information about SBP participation and available benefits, how SBP compares with similar plans in public organizations and private companies, and how large a contribution SBP makes to survivors' incomes. Congress also requested that the assessment consider the feasibility and advisability of having SBP provided by commercial sources.

This report should interest groups and individuals concerned with the adequacy of benefits available to the survivors of service members.

This research was sponsored by Office of the Secretary of Defense and conducted within the Forces and Resources Policy Center of the RAND National Defense Research Institute, a federally funded research and development center sponsored by the Office of the Secretary of Defense, the Joint Staff, the Unified Combatant Commands, the Navy, the Marine Corps, the defense agencies, and the defense Intelligence Community.

For more information on the RAND the Forces and Resources Policy Center, see www.rand.org/nsrd/ndri/centers/frp or contact the director (contact information is provided on the webpage).

Contents

Figures and Tables

Figures

Tables

Summary

Congress requested a review of the Survivor Benefit Plan (SBP) in Section 648 of the National Defense Authorization Act for Fiscal Year 2017 (Pub. L. 114-328). SBP covers service members who are performing in an authorized-duty status—whether active or inactive duty—and die in the line of duty (we refer to this as dying *on duty*), as well as military retirees enrolled in SBP. Retirees are automatically enrolled in SBP at the time of retirement but may choose not to enroll (U.S. Department of Defense [DoD], Defense Finance Accounting Service, 2015a). SBP provides an ongoing benefit to the survivors of members covered by SBP. The SBP benefit is 55 percent of the portion of gross retired pay that the retired enrollee chooses to cover and, for service members who die on duty, 55 percent of gross retired pay computed as 75 percent of their high-36 basic pay (the average of the highest 36 months of basic pay).

Section 648 requires the Secretary of Defense to provide an independent assessment of SBP by a federally funded research and development center and directs that the review (1) describe the purposes of SBP and how it interacts with other federal programs to provide financial stability and resources for survivors, (2) compare benefits under SBP with benefits available to government and private-sector employees, (3) evaluate the effectiveness of SBP in providing survivors with intended benefits, and (4) assess the feasibility and advisability of providing survivor benefits through alternative insurance products commercially available for similar purposes. The summary is organized around these four topics.

Overall, we find that SBP is well structured to provide benefits to survivors of service members who die on duty and military retirees. SBP benefits typically make up a third to a half of survivors' incomes, depending on whether Social Security is also received. SBP benefits generally compare well with those of public and private plans. For widows not receiving Social Security, the percentage with total incomes below the poverty line is typically higher with SBP than for those whose main source of survivor benefits is federal, state, or local government; annuities; or other sources not specified. However, the differences in the percentage are not statistically significant except for one case. Also, this may not indicate a shortcoming of SBP but could derive from prior differences—for instance, lower earnings of the now-deceased spouse of widows receiving SBP compared with widows receiving survivor benefits from other sources—or from differences in the amount of survivor benefit coverage selected. Our data do not include such information, yet we recognize that more-detailed analysis is needed to better understand this and determine whether remedies to the SBP program are warranted. Also, our findings pertain only to widows because the sample of widowers was too small for analysis.

Using commercial sources to provide survivor benefits appears feasible, and, assuming that DoD continues to subsidize SBP, advisability depends on whether the commercial cost of administering SBP and managing the SBP fund, plus DoD's cost of contracting, would be less than in-house costs of administration and managing SBP and on what quality of service would be preferred.

Describe the Purposes of SBP and How It Interacts with Other Federal Programs to Provide Financial Stability and Resources for Survivors

SBP's chief purpose is to provide survivors with a "reasonable level of income" through an annuity (DoD, Under Secretary of Defense for Personnel and Readiness, 2011, p. 735). SBP was established in 1972. It replaced a program created in 1953 under the Uniformed Services Contingency Option Act and known as the Retired Serviceman's Family Protection Plan (RSFPP). This program had several shortcomings. Its premiums were not tax-sheltered; its annuity was not adjusted for inflation; service members had to elect RSFPP before knowing the amount of their retired pay; the premium rate and annuity were subject to change; and the premium was not subsidized, resulting in high costs to enrollees.[1] These factors, in part a product of RSFPP's design to be self-supporting, led to low participation, never exceeding 15 percent. For the vast majority of military retirees, RSFPP was not a successful means of providing survivor benefits.

The legislation creating SBP, 10 U.S.C. 1447–1460b, addressed RSFPP's limitations. According to the law, SBP would be subsidized by DoD, allowing the premiums to be lower. Premium rates would be stable and adjusted for inflation, and enrollment would be done at the time of retirement, with the member knowing what retired pay would be. SBP's participation rate in fiscal year (FY) 2016 was 66 percent of all retirees and 78 percent of the cohort of FY 2016 retirees.

The SBP premium rate depends on the beneficiary category chosen by the member. For instance, the premium for a spouse beneficiary equals 6.5 percent of the base amount. More generally, the premium rate may not exceed 6.5 percent of the gross retired pay. The premium rate is applied to the portion of retired pay chosen to be covered, called the *base amount*, to obtain the premium amount. Upon the death of the SBP enrollee, the eligible survivor receives a benefit equal to 55 percent of the base amount.

Survivors of members who die on duty are eligible for SBP benefits, although members do not pay premiums while on duty. In this case, the base amount is 75 percent of high-36 basic pay, and the SBP benefit is 55 percent of that amount.

In addition to SBP, other benefits are available to survivors. Dependency and Indemnity Compensation (DIC) is a U.S. Department of Veterans Affairs (VA) benefit generally paid to the eligible surviving dependents of a military member who dies while on active duty and to certain survivors of veterans who either had a 100 percent VA disability rating or who died as a result of a service-connected condition. SBP is offset by DIC—that is, DIC is subtracted from SBP. When DIC offsets SBP, survivors are proportionally refunded the SBP premiums that were paid, up to 100 percent. Congress created the Special Survivor Indemnity Allowance (SSIA) to partially offset the offset. Although SSIA had a sunset provision when created, Congress permanently extended SSIA in the National Defense Authorization Act for Fiscal Year 2018 (Pub. L. 115-91).

---

[1]   For a service member who retired at age 45 with a 40-year-old spouse, the cost was 22.8 cents per dollar of coverage when the plan was established. This premium later rose to 25.3 cents per dollar (DoD, Under Secretary of Defense for Personnel and Readiness, 2011, pp. 735–736). SBP today costs 6.5 cents per dollar of coverage.

Other benefits include the DoD death gratuity, life insurance, housing, TRICARE, commissary and exchange use, child care, education assistance, the Survivors Pension, the Annuity for Certain Military Surviving Spouses (ACMSS), the Minimum Income Widow Annuity, tax forgiveness, and Social Security benefits.

In FY 2016, SBP had 1.1 million enrollees and 321,476 annuitants, and 64,169 received DIC and SSIA. Most annuitants were survivors of military retirees, and there were 10,442 annuitants from death on duty. Across all enrolled retirees, the average base amount was 87 percent of retired pay. The base amount has been rising—it was 98 percent for the FY 2016 cohort of retirees. The average monthly annuity for active-duty retiree death SBP annuitants receiving a positive amount (i.e., not entirely offset by DIC) was $1,140. The government liability for SBP in FY 2016 was $2.56 billion, with retirees contributing $1.41 billion. For the FY 2016 cohort of military retirees, the subsidy to SBP was estimated at 44.6 percent of their projected SBP liability.

Compare Benefits Under SBP with Benefits Available to Government and Private-Sector Employees

Defined Benefit Plans

Data from the Bureau of Labor Statistics National Compensation Survey show that nearly 100 percent of defined benefit plan participants in private industry have access to a pre- and postretirement joint and survivor annuity. This was also the case for a vast majority of state and local government employees in defined benefit plans. *Pre- and postretirement* refers to retirement from the labor force and means that the survivor may receive an annuity whether the worker died before or after retiring from the labor force. This is similar to SBP, which provides a survivor annuity whether the member died on duty or was enrolled in SBP after retiring from the military. Like SBP, the default beneficiary is the spouse, and opting out or decreasing the survivor benefit requires the spouse's signed consent.

The legislative basis for these components of private-industry plans comes from two acts. The Employment Retirement Income Security Act of 1974 (Pub. L. 93-406) required qualified plans to offer a qualified joint and survivor annuity (QJSA), which is a life annuity for married couples that guarantees payments for the life of a surviving spouse. To opt out of the QJSA, the Retirement Equity Act (REA) of 1984 established the requirement of written consent witnessed by a plan representative or notary from both the plan participant and the spouse. The REA also established the requirement for pension plans to offer a qualified preretirement survivor annuity, which is a survivor annuity paid out for the life of the surviving spouse.

To fund the survivor benefit, the employee's retirement benefit is reduced by an amount sufficient to cover the actuarial liability of the survivor benefit. This reduction can be thought of as a premium. SBP requires the military retiree to pay an explicit premium. However, the premium paid by the military retiree is less than that needed to fund the liability, with DoD subsidizing the difference.

Other Sources of Survivor Benefits

Defined benefit plans have become less prevalent over time, so it is relevant to describe alternative sources of survivor benefits. These include defined contribution plans; life insurance; workers' compensation for work-related injuries, diseases, and death; and Social Security. The percentage of civilian employees with access to a defined benefit plan, alone or with a defined contribution plan, dropped from 31 to 27 percent from 2009 to 2016. At the same time, access to only a defined contribution plan increased from 40 to 42 percent, while access to a defined contribution plan, alone or with a defined benefit plan, decreased from 55 to 53 percent. This reflects a shift from employers offering both types of plans to employers offering only a defined contribution plan. In 2009, about 18 percent of civilian employees participated in only a defined benefit plan, 28 percent participated in only a defined contribution plan, and 57 percent participated in any retirement plan. In 2016, 14 percent participated in only a defined benefit plan, 31 percent participated in only a defined contribution plan, and 54 percent participated in any retirement plan. Among state and local government employees, 81 percent participated in any retirement plan in 2016, and the majority of these participated in only a defined benefit plan.

Comparison to Federal, State or Local, and Private Plans

We compared SBP with defined benefit plans offered to federal civilian employees and with those plans offered by a select group of public and private employers. The plans are from the Civil Service Retirement System (CSRS), Federal Employee Retirement System (FERS), Los Angeles Fire and Police Pension Fund, Chicago Public Schools, Washington State, Kaiser Permanente, Ford Motor Company United Auto Workers Retirement Plan, and Exxon Mobil. Table S.1 compares plans in terms of the percentage of the final average salary for the retiree annuity and for the survivor annuity. Note, however, that SBP is based on the military retired pay, which depends on high-36 basic pay. Basic pay is about two-thirds of what is known as *regular military compensation*, a general measure of military compensation that is the sum of basic pay, Basic Allowance for Housing, Basic Allowance for Subsistence, and an adjustment for the allowances not being subject to federal income tax. Thus, we describe SBP with respect to *high-36 basic pay* rather than using the term *final average salary*, which is appropriate for retirement plans outside the military.

The comparison shows that SBP's percentage of high-36 basic pay is typically more generous or in line with the selected plans. For instance, the survivor of a military retiree with 20 years of service would receive an annuity equal to 27.5 percent of high-36 basic pay—or 55 percent of gross retired pay, assuming that the member has elected a full base amount. By comparison, the survivor annuity would be 11 percent of final average salary under FERS, 28 percent in the Los Angeles Fire and Police system, and 16 percent at Exxon Mobil. SBP is less generous under the blended retirement system, but those under it would receive DoD contributions to a Thrift Savings Plan, which is a defined contribution plan. The additional available income from the defined contribution plan is not accounted for in the table.

We constructed two sets of detailed examples to illustrate how the *entire set* of survivor benefits compares across the selected plans, including SBP. The first set compares the benefits available after a currently employed individual dies—e.g., after the death of a federal civilian, private-industry worker, or service member on duty. The second set compares benefits available after the death of a military retiree, retired federal civilian employee, or retired private-industry employee. The examples show cumulative benefits and the year-by-year payout of benefits.

When comparing benefits among childless survivors of currently employed individuals, we find that the present discounted value of cumulative benefits over 30 years under SBP ($0.8 million) is greater than those under FERS ($0.7 million) and under a private-industry plan ($0.5 million). When surviving spouses have children, cumulative benefits for the surviving

Table S.1
Comparison of Survivor Benefit Generosity Across Plans

Retirement System	20 Years of Service[a]	30 Years of Service[a]
Military (percentage of high-36 basic pay)		
Current military	27.5	41.3
Blended military (Blended Retirement System)	22.0	33.0
Nonmilitary (percentage of final average salary)		
Civil service (CSRS)	19.9	30.9
Federal employee (FERS)	11.0	16.5
Los Angeles Fire and Police	28.0	52.5
Chicago Public Schools	29.3	44.0
Washington State	0.0[b]	0.0[b]
Kaiser Permanente	14.5	21.8
Ford Motor Company	14.3	21.5
Exxon Mobil	16.0	24.0

[a] Percentages in this column are net of the amount paid for the survivor benefit.

[b] Default is no survivor annuity. Instead, the survivor gets remaining employee contributions plus interest as a lump sum.

family of the service member and private-industry employee are greater than those offered under FERS ($1.1 million versus $0.8 million). The year-by-year payout shows that SBP provides the surviving family with income above the federal poverty line.

When comparing benefits among survivors of retirees, cumulative benefits over 20 years for SBP are generally in line with those provided under FERS and more generous than those of the survivor of the private-industry employee. We have separate examples for an enlisted retiree and officer retiree. In both cases, the service member chooses the default survivor benefit option, and the military retiree has a secondary career as a federal civilian employee. In the enlisted example, SBP benefits ($0.7 million to $0.8 million) are in line with FERS ($0.8 million) and greater than those provided by private industry ($0.5 million). In the officer example, SBP benefits ($1.2 million to 1.4 million) are more generous than those provided by FERS ($1.05 million) and private industry ($0.8 million). Thus, SBP benefits are generally in line with or more generous than those for survivors in the FERS and private-industry examples.

Evaluate the Effectiveness of SBP in Providing Survivors with Intended Benefits

To evaluate effectiveness, we compared the financial status of military and nonmilitary widows with similar observed characteristics. We considered total income, the extent to which survivor benefits contribute to total income, and the percentages of widows below the poverty line and participating in government public assistance programs. The types of income included were wages, Social Security, retirement income other than survivor benefits, survivor benefits, and other income. We divided widows into two groups, those who did receive Social Security and those who did not. A widow is eligible to receive full Social Security benefits if she is at retirement age or reduced benefits at age 60. A widow can get Social Security benefits at any age if she takes care of the deceased's child when that child is younger than age 16 or is disabled (and is therefore receiving Social Security benefits).

The data are from the Current Population Survey Annual Social and Economic Supplement. The sample was limited to widows age 40 and older, but there are few widows at younger ages. We identified military widows as women whose main source of survivor benefits was military benefits, and we grouped other widows based on the main source of their survivor benefits—specifically, VA, company or union, federal government, state or local government, annuities, and other sources. We included a group for widows who did not receive survivor benefits. We used inverse probability weighting of the different groups to make them comparable to widows whose main source of survivor benefits was the military.

We find that fewer than one in five widows reported regular income from survivor benefits other than Social Security. By comparison, two-thirds of military retirees are enrolled in SBP, and their survivors will receive benefits. These findings indicate that, although survivor benefits other than Social Security are relatively uncommon as a source of income for widows in general, a large fraction of military survivors is eligible to receive benefits.

Widows Not Receiving Social Security

Widows who are not receiving Social Security are not old enough or are not taking care of a child younger than age 16. For widows whose main source of survivor benefits was the military, their average age was 61.7, several years away from eligibility for full Social Security benefits. Their average total annual income was about $41,700. This average income was larger than that of similar widows who did not receive survivor benefits (about $30,700); it was comparable to that of widows for whom the main source of survivor benefits was company or union benefits (about $42,300) but somewhat lower than that of widows of federal and state and local government employees (about $48,000 to $50,000). For widows who do not receive Social Security, their survivor benefits were, on average, about half of their total income, so these benefits are a major source of income.

Ideally, in comparing the total annual income of widows receiving SBP with others, we would like to have detailed data on the widows and their deceased spouses, such as their education and labor-force participation. Unfortunately, the available data limit the conclusions we can draw about SBP. Most widows who do not receive Social Security are above the poverty line and do not participate in public assistance programs; about three-fourths of military widows have incomes 50 percent or more above the poverty line. But 15.7 percent of widows for whom their main source of survivor benefits is the military are below the poverty line, a figure that is comparable to the percentage of widows for whom their main source of survivor benefits is a company or union plan or a state or local government plan. However, that figure is higher than the percentage of widows for whom their main source of benefits is federal government benefits. This may not indicate a shortcoming of military survivor benefits but may instead be due to systematic differences in the characteristics of widows and decedents that we do not observe, such as their labor force participation, or differences in the amount of survivor benefit coverage selected. As mentioned, widows receiving SBP are doing well on nearly all measures but this one, though this finding needs to be better understood.

Among widows not receiving Social Security, our findings indicate that, compared with federal widows, military widows have somewhat lower total income, on average, and survivor benefits are a somewhat lower fraction of total income. However, our examples that compare military and federal survivor benefits, such as those shown in Table S.1, indicate that military survivor benefits compare favorably with federal survivor benefits. Thus, it is likely that the higher total income and the higher contribution of survivor benefits to total income among federal government widows compared with military widows is not attributable to more-generous federal survivor benefits but is, instead, attributable to differences in decedent and unobserved widow characteristics.

Widows Receiving Social Security

For widows receiving Social Security, the average age of widows for whom the main source of survivor benefits is the military is 76.4. Their average total annual income is about $40,000. This average income is larger than that of similar widows who did not receive survivor benefits (about $24,000), and it is comparable to that of widows for whom the main source of survivor benefits is company or union benefits or government benefits. The average contribution of survivor benefits to total income is about a third (33.7 percent) for widows for whom the military is the main source of survivor benefits, which is higher than for widows for whom company or union benefits are the main source of survivor benefits (24.9 percent) but less than for widows for whom the main source is federal benefits (44.7 percent).

The percentage of military widows below the poverty line is 3.6 percent, and 90.2 percent have income 50 percent or more above the poverty line. The percentage of widows who are below the poverty line and for whom the main source of survivor benefits is company or union benefits or government benefits is also quite small, about 2 to 3 percent.

Assess the Feasibility and Advisability of Providing Survivor Benefits Through Alternative Insurance Products Commercially Available for Similar Purposes

To assess feasibility, we considered whether insurance products similar to SBP exist in the commercial market and whether those products could incorporate some of the distinctive features of SBP, such as its interaction with DIC. Regarding advisability, commercialization is more likely to be advisable when the price at which commercial providers offer to administer and manage SBP is lower and when the quality of service is at a level satisfactory to DoD. Because the cost information needed to make this assessment is not currently available, our assessment of advisability focuses on some of the factors that could affect the cost of SBP provided by commercial sources.

Feasibility

Commercial sources offer a variety of insurance policies and annuities. The expertise and capability underlying these products indicate that it is feasible for commercial sources to design a product with the features of SBP. SBP is a whole life insurance policy that pays a whole life annuity to the survivor. However, SBP has features that distinguish it from readily available commercial products, and these features would need to be incorporated and recognized. In particular, the premium rate does not depend on the age or health of the insured, benefits are inflation-protected, and benefits are provided to the survivors of members who die on duty even though they pay no premiums. Other distinctive features include the DoD subsidy to SBP, the interaction of SBP with DIC and SSIA, and the effect of commercialization on the level and time pattern of government outlays.

In constructing a commercial SBP product, it would be advantageous for commercial sources to have access to DoD data on retiree and survivor mortality rates and for DoD to share data on retiring service members, SBP enrollees, and survivors.

Another aspect of feasibility is the quality of service that could be provided by commercial sources. Experience with Servicemembers' Group Life Insurance, a VA program provided by a commercial source, suggests that commercial sources for SBP could provide high-quality service.

Advisability

The advisability of DoD contracting for the administration and funding of SBP thus depends on whether commercial sources' cost, plus DoD's contracting cost and subsidy to the commercial provider, would be less than DoD's in-house administration, subsidy, and accrual costs and whether the quality of service would be at a level acceptable to DoD.

Administration costs include keeping track of beneficiary designation, collecting premiums, paying benefits, and resolving day-to-day administrative questions. Benefit payment could be done by a commercial source, as could managing enrollments. Commercialization would involve contracting costs to DoD, and these can include the cost of developing contract specifications and contract implementation, as well as the cost of the oversight of quality and the meeting of contract requirements. DoD would also need to exchange data and clarify responsibilities. The cost of the transition to a commercial source would also need to be considered because the process of migrating SBP to commercial sources would require extensive actuarial calculation to determine DoD's share of the liability, and the commercial sources would have setup costs.

Unlike government provision, for commercialization to be advisable, commercial sources must earn a competitive return on capital, which requires that they earn a higher return on capital than what is earned by the military retirement fund; if commercial sources do not earn a higher return, their costs must be lower (given the quality of service acceptable to DoD). Commercial providers can also face bankruptcy, unlike the government, and bankruptcy may be a possibility during wartime or other instances where claims are unusually high, so survivors might not receive promised benefits. Steps can be taken to mitigate the bankruptcy risk for survivors, such as solvency regulations or reinsurance.

With respect to making SBP more flexible, say by expanding beneficiary designation options and payment options, this could be pursued either by DoD or by commercial providers. Commercial providers may have more flexibility and possibly could accomplish such changes more readily. Today, such changes must often be accomplished by Congress.

Although data are lacking, DoD could get more information about relevant costs by conducting a preliminary competition where firms would submit estimates of what their (unsubsidized) premium rates would be.

Conclusion

Overall, we find that SBP is well structured to provide survivor benefits to service members and military retirees, and SBP benefits compare well with those of public and private plans. The financial status of military widows in terms of average income is broadly comparable to that of nonmilitary widows, especially for widows who receive Social Security; as with other widows who receive survivor benefits, these benefits are a key contributor to their financial status, contributing about half of total income, on average, for younger military widows who do not receive Social Security and about a third of total income for those who do. Using commercial sources to provide survivor benefits appears feasible, yet the advisability of using commercial sources requires information not currently available about internal and external cost and quality of service under different approaches to outsourcing. If SBP is outsourced, we advise continuing DoD's subsidy to SBP because of its importance in keeping premium rates low and enrollment high.

Acknowledgments

At the Office of Compensation (Office of the Under Secretary of Defense for Personnel and Readiness), we thank Jeri Busch, Director; Andrew Corso, Assistant Director of Military Compensation Policy, Retired and Annuitant Pay; Julie Daughety; and Don Svendsen. We are grateful to Rich Allen of the U.S. Department of Defense Office of the Actuary for tabulations of Survivor Benefit Plan participation and cost. Participants in the SBP board meeting in July 2017 provided valuable background information about the Survivor Benefit Plan program and its implementation. At RAND, we appreciate the help provided by Connor Jackson and David Knapp in secondary data analysis. We wish to thank Craig Bond, Lloyd Dixon, and Heidi Golding for their careful reviews of this report.

Abbreviations

ACMSS	Annuity for Certain Military Surviving Spouses
ADFM	active-duty family member
AIME	average indexed monthly earnings
ASEC	Annual Social and Economic Supplement
BAH	Basic Allowance for Housing
BLS	Bureau of Labor Statistics
BRS	Blended Retirement System
CA workers' comp	State of California workers' compensation program
COLA	cost of living adjustment
CPI	consumer price index
CPS	Current Population Survey
CSB	Career Status Bonus
CSRS	Civil Service Retirement System
DEA	Survivors' and Dependents' Educational Assistance
DFAS	Defense Finance and Accounting Service
DIC	Dependency and Indemnity Compensation
DoD	U.S. Department of Defense
DoDAA	Department of Defense Authorization Act
ERISA	Employment Retirement Income Security Act of 1974
FAS	final average salary
FEGLI	Federal Employee Group Life Insurance
FERS	Federal Employee Retirement System

FY	fiscal year
HRS	Health and Retirement Study
IPW	inverse probability weighting
LAFPPF	Los Angeles Fire and Police Pension Fund
MWR	Morale, Welfare and Recreation
NCP	normal cost percentage
NCS	National Compensation Survey
NDAA	National Defense Authorization Act
NIP	Natural Interest Person
OWCP	Office of Workers' Compensation Programs
PDRL	Permanent Disability Retired List
PIA	primary insurance amount
QJSA	qualified joint and survivor annuity
QPSA	qualified preretirement survivor annuity
REA	Retirement Equity Act
RSFPP	Retired Serviceman's Family Protection Plan
SBP	Survivor Benefit Plan
S-DVI	Service-Disabled Veterans Insurance
SGLI	Servicemembers' Group Life Insurance
SNT	Special Needs Trust
SSA	U.S. Social Security Administration
SSIA	Special Survivor Indemnity Allowance
TDRL	Temporary Disability Retirement List
TERA	Temporary Early Retirement Authority
TSP	Thrift Savings Plan
VA	U.S. Department of Veterans Affairs
VGLI	Veterans' Group Life Insurance

## CHAPTER ONE

Introduction

Section 648 of the National Defense Authorization Act (NDAA) for Fiscal Year 2017 (Pub. L. 114-328) calls for a review of the Survivor Benefit Plan (SBP). SBP provides an ongoing benefit to survivors of retired military members enrolled in SBP and to survivors of members who are performing in an authorized-duty status and die in the line of duty. This includes members on active duty; members of the reserves and National Guard on inactive duty, meaning while performing their Inactive Duty Training ("weekend drill"); and other authorized-duty statuses. We shorten these criteria to members who die *on duty*. Section 648 requires the Secretary of Defense to provide an independent assessment of SBP by a federally funded research and development center and directs that the review (1) describe the purposes of SBP and the manner in which it interacts with other federal programs to provide financial stability and resources for survivors, (2) compare benefits under SBP with benefits available to government and private-sector employees. (3) evaluate the effectiveness of SBP in providing survivors with intended benefits, and (4) assess the feasibility and advisability of providing survivor benefits through alternative insurance products commercially available for similar purposes. This report is that review.

Chapter Two describes SBP, its enrollment rate and levels of benefit coverage, and its interaction with other federal programs. Foremost among those programs are the Department of Veterans Affairs (VA) Dependency and Indemnity Compensation (DIC) and Social Security benefits. The chapter also describes other sources of benefits to survivors.

Chapter Three compares SBP with survivor plans in the federal government, selected public organizations (e.g., police and fire), and selected companies in private industry. As the chapter discusses, defined benefit retirement plans include provisions for survivor benefits as mandated by law. However, the prevalence of defined benefit plans has declined, and survivor benefits are more commonly available to today's worker through defined contribution plans, life insurance, workers' compensation death benefits, and Social Security. Chapter Three also includes example computations of survivor benefits available to survivors. One set of examples compares the survivor benefits of members who die on duty with those of federal employees, police, and private-industry employees killed when working. Another set compares the survivor benefits of military and nonmilitary retirees. Several examples have been placed in Appendix C.

Chapter Four evaluates the effectiveness of SBP by comparing the total income of military and nonmilitary surviving widows and the extent to which survivor benefits contribute to total income.[1] In addition to total income, tabulations show the incidence and amount of

---

[1] Note that our findings pertain only to widows because the sample of widowers was too small for analysis.

each type of income contributing to total income. The tabulations categorize widows according to whether they received Social Security and according to their main source of survivor benefits—specifically, the U.S. Department of Defense (DoD), VA, company or union, state or local government, annuity, other sources, and none. Other tabulations show income relative to the federal poverty line.

In Chapter Five, to assess feasibility we consider commercially available insurance products; features of SBP that would need to be incorporated into commercial products, including premium rates that are independent of age and health status; the interaction between SBP and DIC; and the subsidy to SBP. To assess advisability, we consider whether the price at which commercial providers could set up and administer SBP would be lower than the current cost to DoD at a quality of service acceptable to the department.

Chapter Six recaps earlier chapters with respect to the questions asked by Congress.

Appendix A describes other sources of support available to survivors in addition to those described in Chapter One. Appendix B describes the Civil Service Retirement System (CSRS) and FERS, and Appendixes C and D, which are companions to Chapter Three, provide further detailed examples of survivor benefits. Appendix E concerns the estimation of the inverse probability weights that are used in the income comparisons in Chapter Four, and Appendix F presents an example that illustrates the importance of DoD's subsidy to SBP.

## CHAPTER TWO

A Description of SBP and Military Survivor Benefits

SBP provides benefits to eligible survivors of service members who die on duty and survivors of military retirees. This chapter describes SBP in detail, identifies survivor benefit programs that interact with SBP, identifies other sources of benefits available to survivors, and provides a brief legislative history of SBP.

SBP Background and Intent

SBP was established on September 21, 1972, as 10 U.S.C. 1447–1460b. The statutes do not state the purpose and intent of the program, but the Special Subcommittee on Survivor Benefits of the House Armed Services Committee in 1970 described two purposes. First, survivor benefits satisfy a common expectation for labor benefits: "The lack of basic survivor protection, which is a standard feature of most employee fringe benefit programs, public and private, and which is of particular importance to the military man because of his long period of retirement, is a glaring weakness in the singularly outstanding benefits program of the armed forces" (Special Subcommittee on Survivor Benefits, House Armed Services Committee, 1970). That is, military survivor benefits would bring military compensation in line with the compensation packages of public and private employers. Second, retired pay was an earned entitlement, and the government had a "moral obligation" to provide it to retirees and their survivors. The volume *Military Compensation Background Papers* stated that the purpose of SBP is "to establish a program to ensure that the surviving dependents of military personnel who die in retirement or after becoming eligible for retirement will continue to have a reasonable level of income" (DoD, Under Secretary of Defense for Personnel and Readiness, 2011, p. 735). In addition to survivors of military retirees enrolled in SBP, SBP provides for survivors of service members who die on duty.

The surviving spouse of a deceased military member may be eligible for other government assistance programs, including VA DIC, the VA Survivors Pension, Social Security benefits, and other benefits described in Appendix A. SBP, however, is "the only means by which a retired member can ensure that his or her immediate family will be provided with continued government income under any and all circumstances at a level dictated by the member, within established bounds, after the member's death" (DoD, Under Secretary of Defense for Personnel and Readiness, 2011, p. 735).

Table 2.1 shows key figures for SBP in fiscal year (FY) 2016. There were nearly 1.1 million enrollees and approximately 320,000 annuitants. A small fraction of annuitants, 10,442, were survivors of service members who died on duty. The average monthly annuity was about

Table 2.1
FY 2016 Survivor Benefit Plan Overview

Item	Quantity
All SBP enrollees	1,085,769
Paid-up SBP enrollees[a]	143,145
SBP annuitants (including those with DIC offset)	321,476
SBP annuitants (receiving positive SBP annuity)	282,266
Annuitants receiving DIC and SSIA	64,169
Annuitants receiving minimum income annuity	68
Death-on-active-duty annuitants	10,442
Average monthly annuity[b]	$1,140
Participation rate, all retirees	66%
Participation rate, FY 2016 retirees	78%
Average base rate, all retirees	87%
Average base rate, FY 2016 retirees	98%
Estimated subsidy rate, FY 2016 cohort	44.6%
DoD subsidy to SBP, FY 2016	$2.56 billion

SOURCE: Data from DoD, Office of the Actuary, 2017b, 2017c.

NOTE: These figures, unless otherwise noted, also include the 11,314 annuitants from the Reserve Component Survivor Benefit Plan (RC-SBP).

[a] A paid-up enrollee must be at least 70 years old and have paid 360 monthly SBP premium payments.

[b] This is for those receiving a positive annuity (not completely offset by DIC), but it excludes RC-SBP and death-on-active-duty annuitants.

$1,100, or over $13,000 per year. About 64,000 annuitants received DIC and the Special Survivor Indemnity Allowance (SSIA). Overall, two-thirds of all retirees were enrolled in SBP, and the enrollment rate for the FY 2016 cohort of retirees was 78 percent. The overall base rate of retired pay chosen to be covered by SBP (see below) was 87 percent, and for FY 2016 retirees it was 98 percent. DoD's Office of the Actuary reported that the federal government spent $2.56 billion funding the SBP liability during FY 2016, while retirees paid $1.41 billion in premiums (DoD, Office of the Actuary, 2017c). In other words, the government subsidy in the previous fiscal year was 64.6 percent of the SBP cost. However, the Office of the Actuary projected that the future subsidy for service members who retired in FY 2016 will be lower, at 44.6 percent (DoD, Office of the Actuary, 2017b). The remainder of the liability would be funded by SBP premiums.

SBP Details

SBP was established as a subsidized insurance plan that provides an annuity to survivors. It is administered by DoD, and the subsidy is funded as part of DoD's retirement accrual charge.

Members on duty are automatically covered by SBP, and retirees are automatically enrolled but may choose not to enroll.

SBP Annuity Is 55 percent of the "Base Amount" of Retired Pay

The SBP annuity is 55 percent of the base amount of retired pay (DoD, Under Secretary of Defense for Personnel and Readiness, 2011, p. 738). The retiree chooses the base amount from a minimum of $300 per month up to a maximum of gross retired pay per month. The average base amount chosen by cohorts of retirees, as a proportion of retired pay, has increased from 80 percent in 1991 to 98 percent in 2016 (Figure 2.1).

Formulas for Military Retired Pay

There are several retired pay systems for full-time active component members:[1] regular retirement, Career Status Bonus/Redux (CSB/Redux), Blended Retirement System (BRS), Temporary Early Retirement Authority (TERA), and disability retirement (DoD, undated-b). Since the base amount for the SBP annuity is a proportion of retired pay, the retired pay system affects the size of the SBP annuity. The retirement annuities are explained in Table 2.2.

Regular Retirement

Under the regular retirement system,[2] if the member joined the service before September 8, 1980, at retirement, that person receives a monthly annuity of 2.5 percent × years of service × final monthly pay. If the member joined on or after September 8, 1980, at retirement, that

Figure 2.1
Average Base Amount Chosen by FY Cohort

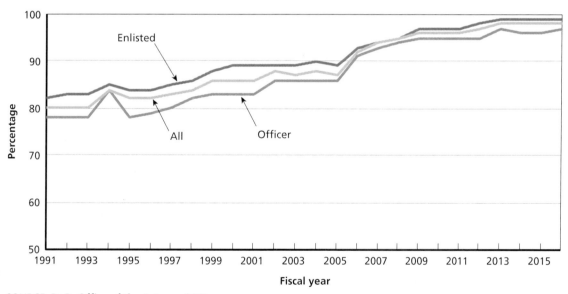

SOURCE: DoD, Office of the Actuary, 2017c.
RAND RR2236-2.1

---

[1] There is also the reserve retirement system.

[2] *Regular retirement* describes any retirement based on longevity for a member of the regular component, as opposed to nonregular retirement or a disability retirement. CSB/REDUX and BRS are both forms of regular retirement. The other existing retired pay systems for regular component members not listed are "final pay" and "high-36."

Table 2.2
Retirement Pay Formulas

Retirement System	Formula
Legacy	2.5% × years of service × high-36
CSB/Redux	(2.5% – penalty) × high-36
BRS	2% × years of service × high-36
TERA	(2.5% × years of service – reduction factor) × high-36
PDRL	max(2.5% × years of service, disability rating) × high-36
TDRL	max(50%, 2.5% × years of service, disability rating) × high-36

NOTES: The formulas are simplifications of retired pay. For instance, CSB/Redux retired pay is not adjusted for cost of living, and BRS includes TSP. PDRL = Permanent Disability Retired List; TDRL = Temporary Disability Retirement List.

person receives a monthly annuity of 2.5 percent × years of service × high-36, where *high-36* is the average of the highest 36 months of basic pay. Both of these annuities are subject to annual consumer price index (CPI) adjustments. For a retirement at 20 years in the regular retirement system, the SBP annuity is 27.5 percent (= 0.55 × 50) of high-36 pay.

CSB/Redux

Members who joined after July 31, 1986, may opt in to CSB/Redux but may no longer do so after December 31, 2017. As under the regular system, the member receives a monthly annuity of 2.5 percent × years of service × high-36; however, the member is penalized 1 percent for each year and 0.8 percent for each month of service under 30 years. Members who opt into CSB/Redux lower their retired pay voluntarily in exchange for a bonus at their 15th year of service. Additionally, CPI adjustments to the retirement annuity are penalized by 1 percent. At age 62, retired pay is reset to 2.5 percent × years of service × high-36 without a penalized multiplier, but future CPI adjustments are still penalized. However, the maximum base amount is not penalized and is calculated as if the member did not choose CSB/Redux. The survivor annuity, however, will still have a 1 percent CPI penalty (DoD, Under Secretary of Defense [Comptroller], 2017).

BRS

From January 1, 2018, to December 31, 2018, members with less than 12 years of service as of December 31, 2017, may opt in to BRS (DoD, undated-c). On and after January 1, 2018, all new accessions will be automatically enrolled in BRS. In BRS, the retiree receives a monthly annuity of 2.0 percent × years of service × high-36 and will have a Thrift Savings Plan (TSP) with an automatic contribution from DoD of 1 percent and matching contributions up to 4 percent of basic pay, for a total match of up to 5 percent. The annuity will be adjusted for cost of living. Upon retirement, the retiree may opt to receive a discounted lump sum in exchange for a 25 percent or 50 percent reduction in retired pay from the date of retirement to his or her full Social Security retirement age, usually 67. At full retirement age, the annuity returns to its full amount.

TERA

Under TERA, members with more than 15 but less than 20 years of service may retire early. A TERA reduction factor decreases the retirement benefit that the member otherwise would have had; the reduction factor depends on length of service (DoD, Defense Finance and Accounting Service [DFAS], 2017b).

Disability Retirement Lists

Service members with a DoD disability rating of 30 percent or more may be placed on the Permanent Disability Retired List (PDRL) and will receive disability retired pay. Disability retired pay is adjusted for cost of living and equals a multiplier × pay base. The multiplier is either 2.5 percent × years of service or the disability percentage rating, whichever is higher, with a maximum multiplier of 75 percent. The pay base is high-36 basic pay if the member joined on or after September 8, 1980, or final basic pay if the member joined before then. Members with a disability rating of 30 percent or more with an unstable condition are placed on the Temporary Disability Retirement List (TDRL). The TDRL formula is the same, but it has a minimum multiplier of 50 percent.

Members on TDRL are eligible for SBP as long as they remain on TDRL. If they return to regular service, they have active-duty coverage. If they move to PDRL, their SBP coverage follows them, with the base amount adjusting to their new retired pay (DoD, Under Secretary of Defense [Comptroller], 2017).

Base Amount for Death on Active Duty

Members on duty are covered by SBP at the full base amount and do not pay premiums. If they die, the base amount is retired pay computed as 75 percent of their high-36 basic pay. This results in an SBP annuity of 41.25 (= 0.55 × 75) percent of high-36 earnings (DoD, Under Secretary of Defense [Comptroller], 2017, p. 46-12). If members die on active duty (but not in the line of duty) and have served more than 20 years, their survivors are (generally) eligible for the SBP annuity they would have received if the member had been retired at that point with full SBP coverage (DoD, Under Secretary of Defense [Comptroller], 2017, p. 46-12; 10 U.S.C. 1448).

Enrollment and Premiums for Retirees

SBP enrollment is at the time of retiring but before the date of retirement. Retiring members are automatically enrolled in SBP but can elect to decline enrollment (DoD, DFAS, 2015a). Enrolled retirees pay premiums that are deducted from retired pay. The premiums are not considered taxable income by the IRS (DoD, DFAS, 2017a). Additionally, when the cost of living adjustment (COLA) or other adjustments to retired pay are made, SBP annuities, premiums, and accrual charges adjust proportionally (DoD, Under Secretary of Defense for Personnel and Readiness, 2011, p. 739). When an SBP enrollee has made 360 months of payments and is age 70 or older, the enrollee is considered "paid up," and premiums cease (DoD, DFAS, 2017c).

The premium rate depends on the beneficiary option the member selects, but the annuity amount is the same for all options—55 percent of the base amount. The member may choose one of the following options: spouse and child, spouse only, child only, former spouse, former spouse and child, or a Natural Interest Person (NIP) (DoD, DFAS, 2015b).

Spouse

If married at retirement, the retiree must have written spousal consent to choose not to enroll in SBP or choose any coverage that does not fully cover the spouse (DoD, DFAS, 2015b). If a spouse does not consent to lower or declined coverage, the spouse will be fully covered under SBP (DoD, Under Secretary of Defense for Personnel and Readiness, 2011, p. 743).

The premium for spouses is 6.5 percent of the base amount (DoD, DFAS, 2015b). The premium for disability retirees is 2.5 percent of the first $337 of the base amount and 10 percent of the remaining base amount, if this is more favorable than the 6.5 percent flat rate (10 U.S.C. 1452[a][1][A][i]). The annuity is paid to the spouse for the remainder of the spouse's life, unless the spouse remarries before age 55, in which case the annuity is terminated. However, if the second marriage ends, the annuity is reinstated.

Child

Children's coverage is based on the age of the retiree and the age of the youngest child. For example, a 50-year-old retiree with a ten-year-old child pays $5.30 per month per $1,000 of the base amount versus $65 per month for an equivalent amount of spouse-only coverage. The premium rate is significantly lower because the SBP annuity is expected to be paid for fewer years to children than to spouses, given age limits. Children must be the member's legal children, unmarried, and under age 18 (or under age 22 if they are unmarried full-time students) to be eligible for the annuity. An incapacitated child is eligible indefinitely, as long as the child is unmarried and the incapacitation occurred prior to age 18 (or age 22 if a full-time student). In this case, members may arrange for their annuities to be deposited in a Special Needs Trust (SNT) (DoD, DFAS, 2016b). The premiums for child coverage cease when children are no longer eligible for the annuity (10 U.S.C. 1452). If paid, the annuity is divided among all eligible children (10 U.S.C. 1450). Spouse and child coverage offers the same annuity amount but allows the annuity to be paid to the eligible children in the event that the spouse is unable to receive it because of death or early remarriage.

NIP

The NIP election can be made by an unmarried retiree with no eligible dependents. If the NIP is not related or is a first cousin or more distantly related, the member must prove that the NIP has a financial dependency. NIP differs from other election options in a few ways. First, the member must choose full retired pay as the base amount, and the premium is 10 percent of the base amount plus 5 percent for every five years the NIP is younger in age than the retiree, not to exceed 40 percent in total (10 U.S.C. 1452). Second, coverage may be canceled at any time (DoD, DFAS, 2015b), and the member may change his or her election, if desired, within one year of gaining a spouse or a child (DoD, DFAS, 2016a). Third, if the beneficiary dies, the retiree can elect a new one within 180 days (DoD, Under Secretary of Defense [Comptroller], 2017, p. 43-5). Finally, if the member was medically retired, the insurable interest will receive an annuity only if the member lives for more than one year after retirement (DoD, Under Secretary of Defense [Comptroller], 2017, p. 43-20).

Former Spouse

SBP premiums and coverage are the same for a former spouse as for a current spouse. Former spouse coverage can be voluntarily chosen, even if the member has remarried a different spouse. DFAS requires that retirees notify current spouses of voluntary SBP coverage of former spouses. If the divorce takes place after retirement, the member may elect coverage for the former spouse but must do so within one year of the divorce decree (DoD, DFAS, 2015b). Courts can also order a military member to elect former-spouse coverage, and the former spouse can trigger the coverage through DFAS if he or she acts within a year of the court order.

Other Opportunities to Change Coverage

Except in special circumstances, such as those outlined above, SBP members cannot change their plans after retirement. However, there are some exceptions. With spousal consent, a member has a one-time opportunity to cancel, but not otherwise change, coverage between 25 and 36 months after retirement (DoD, DFAS, 2016a). If this occurs, there is no refund of payments received, and the member is barred from future SBP enrollment. A member may also add child coverage for additional children, unless the member had children at retirement and opted not to cover them at that time. Spousal coverage may be added because of marriage or remarriage or removed because of death or divorce.

There have been a few "open seasons" mandated by Congress that allowed service members to change their coverage. These open seasons are rare and occur only when Congress determines that they are appropriate. The most recent open season was in 2005 (DoD, Under Secretary of Defense for Personnel and Readiness, 2011, p. 748).

Interaction Between SBP and VA Benefits

We describe two types of interaction between SBP and VA benefits. The first relates to VA disability compensation and concerns the payment of SBP premiums, and the second relates to VA DIC.

SBP Premiums Deducted from VA Compensation

VA pays disability benefits to veterans with "disabilities from a disease or injury incurred or aggravated during active military service" (VA, 2017c). VA disability benefits can offset military retirement benefits.[3] In instances of severe disability, where VA disability compensation is close to or exceeds a member's retired pay, little or no retired pay might remain after being offset. As a result, SBP premiums cannot be deducted from retired pay in the normal process. However, payments can be automatically deducted from the VA compensation (DoD, DFAS, 2017c).

DIC

The purpose of DIC is "to authorize a payment to the surviving dependents of a deceased military member partially in order to replace family income lost due to the member's death and partially to serve as reparation for the death" (DoD, Under Secretary of Defense for Personnel and Readiness, 2011, p. 693). An eligible surviving spouse or child may receive DIC from VA in addition to SBP if the military member

- died on active duty (or on active-duty training or inactive-duty training)

---

[3]   However, a regular retiree with a VA disability rating of 50 percent or more is entitled to concurrent retirement and disability pay (DoD, DFAS, 2013).

- died from a service-related cause
- died with a VA-rated 100 percent disability for ten years prior to death, disability rated postretirement at 100 percent for five years prior to death, or at 100 percent one year prior to death if the member was a former prisoner of war (VA, 2017g).

The spouse will receive DIC as long as he or she does not remarry before age 57 (with some caveats). The child will receive DIC only if he or she is not already included in the DIC amount going to the spouse, is unmarried, and is under 18 or between ages 18 and 23 if a full-time student.

For spouses, the basic amount of DIC was $1,257.95 per month as of December 2016, plus an additional $311.64 per dependent child and a two-year flat-rate monthly transition allowance of $270 if there are any dependent children (VA, 2017g). In cases where there is only a child recipient, the rates are $488 for one child; $701 for two children; and $915 for three children, plus $174 for each additional child (38 U.S.C. 1313).

If a surviving spouse is entitled to VA Aid and Attendance, the spouse will receive an additional $311.64 per month. Spouses are entitled to Aid and Attendance if they are another person's help with very basic daily activities, if they are bedridden, if they are in a nursing home because of a disability, or if they have severely diminished eyesight (VA, 2015).

If a surviving spouse is housebound, that person will receive an additional $145.99 per month. A surviving spouse is entitled to this if he or she is "substantially confined to immediate premises because of a permanent disability" (VA, 2015).

If the deceased veteran was entitled to receive compensation for a VA-rated disability of 100 percent for at least eight continuous years prior to death and if the surviving spouse was married to the veteran that entire time, the spouse will receive an additional $267.12 per month.

If the DIC entitlement is less than the maximum SBP benefit for which the annuitant was eligible, the SBP annuity will then be equal to the difference between this amount and the DIC annuity (DoD, Under Secretary of Defense for Personnel and Readiness, 2011, p. 739). In other words, DIC offsets SBP dollar for dollar. However, DIC is nontaxable and SBP is, so this might result in a net increase in wealth for the annuitant. When SBP is offset by DIC, the spouse is refunded the SBP premiums paid by the retiree in proportion to the offset, up to 100 percent (DoD, Under Secretary of Defense for Personnel and Readiness, 2011, p. 739).

If an SBP-annuitant spouse who had been affected by the DIC offset later loses DIC entitlement because of remarriage after age 55, the spouse will receive the original SBP annuity as if the offset had never occurred. However, the spouse must pay back the refund for the SBP premiums (10 U.S.C. 1450).

Members enrolled in SBP may cancel their coverage if they have a service-connected disability that is rated 100 percent for ten or more continuous years or rated 100 percent for at least five years postretirement (DoD, Under Secretary of Defense [Comptroller], 2017, p. 43-20). Under these conditions, their deaths are deemed service-related, and their surviving spouses will receive DIC annuities for life. If the member cancels SBP coverage, the spouse will receive a refund of all SBP premiums.

SSIA

SSIA offsets the DIC offset. If a surviving spouse is entitled to the SBP annuity, but it is offset in part or in total by DIC, then the spouse will receive $310 per month in SSIA. Congress permanently extended SSIA in the FY 2018 NDAA (Pub. L. 115-91).

Other Sources of Benefits and Support Available to Survivors

In addition to DIC and SSIA, survivors may receive other benefits and have access to other sources of monetary support. These are described in Appendix A and include the DoD Death Gratuity, Servicemembers' Group Life Insurance (SGLI), Veterans' Group Life Insurance (VGLI), Service-Disabled Veterans Insurance (S-DVI), housing, health care, financial assistance for education, commissary and exchange use, child care, burial, Social Security, unpaid pay and allowances, tax forgiveness, Parents' Dependency and Indemnity Compensation, Survivors Pension, Minimum Income Widow Annuity, and Annuity for Certain Military Surviving Spouses (ACMSS).[4]

SBP History

The Contingency Option Plan, the first program with aims similar to those of SBP, was enacted by the Uniformed Services Contingency Option Act of 1953.[5] This was a voluntary, actuarially fair plan that reduced retired pay by a set proportion in return for a survivor annuity (DoD, Under Secretary of Defense for Personnel and Readiness, 2011, p. 735). However, it had several shortcomings that appear to have dissuaded military members from participating. The money withheld from retired pay was taxable, the survivor annuity was not adjusted for inflation, the opt-in choice had to be made before knowing the amount of retired pay, the premium rate and annuity were subject to change after opt-in, and the premium rate was high (DoD, Under Secretary of Defense for Personnel and Readiness, 2011, p. 735). Although Congress improved the plan over the next 25 years, the Contingency Option Plan, later known as the Retired Serviceman's Family Protection Plan (RSFPP), never achieved more than 15 percent participation (Special Subcommittee on Survivor Benefits, House Armed Services Committee, 1970). RSFPP was terminated in 1972 and replaced by SBP.

SBP was subsidized, and as a result SBP premiums were significantly lower (DoD, Under Secretary of Defense for Personnel and Readiness, 2011, p. 737) and the participation rate was higher. The target participation rate for SBP was 85 percent (DoD, Under Secretary of Defense for Personnel and Readiness, 2011, p. 737). Figure 2.2 shows the SBP participation rate by retirement cohort from 1991 to 2016 for officers and enlisted. The combined rate was 60 percent in 1990, reached its peak of 81 percent in 2010, and was 78 percent in 2016. The officer participation rate has consistently been higher than the enlisted rate. The increase in the overall

---

[4] The National Military Family Association (2008) has prepared a guide to survivors' benefits.

[5] This section is largely based on DoD, Under Secretary of Defense for Personnel and Readiness (2011).

Figure 2.2
SBP Enrollment by FY Cohort

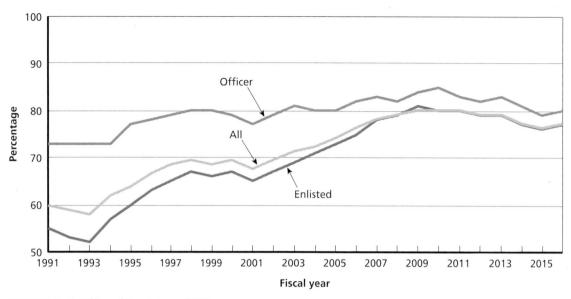

SOURCE: DoD, Office of the Actuary, 2017c.
NOTE: There was a methodology change in 2012.
RAND *RR2236-2.2*

rate was largely driven by the growing enrollment of enlisted members, whose enrollment rate converged toward that of officers.[6]

The SBP annuity was initially offset by Social Security. Until 2008, the SBP annuity of a widow at age 62 with no children was reduced "by the lesser of the Social Security survivor benefit that would be paid based solely on the member's active military service after December 31, 1956, or 40 percent of the amount of the annuity that would otherwise be payable" (DoD, Under Secretary of Defense for Personnel and Readiness, 2011, p. 739). The Survivor Benefit Plan Amendments of 1985 in the Department of Defense Authorization Act (DoDAA) of 1986 (Pub. L. 99-145) made several substantial changes to SBP with the aim of simplifying it and making it fairer. The biggest change was in how Social Security offsets were handled. The DoDAA of 1985 had removed the Social Security offset when the Social Security benefit to the spouse was from the surviving spouse's earnings. But this was "rendered ineffective" by the DoDAA of 1986 (DoD, Under Secretary of Defense for Personnel and Readiness, 2011, p. 741), in which Congress established a two-level system. The survivor would receive 55 percent of the member's retired pay and, at and after age 62, would receive 35 percent. The FY 1990 and FY 1991 NDAAs (Pub. L. 101-189 and Pub. L. 101-510) established the Supplemental Survivor Benefit Plan, which was designed to be actuarially neutral. Under it, SBP enrollees with maximum coverage could opt to provide a supplemental annuity that replaced the 55/35 Social Security offset, so spouses could receive a 40, 45, 50, or 55 percent annuity for the rest of their lives. The Social Security offset was terminated in the FY 2005 NDAA (Pub. L. 108–375), which eliminated the 55/35 Social Security offset step-wise to FY 2008.

---

[6] We do not know the reason for this. One possibility is that enlisted members have become more aware that SBP is an insurance bargain because of the DoD subsidy, and their awareness might have grown through changes in time-of-retirement financial counseling about enrolling in SBP and through information available on the internet.

The FY 1987 NDAA (Pub. L. 99-661) made several revisions to SBP (DoD, Under Secretary of Defense for Personnel and Readiness, 2011, p. 744). In divorce cases, state courts would now be able to order members to enroll in SBP for a former spouse. The age at which survivors could marry a new spouse while still retaining their SBPs was decreased from 60 to 55. If a retirement-eligible active-duty member died without a spouse, or if the spouse later died, dependent children were now authorized to receive survivor benefits. Before this, orphans would have received the benefit only if the spouse and member died "as a result of a common accident" (DoD, Under Secretary of Defense for Personnel and Readiness, 2011, p. 744). The act eliminated the 55/35 Social Security reduction for incapacitated dependent children when they reached age 62.

Other minor changes to SBP were made in the 1980s. In 1983, SBP was modified to allow former spouses to be designated as beneficiaries (DoD, Under Secretary of Defense for Personnel and Readiness, 2011, p. 740). In 1984, SBP was amended to allow payments to be authorized when the retired participant is missing (DoD, Under Secretary of Defense for Personnel and Readiness, 2011, p. 741). In 1985, Congress changed how coverage costs for SBP were calculated, lowering costs for SBP participants. Congress had aimed for a 40 percent DoD subsidy, but the level had decreased to 28 percent because the formula had not been updated to account for increases in military basic pay (DoD, Under Secretary of Defense for Personnel and Readiness, 2011, p. 742). (The current SBP subsidy is 44.6 percent.) In the same act, the FY 1986 NDAA, the SBP amendments gave more power to spouses; the service member could not defer full coverage for the spouse without the spouse's consent, unless this spouse was from a new marriage (DoD, Under Secretary of Defense for Personnel and Readiness, 2011, p. 743).

The FY 1990 and FY 1991 NDAAs (Pub. L. 101-189 and Pub. L. 101-510) lowered the SBP spousal coverage premium to its current flat rate of 6.5 percent of the base amount (DoD, Under Secretary of Defense for Personnel and Readiness, 2011, p. 746). Like the SBP Amendments of 1985, this was done to adjust the cost-sharing ratio and increase enrollment.

The FY 1999 NDAA (Pub. L. 105-261) established that SBP participants, starting in 2008, would reach "paid-up SBP" status when they had made payments for 360 months and were at least 70 years of age (DoD, Under Secretary of Defense for Personnel and Readiness, 2011, p. 767).

There have been three substantial changes to NIP coverage, which is also called *insurable interest persons*. An insurable interest is someone other than a spouse or child whom the retiree lists as the beneficiary. In the FY 1995 NDAA (Pub. L. 103-337), insurable interest coverage was changed so that it can be canceled at any time (Pub. L. 103-337).[7] In the FY 2003 NDAA (Pub. L. 108-136), insurable interest coverage rules changed such that coverage is revoked if a medically retired member dies because of disability-connected reason within one year of retirement (Pub. L. 108-136).[8] In the FY 2007 NDAA (Pub. L. 109-364), NIP coverage was made more flexible. If the insurable interest beneficiary dies, a retiree may elect a new insurable interest within 180 days (Pub. L. 109-364).[9]

---

[7] Specifically, see Pub. L. 103-337, Div. A, Title VI, §638, Title XVI, §1671(d)(2), 108 Stat. 2791, 3015.

[8] Specifically, see Pub. L. 108-136, Div. A, Title VI, §§644(a), (b), 645(a), (b)(1), (c), November 24, 2003, 117 Stat. 1517–1519.

[9] Specifically, see Pub. L. 109-364, Div. A, Title VI, §§643(a), 644(a), Title X, §1071(a)(8), October 17, 2006, 120 Stat. 2260, 2261, 2398.

The FY 2008 NDAA (Pub. L. 110-181) established SSIA to offset the DIC offset to SBP (DoD, Under Secretary of Defense for Personnel and Readiness, 2011, p. 749). The FY 2015 NDAA (Pub. L. 113-291) gave military members the option to direct deposit their annuity for incapacitated children into an SNT (DoD, DFAS, 2016b).

The FY 2017 NDAA (Pub. L. 114-328), which mandated this study, made changes for retired active-duty SBP members. SBP premium payment rules were modified so that members could pay them from combat-related special compensation (CRSC), if necessary (Kamarck et al., 2017, p. 9), and SSIA was extended to May 31, 2018.

The FY 2018 NDAA (Pub. L. 115-91) made SSIA permanent. Also, Section 622 clarified that BRS retirees who opt for a lump-sum payment of a portion of their retired pay do not pay for SBP premiums from the lump sum. The premiums are paid from the remaining retired pay. Also, the full base amount is considered to be the retired pay that would have been received without taking the lump sum.

## CHAPTER THREE

How Do SBP Benefits Compare with Survivor Benefits Available to Government and Private-Sector Employees?

We discuss the prevalence and types of work-related benefits providing income security to survivors and compare the SBP program with survivor benefits offered outside of active-duty military. SBP pays an annuity through the military retirement system's defined benefit plan; therefore, the first section describes defined benefit plans and compares them with SBP. Next, we use published tabulations showing that defined benefit plans have declined over time in private industry, so fewer employees can rely on them as a means of providing survivor benefits. However, other work-related benefits are available, including employer-sponsored defined contribution plans, life insurance, workers' compensation programs, and Social Security. We compare SBP with survivor benefits available to federal civilian employees, selected private-industry employees, and selected local public employees. The comparison is in two parts. We first compare survivor benefit generosity across plans and then present detailed examples comparing the set of benefits available to survivors covered under SBP with the set offered to analogous civilian employees.

Defined Benefit Plans

Existing military retirement systems all contain a defined benefit plan, so our discussion begins with defined benefit plans offered by public and private employers, and we first distinguish between *defined benefit* and *defined contribution plans*. A defined benefit plan is funded by the employer, sometimes also with contributions by the employee. The employer assumes the responsibility to fund the plan's liability (accrued benefits owed) and pays an annuity to eligible retirees and their surviving spouses for the remainder of their lives. Under a defined contribution plan (e.g., 401[k], 403[b]), the employer (and often the employee) makes ongoing contributions to an investment account owned by the employee. The balance from this investment account provides income for the employee in retirement and for the surviving spouse after the employee dies. The defined benefit plan provides retirement and survivor annuities with certainty, assuming the employer has funded the liability. The defined contribution plan's contributions are owned with certainty by the employee, but the rate of return on the fund is subject to risk, implying uncertainty in the annuity stream that will be available in retirement. Also, the amount available to the surviving spouse will depend on how much has already been paid out.

To understand how survivor annuities provided by nonmilitary defined benefit plans compare with SBP, it is helpful to understand the rules governing the provision of survivor annuities to employees in the private sector. Federal legislation requires defined benefit plans to offer survivor annuities. The Employment Retirement Income Security Act (ERISA) of 1974 and Retirement Equity Act (REA) of 1984 require defined benefit plans to offer a qualified joint and survivor annuity (QJSA) and a qualified preretirement survivor annuity (QPSA).[1] QJSA is a life annuity for married couples that guarantees payments for the life of a surviving spouse. These payments are generally taxable.[2] QJSA is required to be at least 50 percent, but not greater than 100 percent, of the actuarial equivalent of the single annuity for the life of the participant. Plan participants default into QJSA but can waive it during the 180-day period ending on the annuity start date. QPSA requires pension plans to offer a survivor annuity equal to at least 50 percent of the account balance at the date of death of a vested plan participant and is an annuity paid out for the life of the surviving spouse. QPSA is required to begin no later than the date at which the plan participant would have reached the plan's early retirement age. Similar to the QJSA, plan participants default into QPSA and can opt out with written consent from both the plan participant and spouse.[3]

These survivor annuity requirements apply to almost all defined benefit plans but few defined contribution plans. In addition, these requirements generally do not apply to federal, state, and local government plans, including military SBP.

QJSAs and QPSAs are the private-industry equivalent to SBP, and SBP has similarities to them. Like QPSA, SBP pays preretirement benefits if the member's death occurs before the member would have retired from the military. As noted, defined benefit plans must contain a QJSA "as the only form of benefit unless the participant and spouse, if applicable, consent in writing to another form of benefit payment,"[4] and the employee can choose the survivor benefit level similar to SBP (IRS, 2017). The spouse of a military retiree is covered by SBP at the maximum level unless the spouse agrees in writing to a lesser amount or to not be covered by SBP. With respect to funding survivor benefits, if we assume that an employer's contribution to a defined benefit plan is the same regardless of whether a worker is married, then to fund the survivor benefit, the married employee's retirement benefit must be reduced by an amount sufficient to cover the actuarial liability inclusive of the survivor benefit. This reduction can be thought of as a premium for the survivor benefit. SBP requires the military retiree to pay

---

[1] See 29 U.S.C. 1055 for details on which plans are required to offer a qualified joint and survivor annuity. The survivor annuities mandated by ERISA and REA do not need to be provided unless the participant and spouse have been married for the one-year period ending on the earlier of (1) the participant's annuity starting date and (2) the date of the participant's death. The Pension Protection Act of 2006 (Pub. L. 109–280) created an additional survivor annuity requirement. It requires pension plans to offer a qualified, optional survivor annuity for those who opt out of the QJSA and was effective for plan years beginning on or after January 1, 2008. The optional survivor annuity is designed to give married couples more options in terms of the generosity of the joint and survivor annuity. Specifically, the optional survivor benefit amount is based on QJSA. The plan must offer a 75 percent survivor annuity option if QJSA provides a survivor annuity of less than 75 percent, and the plan must offer a 50 percent survivor annuity option if QJSA provides a survivor annuity of 75 percent or greater.

[2] See IRS Publication 575, "Pension and Annuity Income," for details.

[3] The period in which a participant can opt out of a QPSA begins on the first day in the plan year when the participant reaches age 35 and ends on the date of the participant's death. If the participant is separated from the employer, then the period in which a participant can opt out of the QPSA begins no later than the date of separation.

[4] This IRS (2017) webpage adds, "The amount paid to the surviving spouse must be no less than 50% and no greater than 100% of the amount of the annuity paid during the participant's life. Alternatively, a participant who waives a QJSA may elect to have a qualified optional survivor annuity (QOSA). The amount paid to the surviving spouse under a QOSA is equal to the certain percentage (as chosen) of the amount of the annuity payable during the participant's life."

an explicit premium, but DoD subsidizes SBP. Therefore, the premium paid by the military retiree is less than that needed to fund the liability, with the subsidy making up the difference.

When a member dies on duty, the SBP annuity is computed based on what the member's retirement benefit would have been at that time (see Chapter Two).[5] Although the exact amount of the annuity depends on specifics, it is likely that the SBP annuity will often be larger than a QPSA annuity. The QPSA annuity must be at least 50 percent of the account balance at the date of the death of a vested plan participant. The account balance could be quite low for a low-tenure worker because there would be few years in which contributions were being made to the defined benefit plan, which would result in a small survivor annuity. In contrast, SBP values for the survivors of members who die on duty are calculated as if they had retired and had a 75 percent multiplier of high-36 basic pay on the date of death and the members had paid no SBP premiums. QPSAs provided to private-industry employees may be considered as being partially funded by employees if their defined benefit plan requires an employee contribution.

Table 3.1 shows access to joint and survivor annuities among workers participating in a defined benefit plan for the most recent year of the National Compensation Survey (NCS).[6] These data are split by whether the defined benefit plan is traditional or nontraditional. According to the BLS, "traditional plans calculate benefits as a percent of terminal earnings, as a percent of career earnings, as the dollar amount per month for each year of service, and as a percent of employer and employee contributions. Cash balance and pension equity plans are classified as non-traditional plans" (BLS, 2017). Nontraditional plans provide payments as a lump sum at retirement; the lump sum may be converted into an annuity.

As seen in Table 3.1, nearly all defined benefit plan participants in private industry have access to a pre- and postretirement joint-and-survivor annuity, demonstrating that most of these plans adhere to federal law. Plans not offering a QJSA or QPSA might represent noncompliance or be plans that are not subject to the requirements. The table also shows that a vast majority of state and local government employees in defined benefit plans have access to a QJSA or QPSA.

Defined Benefit Plans Have Become Less Prevalent over Time

Between 1975 and 2004, when the BLS revised its data series, the percentage of participants in private pension plans who were enrolled in defined benefit instead of defined contribution plans decreased from 71 percent to 28 percent (Employee Benefit Security Administration,

---

[5] "Members who die on active duty are generally assumed to have retired with full disability on the day they died and to have elected full SBP coverage for spouses, former spouses, and/or children. If it is more beneficial for the survivors to have elected child only because of Dependency and Indemnity Compensation (DIC) offsets, the family has the option to make that election instead. If the death does not occur in the line of duty, the SBP benefit is based on the member's years of service, rather than assuming a full disability retirement. Insurable interest elections may be applicable in some cases" (DoD, Office of the Actuary, 2017a). Disability retired pay for full (100 percent) disability is 75 percent of retired basic pay.

[6] The Bureau of Labor Statistics (BLS) provides information about the incidence and provision of employee benefits in the NCS. The NCS data are nationally representative of civilian workers, which include private-industry and state and local government employees. The data are collected in three steps: (1) probability sample by geography, (2) probability sample of establishments within sampled areas, and (3) a probability sample of occupations within sampled establishments. The BLS NCS covers years 2007 through 2016. From 1985 through 2006, the BLS administered the Employee Benefits Survey to track access to and participation in various employer-provided benefits. The survey questions are not necessarily the same as those used in the NCS.

Table 3.1
Defined Benefit Plan Features, Among Workers Participating in the Plans

	Traditional Defined Benefit Plan		Nontraditional Defined Benefit Plan	
	Access to Plans with Postretirement Joint and Survivor Annuity	Access to Plans with a Preretirement Joint and Survivor Annuity	Access to Plans with Postretirement Joint and Survivor Annuity	Access to Plans with a Preretirement Joint and Survivor Annuity
Private-industry employees, 2014	100%	99%	100%	93%
State and local government employees, 2016	95%	89%	Not reported	Not reported

SOURCES: Perez and Groshen, 2015; BLS, 2017.

NOTES: Defined benefit plans classified as traditional are those with benefits calculated as a percentage of terminal earnings, as a percentage of career earnings, as the dollar amount per month for each year of service, and as a percentage of employer and employee contributions. Defined benefit plans classified as nontraditional are plans that provide payments as a lump sum at retirement, and the lump sum may be converted into an annuity, including cash balance and pension equity plans. In 2014, 67 percent of private-industry employees participating in a defined benefit plan had a traditional plan, and 33 percent had a nontraditional plan. In 2016, 98 percent of state and local government employees participating in a defined benefit plan had a traditional plan, and 2 percent had a nontraditional plan.

2016). The implication is that fewer workers can rely on defined benefit plans as a source of survivor benefits, while more workers will rely on defined contribution plans.

The BLS records the percentages of workers with access to and participating in employer-sponsored retirement benefit plans. These statistics are also available separately for defined benefit and defined contribution plans. *Access* is defined as being available for use by the employee. Employees are considered participants if they have paid any required contributions and have fulfilled applicable service requirements.

Private Employers Are More Likely to Offer Defined Contribution Plans

Figure 3.1 depicts the percentages with access to employer-sponsored retirement benefit plans among civilian employees, in 2009 (the end of the recession in the United States) and 2016. Almost 70 percent of workers had access to any retirement plan, and 54 percent participated in a plan, in 2016; both percentages were only slightly higher in 2009. The shift from defined benefit to defined contribution plans experienced in the decades before the recession continued. The percentage of civilian employees with access to a defined benefit plan, alone or with a defined contribution plan, dropped from 31 to 27 percent over the seven years. At the same time, access to only a defined contribution plan increased from 40 to 42 percent, while access to a defined contribution plan, alone or with a defined benefit plan, decreased from 55 to 53 percent. This reflects a shift from employers offering both types of plans to employers offering only a defined contribution plan. In 2009, about 18 percent of civilian employees participated in only a defined benefit plan, 28 percent participated in only a defined contribution plan, and 57 percent participated in any retirement plan. In 2016, 14 percent participated in only a defined benefit plan, 31 percent participated in only a defined contribution plan, and 54 percent participated in any retirement plan.

Table 3.2 shows that there are substantial differences in the availability and type of retirement plans for private-industry versus state or local government employees. Two-thirds of private-industry employees had access to at least one retirement plan, and one-half participated

Figure 3.1
Access to and Participation in Retirement Benefit Plans, Civilian Employees

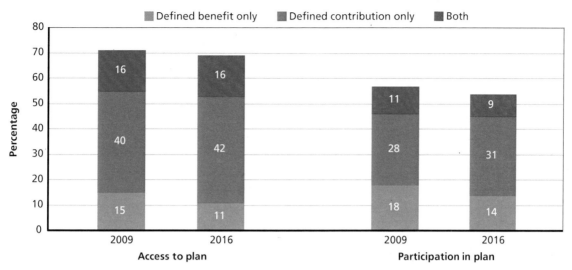

SOURCES: Perez and Groshen, 2016; Solis and Hall, 2009.
RAND RR2236-3.1

Table 3.2
Access to and Participation in Retirement Benefit Plans, by Type of Civilian Employer, 2016

	Private Industry		State or Local Government	
	Access to Plan	Participation in Plan	Access to Plan	Participation in Plan
Defined benefit plan	4%	5%	57%	66%
Defined contribution plan	48%	34%	5%	6%
Both plan types	14%	10%	28%	9%
Any plan	66%	49%	90%	81%

SOURCE: Perez and Groshen, 2016.

in a plan in 2016. Defined benefit plans were offered to only 18 percent of these employ-ees, mostly in combination with defined contribution plans. Almost half of private-industry employees had access to only a defined contribution plan.

In contrast, a substantially larger share of state and local government employees had access to and participated in an employer-sponsored retirement plan. Almost all of these work-ers had access to a defined benefit plan, and about one-third of them also had access to a defined contribution plan. Individuals eligible for both types of plans often chose to participate in only the defined benefit plan. As a result, more than 90 percent of public-employee plan participants were covered by a defined benefit plan. Only 12 percent of these defined benefit plan participants also had a defined contribution plan.

Many Defined Benefit Plan Participants Are in Plans Closed to New Employees

For the NCS, the BLS reports statistics on the percentages of defined benefits plans that are open and frozen among workers who participate in these plans. Open plans are those that allow new employees to participate. Frozen plans can be subject to a soft or a hard freeze. A soft freeze is one in which new employees are not allowed to participate but at least some existing participants continue to accrue benefits. A hard freeze is when new employees are not allowed to participate and existing participants stop accruing benefits on the date the plan is frozen.

Figure 3.2 shows the percentages of private-industry and state or local government employees in defined benefit plans with a soft or a hard freeze in 2016. About one-quarter of private-industry employees participating in defined benefit plans were in plans with a soft freeze, and half as many were in plans with a hard freeze. More than three-quarters of frozen-plan participants were in plans that were closed to new workers or stopped accruing benefits more than five years earlier (Perez and Groshen, 2016). Almost nine in ten of these workers reported that their employer offered alternative plans. The most common alternative was a defined contribution plan, reported by 35 percent (Perez and Groshen, 2016).

More state and local employees—almost 60 percent—were in frozen retirement plans. All of them were in plans with a soft freeze. All had employers that offered an alternative option, with 94 percent reporting that their employer offered a modified version of the existing defined benefit plan and 17 percent reporting access to a new defined contribution plan (Perez and Groshen, 2016).[7]

Other Work-Related Resources Providing Income for Survivors

Defined benefit plans are becoming less common, and fewer than a quarter of civilian employees participated in a defined benefit plan in 2016. Therefore, we describe other employer-sponsored

Figure 3.2
Open and Frozen Plans Among Civilian Employees Participating in Defined Benefit Plans, 2016

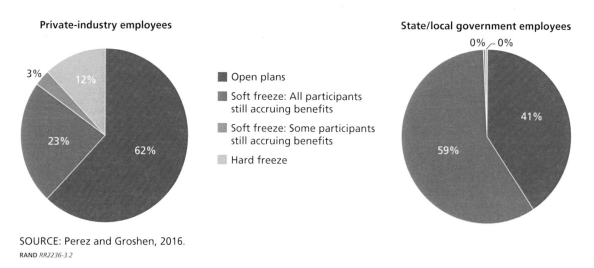

SOURCE: Perez and Groshen, 2016.
RAND *RR2236-3.2*

---

[7] Employers may offer more than one alternative, so the percentages of employees participating in each alternative are not additive.

and work-related resources providing income for surviving spouses—namely, defined contribution plans, life insurance, workers' compensation, and Social Security.

Defined Contribution Plans

Married participants with employer-sponsored defined contribution plans, such as a 401(k), usually name their spouses as the beneficiaries of the accounts. In general,[8] spouse beneficiaries may withdraw the account balance as a lump sum or roll over the account balance into their own retirement plans. The income tax treatment, early-withdrawal penalties, and required minimum distributions vary across the different options and by whether the employee contributions were pre- or after-tax, as summarized in Table 3.3.

The size of the balances of defined contribution accounts indicates the potential magnitude of this resource to surviving spouses. To examine these balances, we use the RAND Health and Retirement Study (HRS) data set.[9] HRS is a longitudinal, representative survey of individuals over age 50. The RAND HRS data (from 2016) are a version of HRS data containing a subset of variables that are harmonized across years 1992 through 2014 and reported at the individual level. The HRS allows us to infer military retiree status and ask detailed questions about income and assets, including employer-sponsored defined contribution balances. Nonmilitary individuals are defined as respondents who are not veterans and, among married respondents, restricted to those couples who do not report any veteran or military pension income. Military retirees are defined as respondents who are veterans with at least 15 years of military service (based on variables that report the years when the individual entered and

Table 3.3
Distribution Options Among Employer-Sponsored Defined Contribution Plans for Surviving Spouses

Distribution	Pay Income Tax	10% Early-Withdrawal Penalty If Under Age 59.5	Subject to Required Minimum Distributions
Pretax contributions			
Withdraw balance as lump sum	Yes	No	N/A
Roll over balance into own traditional IRA	No income tax owed to roll over account; distributions are subject to income tax	Yes	Based on survivor's age
After-tax contributions (Roth)[a]			
Withdraw balance as lump sum	No	No	N/A
Roll over balance into own Roth IRA	No	Yes	No

NOTES: Estate tax may be owed if the total combined value for all accounts associated with the estate exceeds the federal lifetime gift and estate exclusion amount. In 2017, this limit was $5,490,000. N/A = not applicable.
[a] No income tax is owed if the account had been opened for at least five years.

---

[8]   Each plan has its own set of rules, as dictated by the plan administrator. Certain plans allow the beneficiary to keep the account in the deceased person's name or to establish an "inherited" account.

[9]   The HRS is sponsored by the National Institute on Aging (grant number NIA U01AG009740) and is conducted by the University of Michigan. The sources for the HRS data are the 1992–2010 HRS Core Fat Files (HRS, 2017); RAND HRS Data, Version P (RAND Corporation, 2016); and Gustman, Steinmeier, and Tabatabai, 2014.

exited the military) who meet at least one of the following criteria: (1) Report a military pension that started within two years of leaving active-duty service, and the military pension is not unrealistically small; (2) report a nonmilitary pension that started within two years of leaving active-duty service, and the nonmilitary pension is not unrealistically small; and (3) military pension benefits started when veteran was between ages 37 and 50, and the military pension is not unrealistically small. A pension is not unrealistically small if the median reported pension benefit income amount across waves (excluding those with zero reported pension benefit income) is greater than the 75th percentile of the annualized lowest gross monthly military pension paid to an E-5 who retired within two years of the respondent's exit from active duty. Criterion 2 is meant to capture military pensions that may have been misreported as civilian pensions.

While the HRS provides a valuable source of information about the income and wealth of older Americans, it has some limitations for the purposes of our analysis. The sample size of military retirees is small, and questions about defined contribution retirement accounts apply only to those who are currently employed or reported information about employer-sponsored retirement accounts when they were first interviewed. The HRS asks respondents about their three previous jobs where they were employed for at least five years and that provided pension benefits, and respondents report the current account balances in defined contribution accounts from their current primary employer. Gustman, Steinmeier, and Tabatabai (2014) tracked these variables across HRS waves 1 through 10 and generated variables for the defined contribution wealth from a respondent's current or last job and previous jobs.

Averages of accumulated defined contribution wealth are presented in Table 3.4 for male respondents who have a positive defined contribution wealth (sum from current and previous jobs).[10] The sample sizes of nonmilitary individuals and military retirees are small, so the data for these individuals reported in Table 3.4 are subject to noise, as indicated by the large reported standard deviations. Note that 26 percent of nonmilitary men and 17 percent of male military retirees have positive accumulated wealth from defined contribution plans.

Table 3.4 provides evidence that military retirees may have lower average defined contribution balances than nonmilitary retirees do, both overall and when split by educational attainment. However, military retirees are typically age 40 or older when they retire, and the HRS is for individuals age 50 or older. Also, the military retirement system did not have a defined contribution plan. The difference in accumulated defined contribution wealth is therefore at least partially attributable to fewer years during which the military retiree could participate in a defined contribution plan. Also, the military retiree is receiving military retired pay, which is not included in the wealth shown in the table.

Life Insurance

Life insurance benefits that are paid out as a lump sum are generally not subject to income tax, while benefits paid out in installments are partially taxed.[11] Using NCS data, we tabulated the percentages of private-industry employees and state and local government employees par-

---

[10] For respondents who were interviewed more than once, we kept the observation from the most recent wave. The table includes respondents from HRS waves 1–10 who were interviewed in 1992 through 1995 and biennially from 1996 through 2010. Respondents with reported accumulated defined contribution wealth greater than the 99th percentile were top coded at the 99th percentile.

[11] See IRS Publication 525, "Taxable and Nontaxable Income," for details.

Table 3.4
Average Accumulated Defined Contribution Wealth, Men

	Nonmilitary	Military Retiree
Average	$183,440	$147,455
	(291, 831)	(166, 555)
By educational attainment		
Less than four years of college	$121,691	$111,081
	(215, 864)	(156, 405)
At least four years of college	$256,808	$175,107
	(348, 165)	(171, 553)
Unweighted observations	1,501	48
Weighted observations	9,728,601	231,089

NOTES: Our tabulations were done using the HRS (HRS, 2017; RAND Corporation, 2016; Gustman, Steinmeier, and Tabatabai, 2014). Statistics are weighted by respondent weights. Account balances are in 2015 dollars. Standard deviations are in parentheses. Accumulated defined contribution wealth variables were created by Gustman, Steinmeier, and Tabatabai (2014). Waves 1–10 include interview years 1992–1995 and biennially from 1996 through 2010. *Nonmilitary* means married respondents who are not veterans and in which the couple do not report any veteran's or military pension income. Military retirees are defined as respondents who are veterans with at least 15 years of military service (based on variables reporting the years when the individual entered and exited the military) who meet at least one of the following criteria: (1) report a military pension that started within two years of leaving active-duty service, and the military pension is not unrealistically small; (2) report a nonmilitary pension that started within two years of leaving active-duty service, and the nonmilitary pension is not unrealistically small; and (3) military pension benefits started when the veteran was between the ages 37 and 50, and the military pension is not unrealistically small. A pension is not unrealistically small if the median reported pension benefit income amount across waves (excluding zeros) is greater than the 75th percentile of the annualized lowest gross monthly military pension paid to an E-5 who retired within two years of the respondent's exit from active duty.

ticipating in employer-provided life insurance plans between 2007 and 2016. Rates of participation were stable across this period, with rates being higher among state and local government employees than those for private-industry employees. In 2016, 78 percent of state and local government workers and 54 percent of private-industry workers participated in employer-provided life insurance. Among those with access to the benefit, at least 96 percent of both groups of workers participated in each year, suggesting that workers are very likely to participate in life insurance if it is offered by their employers.

The NCS contains information about the benefit structure of life insurance plans among those with access. In general, life insurance benefits are set as a fixed amount or calculated as a fixed multiple of annual earnings. Figure 3.3 shows the percentages of workers, among those with access to life insurance plans, by benefit structure in 2016. Among private-industry employees with access to an employer-sponsored life insurance plan, 62 percent had access to a plan paying a fixed multiple of annual earnings, and 34 percent had access to a plan paying a fixed amount. Among state and local government employees with access to an employer-sponsored life insurance plan, 38 percent had access to a plan paying a fixed multiple of annual earnings, while 52 percent had access to a plan paying a fixed amount. The median multiple of earnings among employees with access to fixed multiple of earnings life insurance plan was 1.0 for private-industry employees and 1.5 for state and local government employees. The median maximum benefit was $250,000 among private-industry employees and $100,000 among state

Figure 3.3
Life Insurance Benefit Structure, Among Employees with Access to Life Insurance Plans, 2016

SOURCE: Perez and Groshen, 2016.
NOTE: "Other" includes life insurance plans that calculate benefits as a variable multiple of earnings, offer a
variable dollar amount payment, or use some other benefit calculation.
RAND RR2236-3.3

and local government employees (Perez and Groshen, 2016).[12] Among workers with access to
a flat-amount life insurance plan, which is a plan that provides a fixed life insurance benefit
amount, the median maximum benefit was $20,000 in 2016 for both private-industry and
state and local government employees (Perez and Groshen, 2016).

A limitation of NCS data is that they apply only to current workers, so we use HRS data
to obtain the percentage of individuals age 50 or older covered by life insurance, regardless of
whether it is provided through their employers and regardless of whether they are employed.
These statistics are weighted, restricted to married men, and calculated for military retirees
and nonmilitary respondents.[13] The data show that 65 percent of nonmilitary respondents and
84 percent of military retirees had life insurance. One reason the military retiree percentage
could be higher than the nonmilitary respondents' percentage is if military retirees include
SBP in responding to the question about life insurance, in addition to other life insurance. Earlier, Table 2.1 showed that 66 percent of all military retirees in FY 2016 were enrolled in SBP.

The percentage of military retirees with life insurance is much higher than the employer-
sponsored life insurance participation rates in NCS data. However, in the NCS data, we cannot
ascertain whether workers have life insurance plans outside of their employers.

Workers' Compensation

Workers' compensation programs are another source of income security for survivors, specifically survivors of an employed family member. These programs provide insurance against
work-related injuries, diseases, and deaths. All states and the District of Columbia offer their

---

[12] The median maximum benefit is restricted to plans where a maximum benefit amount is imposed. Among private-industry employees with access to a fixed-multiple-of-earnings life insurance plan, 70 percent had access to plans with a maximum benefit amount in 2016. Among state and local government employees with access to a fixed-multiple-of-earnings life
insurance plan, 54 percent had access to plans with a maximum benefit amount in 2016.

[13] For respondents who were interviewed more than once, we kept the information from the most recent interview wave.
We used data for respondents from waves 1 through 12, which cover years 1992 through 1995, and, biennially, 1996
through 2014.

own workers' compensation programs, and, with the exception of Texas, participation in workers' compensation is required for most private-industry employers. Both cash and medical benefits are offered through these programs, and the generosity of benefits varies across states. In January 2016, maximum weekly death benefits ranged from $432.60 in Idaho to $1,628 in Iowa, for example, and states have different rules regarding how long survivors may receive benefits (Baldwin and McLaren, 2016). Certain groups of workers, including federal civilian employees, have their own workers' compensation program other than those offered by states. In 2014, an estimated 91 percent of the employed U.S. workforce was covered by workers' compensation (Baldwin and McLaren, 2016). Workers' compensation benefits, including death benefits, are not subject to income tax.

Social Security

Social Security survivor benefits are described in Appendix A and summarized in Appendix Table B.5. Table 3.5 provides the number of survivors, by type of beneficiary, as of December 31, 2016. In total, there were 6.0 million individuals receiving Social Security survivor benefits, of which 4.1 million were surviving spouses and 1.9 million were surviving children. The Social Security Administration (SSA) estimated that total benefits paid to surviving children and surviving spouses (includes aged and disabled widows and widowers) were $19.8 billion and $95.8 billion, respectively, in 2016 (SSA, undated-a).

Table 3.5
Beneficiaries of Social Security Survivor Benefits, December 31, 2016

Beneficiaries	Number of Beneficiaries
Widows and widowers	
Aged	3,744,962
Young	132,757
Disabled	259,207
Total	4,136,926
Children	
Minor	1,179,370
Disabled	654,531
Students	59,058
Total	1,892,959
Parents	1,208
Total	6,031,093

SOURCE: SSA, undated-b.

NOTES: To be eligible for Social Security survivor benefits, an "aged" widow or widower must be at least 60 years old, and a "young" widow or widower must have a child under 16 or a disabled child in his or her care. Disabled widows and widowers must meet disability requirements and be at least 50 years old. A minor child is a child under 18. A disabled child is a child disabled before the age of 22. A student child is a high school student under age 19. A parent is a parent of the deceased worker that must have been dependent on the deceased worker and be at least 62 years old.

Comparing SBP with Other Programs: Introduction

To understand how SBP compares with other programs, we conducted narrow and broad comparisons. We first compare SBP with survivor benefits plans offered to federal civilian employees through the federal CSRS and the Federal Employee Retirement System (FERS), as well as with those offered by selected public and private employers. We then present examples comparing the amounts from the set of benefits available to those covered by SBP—SBP along with other death-related benefits—with the amounts from the set of benefits available to analogous nonmilitary employees covered under other survivor plans.

Comparing SBP with Other Programs: Survivor Benefit Generosity

In this section, we compare the generosity of the survivor benefit annuity of SBP under the regular retirement and BRS with FERS, CSRS, and selected public and private defined benefit plans. Each defined benefit plan is based on the employee's retirement annuity, in which the annuity formula depends on final average salary (FAS) or, for the military, high-36 basic pay, service tenure, and benefit rate. The definition of *FAS* varies across the plans (see Tables B.5 and B.6). In Tables 3.6 and 3.7, we consider two cases: survivor benefits available to a retiree with 20 years of service and those available to a retiree with 30 years of service. To get a sense of how generosity varies across the plans, we use the SBP multiplier to compare the FAS multiplier for the retiree and, separately, for the survivor, in the nonmilitary plans. The multiplier is the percentage applied to FAS to calculate the benefit. The SBP multiplier applies to the high-36 basic pay.[14] The comparison assumes that a retiree would choose the default survivor benefit option and that the survivor benefit option is calculated using the entire retirement annuity as the base amount. The multipliers for the retiree's retirement benefit include required premium costs and reductions to the annuity to pay for the default survivor benefit option.

There are a few caveats. First, employers may offer other benefits, such as a defined contribution plan or life insurance. The other benefits are not captured here. As a result, employees with a less generous defined benefit plan may have access to other benefits that put them on equal or even better financial standing than employees with a more generous defined benefit plan. Second, salary differences across employers would affect FAS levels. Third, if a military retiree has a second career, then he or she would potentially have access to survivor benefits and income protections through the second job, in addition to SBP. Fourth, the private and local public plans included in the comparison discussed and included in Table 3.7 are illustrative and were chosen because they offer an employer-sponsored defined benefit plan with publicly available details. While these plans may not necessarily be representative of a typical private-sector employee, their default survivor annuity options range widely from no survivor annuity to a survivor annuity equal to 75 percent of the retiree benefit. We hope that this range of generosity covers the spectrum of survivor benefits offered to employees outside federal service.

Table 3.6 compares SBP with CSRS and FERS. Under all three, survivor benefits are adjusted for cost-of-living increases. CSRS is being phased out and applies only to employees

---

[14] Basic pay is about two-thirds of regular military compensation, a general measure of military compensation that is the sum of basic pay, Basic Allowance for Housing (BAH), Basic Allowance for Subsistence, and an adjustment for the allowances not being subject to federal income tax. Thus, we describe SBP with respect to high-36 basic pay, recognizing that this is less than regular military compensation. We use FAS for retirement plans outside the military.

Table 3.6
Survivor Benefit Annuity Generosity SBP Versus Federal Civilian

	Military Survivor Benefit	Military SBP Under BRS	CSRS	FERS
Pension calculation	Entered service after September 7, 1980: 2.5% × years of service × high-36	Opt into BRS: 2% × years of service × high-36, plus TSP matching up to 5% of basic pay	Age 62+ and 5 years of service, age 60+ and 20 years of service, or age 55+ and 30 years of service First 5 years: 1.5% of high-3 Second 5 years: 1.75% of high-3 All years over 10: 2% of high-3	Age 62 or older at separation with 20 or more years of service = 1.1% × high-3 average salary × years of service Under age 62 at separation for retirement or age 62 with less than 20 years of service = 1% × high-3 average salary × years of service
Default survivor benefit option	55%	55%	55%	50%

	Percentage of High-36 Basic Pay[a]		Percentage of FAS[a]	
Example 1: annuitant with 20 years of service				
Retiree	46.8%	37.4%	32.4 to 35.1%	19.8%
Survivor	27.5%	22.0%	19.9%	11.0%
Example 2: annuitant with 30 years of service				
Retiree	70.1%	56.1%	50.4 to 54.6%	29.7%
Survivor	41.3%	33%	30.9%	16.5%

NOTE: The high-3 average salary is the average of the highest average basic pay earned during any three consecutive years of service.

[a] The percentage multiplied by high-36 basic pay (military) or FAS (nonmilitary) to calculate the benefit. The percentage is net of the cost of premiums or reductions in pension benefit from selecting the default survivor benefit option. For military SBP both with and without BRS, the pension benefit is reduced by 6.5 percent—e.g., 50 percent is reduced to 48.75 percent. For CSRS, the annual pension benefit is reduced by 2.5 percent of the first $3,600, plus 10 percent of the annual pension benefit amount over $3,600. The range presented for the FAS multiplier assumes a 2.5 to 10.0 percent reduction in pension benefit. For FERS, the pension benefit is reduced by 10 percent.

who entered federal civilian service before January 1, 1984.[15] FERS covers employees who entered federal civilian service on or after January 1, 1984.[16] CSRS includes only a defined benefit. By design, FERS has a less generous defined benefit plan than CSRS does but includes

---

[15] Employees covered by CSRS had the opportunity to change over to the FERS system during 1987 and 1998 open seasons.

[16] The FERS system also includes employees hired after December 31, 1986, with less than five years of creditable service or who transferred to the FERS system during open season. *Creditable service* means civilian and military service for which deductions or deposits are in the former employee's retirement account, civilian service for which the survivor makes a deposit, or military service performed before 1957.

Table 3.7
Survivor Benefit Annuity Generosity SBP Versus Select Public and Private-Employer Plans

	Military Survivor Benefit	Military SBP Under BRS	Los Angeles Fire and Police Pension	Chicago Public Schools	Washington State Employees	Kaiser Permanente Employee Pension Plan	Ford Motor Company United Auto Workers Retirement Plan	Exxon Mobil Pension Plan
Pension calculation	Entered service after September 7, 1980: 2.5% × years of service × high-3	Opt into BRS: 2% × years of service × high-3, plus TSP matching up to 5% of basic pay	Years-of-service percentage × FAS; Years-of-service percentage starts at 40% for 20 years, increases 3 percentage points per year for years 21–25, increases 4 percentage points per year for years 26–30, increases 5 percentage points per year for years 31–33	2.2% × FAS × years of service	2% × FAS × years of service	1.45% × FAS × years of service	Annuity (ranges from $53.55 to $54.30) × years of service (depending on employee class, benefit rates apply to retirement after October 1, 2010)	(1.6% × FAS × years of service) – Social Security offset; Social Security offset is 1.5% of estimated Social Security benefit × pension service (up to a max of 33.33 years)
Default survivor benefit option	55%	55%	70%	66.67%	0[a]	50%	65%	50%
	Percentage of High-36 Basic Pay[a]		Percentage of FAS[a]					
Example 1: annuitant with 20 years of service								
Retiree	46.8%	37.4%	40.0%	40.5 to 43.6%	40.0%	26.1 to 27.6%	20.9%	28.8 to 30.4%[c]
Survivor	27.5%	22.0%	28.0%	29.3%	0.0%[b]	14.5%	14.3%	16.0%
Example 2: annuitant with 30 years of service								
Retiree	70.1%	56.1%	75.0%	60.7 to 65.3%	60.0%	39.6 to 41.8%	31.4%	43.2 to 45.6%[c]
Survivor	41.3%	33.0%	52.5%	44.0%	0.0%[b]	21.8%	21.5%	24.0%

NOTE: Calculations are based on our interpretation of plan descriptions and are simplified for illustrative purposes.

[a] The percentage multiplied by high-36 basic pay (military) or FAS (nonmilitary) to calculate the benefit. The percentage is net of the cost of premiums or reductions in pension benefit from selecting the default survivor benefit option. For military SBP both with and without BRS, the pension benefit is reduced by 6.5 percent. There is no premium to Los Angeles Police Department annuitants if they select the default survivor benefit option. For Chicago Public School annuitants, the default survivor benefit is funded through an employee payroll contribution equal to 1 percent of salary. As a result, the cost calculated as a reduction to pension benefits depends on the annuitant's earnings history and length of time that pension benefits are paid out. Using a sample earnings profile for Chicago Public School teachers from Knapp et al. (2016), we assume the cost would translate to a 1 to 8 percent reduction in pension benefits, which corresponds to the annuitant receiving pension benefits for 5 to 30 years. The Kaiser Permanente and Exxon Mobil annuitants' pensions are actuarially reduced when the default survivor benefit option is selected. For comparison, we assumed that the reduction ranged from 5–10 percent, which roughly covers the range of reductions for other plans presented here. The Ford Motor Company's annuitant pension is based on hourly rates published in United Auto Workers Local 387 (2007) and is reduced 5 percent when the default survivor benefit option is selected.

[b] Default is no survivor annuity. Instead, the survivor gets remaining employee contributions plus interest as a lump sum.

[c] Excludes Social Security offset.

the addition of a defined contribution plan (TSP) and Social Security. Details about CSRS and FERS survivor benefits are in Appendix B.

The default survivor benefit is 55 percent of the retirement annuity for SBP and CSRS and 50 percent for FERS. These percentages are equal or close to one another. Thus, measured in terms of the default survivor benefit percentage, SBP appears comparable to the federal programs. But this measure of comparability does not account for differences in the generosity of the defined benefit retirement annuity across programs. When we account for these differences, the multiplier is larger for military retired pay than for either FERS or CSRS. For example, for 20 years of service, the multiplier is 46.8 percent[17] for the military retiree net of the SBP premium (37.4 percent under BRS) but only 32.4 to 35.1 percent for CSRS[18] and 19.8 percent for FERS. The multiplier for the survivor is 27.5 percent for the military survivor[19] (22 percent under BRS), but 19.9 percent for CSRS, and 11 percent for FERS.[20]

A broadly similar result is found when we compare SBP with a selected set of local government and private-sector survivor benefits. Table 3.7 compares the generosity of the SBP annuity with those offered by the Los Angeles Fire and Police Pension Fund (LAFPPF), Chicago Public Schools, Washington State, Kaiser Permanente, Ford Motor Company United Auto Workers Retirement Plan, and Exxon Mobil. Many of these employers have provided different defined benefit plans to their workers depending on which plan details were publicly available when an employee was hired. The plans summarized here apply to the most recent cohort of employees. Benefits provided by LAFPPF, Chicago Public Schools, and Washington State are documented as being adjusted for cost of living or subject to annual increases to account for inflation.[21] More information about each plan is in Table B.6.

With the exception of the Washington State employee pension plan, SBP and the other public and private plans in Table 3.7 provide a survivor annuity as the default option for married participants. Kaiser Permanente and Exxon Mobil have a default survivor annuity of 50 percent of the retiree annuity. Ford Motor Company has a default of 65 percent, Chicago Public Schools has a default of 66.67 percent, and LAFPPF has a default of 70 percent. As mentioned, the default survivor option for SBP is 55 percent, so these alternative plans appear to provide a better benefit. But once we account for differences in the computation of the retirement annuity, SBP is generally similar to or better than these other plans.

Specifically, for 20 years of service, the multiplier is 46.8 percent under the regular retirement system, which is higher than multipliers of all other plans. The 37.4 percent multiplier under BRS is in line with the other plans. The FAS multiplier for the other plans ranges from

---

[17] The retired pay multiplier at 20 years of service is 50 percent. The SBP premium is 6.5 percent, leaving a net multiplier of 46.75 percent—50 × (1 − 0.065)—or 46.8 percent rounded.

[18] For CSRS, the annual pension benefit is reduced by 2.5 percent of the first $3,600, plus 10 percent of the pension benefit amount over $3,600. The range presented for the FAS multiplier assumes a 2.5 to 10 percent reduction in pension benefit.

[19] 55 percent of the retired pay multiplier of 50 percent = 27.5 percent.

[20] Similarly, for 30 years of service, the multiplier net of the SBP premium is 70.5 percent for the military retiree (56.1 percent under BRS), 50.4 to 54.6 percent for CSRS, and 29.7 percent for FERS. Because the retired pay multiplier (before reductions in premiums are included) is larger for military retirement benefits, the multiplier for the military survivor is 41.25 percent (33 percent under BRS), compared with 30.9 percent for CSRS, and 16.5 percent for FERS.

[21] Documentation about inflation protection could not be found online for Kaiser Permanente, Ford Motor Company, or Exxon Mobil. This does not necessarily mean that benefits are not inflation-protected.

20.9 percent for Ford Motor Company United Auto Workers to 43.6 percent for the Chicago Public School system. Assuming that retirees choose the default survivor benefit option, a survivor of a military retiree would receive 27.5 percent of final basic pay (22 percent under BRS). This is roughly the same (or smaller in the case of BRS) as the rates for a survivor of a Los Angeles police officer or firefighter (28 percent) and of a former Chicago Public School employee (29.3 percent). A Washington State employee plan (plan 3) has a defined benefit component and a defined contribution component (see Washington State Department of Retirement Systems, 2016). The plan does not offer a survivor annuity as the default option but instead refunds remaining employee contributions in the defined contribution component, plus interest, as a lump sum. The retiree has an option to purchase a joint and survivor annuity of 50 percent, 67 percent, or 100 percent of the retirement annuity.

For a military retiree with 30 years of service, his or her pension net of the SBP premium is 70.1 percent of high-36 basic pay under the regular retirement system (56.1 percent under BRS). A retiree of the Los Angeles Fire or Police Department would receive a pension equal to 75.0 percent of FAS. The FAS multiplier for the other plans ranges from 31.4 percent for Ford Motor Company to 65.3 for Chicago Public Schools. The default FAS multiplier for the survivor annuity is 52.5 percent for LAFPPF, 44.0 percent for Chicago Public School, and 41.3 for the regular military retirement system (33.0 percent under BRS). The military percentages are higher than those for the Ford Motor Company, Kaiser Permanente, and Exxon Mobil. The same comments as above apply to the Washington State employee plan.

Thus, judging by the multiplier for survivor benefits, SBP is typically more generous or in line with the selected plans. SBP is less generous under BRS, but BRS has a TSP with DoD (and member) contributions. The additional available income from the defined contribution plan is not accounted for in this comparison.

SBP's multiplier is more than twice as large as that for FERS under the regular retirement system and exactly twice as large under BRS. This does not necessarily mean that FERS survivors are worse off compared with survivors of military retirees in the regular retirement system, given that FERS survivors may have access to TSP account balances. However, survivors under BRS will also have access to TSP account balances and, as seen, have higher multipliers than do FERS survivors.

Comparing SBP with Other Programs: Detailed Examples

The percentage comparisons in Table 3.7, while useful, give a partial view of how military survivor benefits compare with benefits available to nonmilitary survivors. First, SBP beneficiaries may be eligible for benefits in addition to SBP, and the same is true for nonmilitary survivor benefit programs. Second, as is clear from the descriptions of SBP in Chapter Two and of the private- and public-sector plans in Appendix B, survivor benefit plans have multiple features that make comprehensive comparisons of programs challenging. Third, the percentages, of course, do not show benefit amounts. To address these issues and provide a more comprehensive comparison of the set of benefits available, we constructed examples of the one-time and ongoing benefits that survivors would receive, incorporating the multiple sources of possible benefits for which the survivor may be eligible.

We consider two sets of examples. The first set compares benefits available after a *currently employed* individual dies. These examples are meant to provide comparisons of survivor benefits for a military member who dies on duty relative to employees who die while employed for other organizations. The second set focuses instead on retirees and compares benefits available after the death of a *retired* employee or a military retiree. For each set of examples, we describe the assumptions and the types of benefits a survivor would receive and then compare the SBP beneficiary with nonmilitary counterparts.

Examples of current-employee deaths include the following:

- enlisted service member
- federal civilian employee under FERS, enlisted equivalent
- private-industry employee, enlisted equivalent
- Los Angeles police officer, enlisted equivalent (see Appendix D).

Examples of annuitant deaths include the following:

- officer annuitant under regular retirement plus federal civilian service under FERS
- officer annuitant under BRS plus federal civilian service under FERS
- FERS annuitant, officer equivalent
- private-industry annuitant, officer equivalent
- enlisted annuitant under regular retirement plus federal civilian service under FERS
- enlisted annuitant under BRS plus federal civilian service under FERS
- FERS annuitant, enlisted equivalent
- private-industry annuitant, enlisted equivalent
- officer annuitant, SBP and DIC optimization examples (see Appendix D)—specifically,
  - officer annuitant under regular retirement, one child
  - officer annuitant under regular retirement, two children.

To depict the benefits available to survivors in the examples, we assume a pay profile for the employee on which the retirement benefit—and therefore the survivor benefit—is based. For the civilian pay profile for enlisted personnel, we use the median wage by years of service for full-time male workers with associate's degrees. For officers, we use the 80th percentile wage for full-time male master's degree holders in management occupations. The data on civilian pay are from the U.S. Census Bureau. In examples where a survivor receives Social Security survivor benefits, we use SSA's detailed online calculator.[22] We assume that the deceased did not have any other employment except for that described and assume that the surviving spouse would not experience any reduction in benefits owing to his or her own employment or employment history. We further assume that the annuity streams are inflation-protected and that the amounts are in 2017 dollars. When we compare year-by-year annuity streams, we do not discount them to compare them with the 2017 federal poverty line. This comparison allows us to get a sense of how the survivor's financial well-being changes as a result of the death and the adequacy of survivor benefits in providing support. Further, we provide the present discounted value of the stream of income to compare the value of aggregate survivor benefits with the survivor across the examples.[23]

---

[22] To access the online calculator, see SSA, 2017.

[23] For these examples, we used a discount rate of 6 percent, which was the estimated personal discount rate at entry or accession for officers in previous RAND studies (Asch, Hosek, and Mattock, 2014; Mattock, Hosek, and Asch, 2012). Our main findings are robust to choosing both lower and higher discount rates. For example, the result that military survivor benefits are in line with or more generous than survivor benefits provided by FERS or to survivors of the private-industry employee remains unchanged if we use a 0 percent personal discount rate or a 20 percent personal discount rate.

Current-Employee Death Examples

These examples compare the benefits for survivors of an enlisted member who is killed in action with those of a FERS-eligible employee and a private-industry employee who die from a work-related injury. Because the FERS-eligible employee and private-industry employee die from a work-related injury, their survivors are eligible to receive death benefits through workers' compensation. We show examples for two cases: surviving spouse with no children and surviving spouse with one child age one and one child age three. In each case, we show estimates of annual total benefits for 30 years following the death. Thirty years is long enough to see how survivor benefits evolve as children get older. Table 3.8 includes a summary of assumptions and types of survivor benefits available for each example. Detailed descriptions of the benefits and assumptions are in Appendix C.

For the enlisted member example, we assumed that the member was born on January 1, 1994, entered military service at age 20, and died in 2017 after three years of service. We chose to have the military service member die after three years based on 2007 DoD actuary tables showing that the highest death rates for most non–retirement-eligible enlisted service members were in the age range 18–23 (DoD, Office of the Actuary, 2008). Because the enlisted pay profile assumes an entry age of 20, we assume that the enlisted member dies after three years of service to obtain a high-36 average salary at age 23. Because the enlisted member was killed in action, the surviving spouse is eligible for DIC, which is estimated to be greater than SBP in the example. As a result, DIC offsets the SBP amount completely, and the spouse receives DIC each year and, in addition, receives SSIA each year to compensate for the offset. In the examples with children, the surviving family would also receive an additional DIC allowance

Table 3.8
Current-Employee Death Summary of Assumptions and Benefits

	Enlisted	Federal FERS	Private Industry
Date of birth	1/1/1994	1/1/1987	1/1/1987
Date entered employment	1/1/2014	1/1/2007	1/1/2007
Years of service	3	10	10
Date of death	1/1/2017	1/1/2017	1/1/2017
Cash annuity	DIC, SSIA, Social Security	OWCP, Social Security	California workers' compensation, Social Security
Cash lump sum	BAH, death gratuity, SGLI, unpaid pay/allowances, tax forgiveness, Social Security	Refund of FERS contributions, FEGLI, OWCP benefits, Social Security	California's workers' compensation, life insurance, Social Security
Other resources	*Marine Gunnery Sergeant John David Fry Scholarship or DEA, burial, childcare, TRICARE, and other minor benefits*	TSP (assume lump sum distribution), *federal employee health benefits*	Defined contribution plan (assume lump sum distribution)

NOTES: Italicized benefits are not included in the figures. DEA = Survivors' and Dependents' Educational Assistance; OWCP = Office of Workers' Compensation Programs (U.S. Department of Labor); FEGLI = Federal Employee Group Life Insurance.

per year per dependent child under age 18 and a flat-rate DIC transition allowance for two years. Survivors of the enlisted member would be eligible to receive Social Security survivor benefits. The lump-sum benefits include BAH,[24] the death gratuity, SGLI, unpaid pay and allowances, and tax forgiveness. The largest cash lump sum benefits come from the death gratuity ($100,000) and the SGLI payout ($400,000).

The federal FERS-eligible employee and private-industry employee are born on January 1, 1987, begin working at age 20, and die after ten years of service. For these examples, we assume that the employee had ten years of service rather than three as in the enlisted example to try to demonstrate the differences in risk between military and nonmilitary jobs. Further, we hold the date of death constant across all the examples so that the survivor benefit comparison can be made across the same set of years.

The survivors of the FERS-eligible employee are assumed to receive federal workers' compensation death benefits through OWCP instead of survivor benefits through FERS, since OWCP benefits are estimated to be greater than those from FERS, and survivors must choose between the two sources of benefits. Survivors of the FERS-eligible employee would also be eligible to receive Social Security survivor benefits. We assume that the federal employee was killed during work with the military in a contingency operation and is eligible to receive the OWCP death gratuity. The largest cash lump sum benefits come from the OWCP death gratuity ($100,000) and the life insurance payout from FEGLI ($110,000). In terms of other cash lump-sum benefits, we include the refund of FERS employee contributions and other OWCP lump-sum benefits. In addition, we assume that the survivor would cash out the deceased employee's TSP account balance, which is estimated to be about $50,000.

The private-industry employee is assumed to be covered by the State of California workers' compensation program (CA workers' comp), and the survivors would receive cash annuity benefits from CA workers' comp and Social Security. In addition, the survivor would receive a burial-expense allocation through CA workers' comp, the Social Security lump-sum payment, and a life insurance payout. We assume that the private-industry employee had life insurance of $250,000, which is the median maximum for private-industry employees with access to a fixed-multiple-of-earnings life insurance benefit plan, as reported by BLS. Finally, survivors of the private-industry employee are assumed to cash out the deceased employee's defined contribution account balance, estimated to be about $34,000.

Figure 3.4 depicts the one-time payment in the year of death and the cumulative benefits over 30 years across the three examples for the case of a surviving spouse and no dependent children. Survivors of the enlisted member receive the largest payout in the year of death, at about $0.5 million. Survivors of the FERS-eligible employee and private-industry employee receive a one-time payment of about $0.3 million in the year of death. As noted, the 30 years of cash benefits shown in the figure are discounted.

Figure 3.5 shows annuity payments year by year over 30 years. Across all three examples, the survivor would receive annual cash annuity payments greater than the federal poverty line for a one-person household ($12,060 in 2017). The annuity for a surviving spouse of an enlisted member is less than that for a FERS survivor. The annual cash annuity for the survivors of the enlisted member and FERS-eligible employee is equal to 156 percent and 219 percent of the federal poverty line percentage, respectively. However, when we examine cumula-

---

[24] Although BAH is monthly, the survivor receives BAH (or on-base housing) for a one-year period, so, for simplicity, we count it as a lump sum.

Figure 3.4
Current-Employee Death Comparison of Survivor Benefits 30 Years After Death, No Children

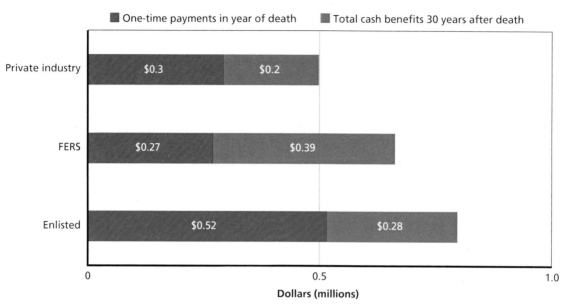

NOTE: Benefits are discounted using an annual discount rate of 6 percent.
RAND RR2236-3.4

Figure 3.5
Current-Employee Death Annuity Comparison, No Children (2017 Dollars)

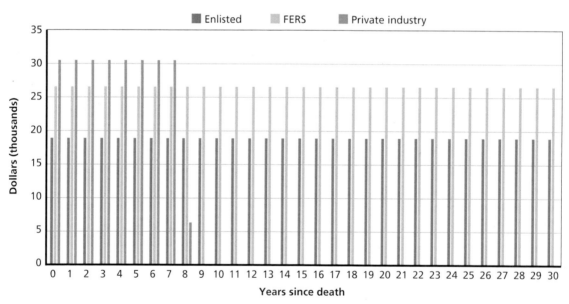

RAND RR2236-3.5

tive discounted benefits over a 30-year period, including the lump-sum payments in the year of death, in Figure 3.4, total benefits under SBP ($0.80 million) are greater than those provided by FERS ($0.66 million). The annuity paid to a surviving spouse of a private-industry employee is greater than that paid to the surviving spouse of the enlisted member in the first seven years (Figure 3.5). These are the CA workers' comp installment payments. Once they are completed, the surviving spouse does not receive a cash annuity until reaching full retirement age, which occurs beyond 30 years after the employee's death. During the first seven years in which the survivor receives full CA workers' comp payments, those payments equal more than 250 percent of the federal poverty line. Comparing total cumulative benefits over 30 years (Figure 3.4), benefits for the enlisted spouse are more generous than those for the spouse of the private-industry employee, $0.80 million versus $0.50 million.

The ranking of benefits is robust to the choice of survival period. For example, if we shorten the survival period to 15 years, total military survivor benefits ($0.72 million) are greater than those provided by FERS ($0.56 million), which in turn is greater than those provided to survivors of the private-industry employee ($0.50 million). If we increase the survival period to 70 years, military, FERS, and private-industry survivor benefits are $0.85 million, $0.73 million, and $0.50 million, respectively.

Figures 3.6 and 3.7 present benefits in 2017 dollars for a surviving spouse with two children, age one and age three, in the year of death. The one-time payments in the year of death are the same as those estimated for a surviving spouse with no children. Focusing on annual benefits, Figure 3.7 shows reductions in benefits for survivors of the enlisted member, FERS-eligible employee, and private-industry employee in years 15 and 17. These reductions reflect lower total family Social Security survivor benefits available when children turn age 16 and 18. Additionally, children age out of dependent benefits under SBP benefits, federal workers'

Figure 3.6
Current-Employee Death Comparison of Survivor Benefits 20 Years After Death, Two Children

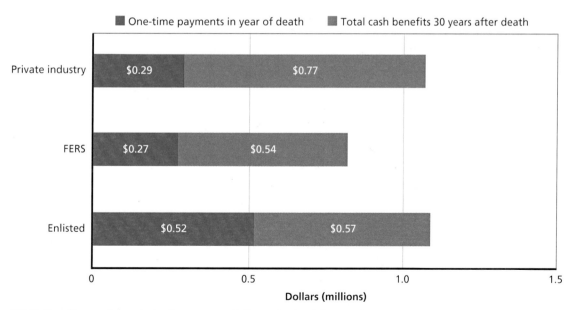

NOTE: Benefits are discounted using an annual discount rate of 6 percent.
RAND RR2236-3.6

Figure 3.7
Current-Employee Death Survivor Annuity Comparison, Two Children (2017 Dollars)

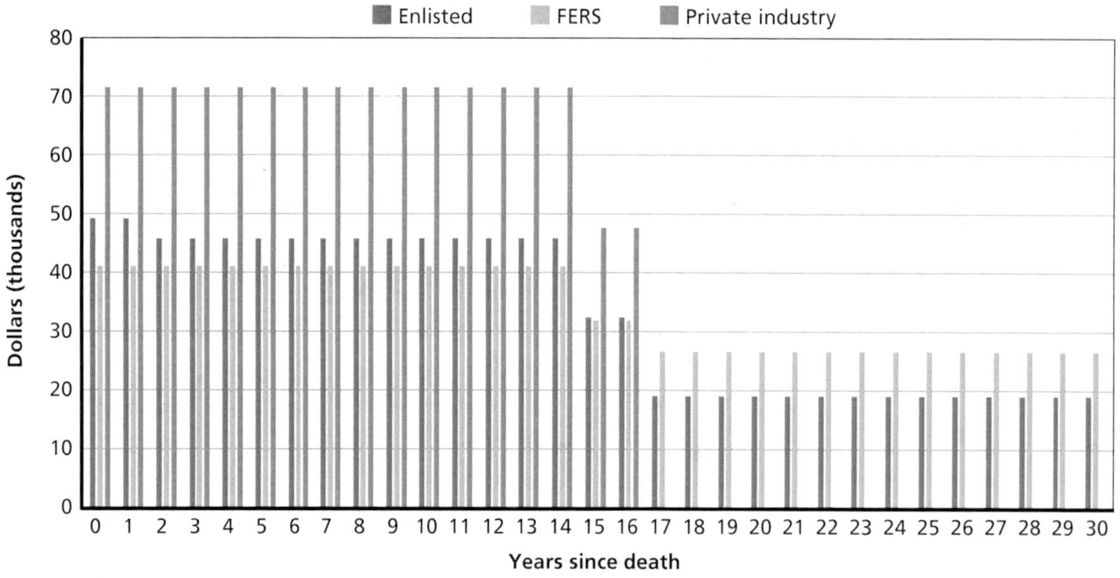

RAND RR2236-3.7

compensation death benefits, and CA workers' comp, which corresponds to the reduction in benefits in year 17.

The annuity for survivors of the FERS-eligible employee is the least generous until year 15, when the cash annuity becomes roughly equal to that offered to survivors of the enlisted member. In year 17, the cash annuity for the FERS survivor exceeds the annuity for the survivor of the enlisted member. Because we assume that survivors of the FERS-eligible employee would opt for OWCP benefits, these differences are due to differences between the benefits offered under OWCP and SBP.

For the enlisted and FERS examples, the surviving family's annual annuity exceeds the federal poverty line each year. For the survivor of the enlisted member, the survivor annuity ranges between about 150 to 240 percent of the federal poverty line. For the survivor of the FERS-eligible employee, the survivor annuity ranges between about 200 to 220 percent of the federal poverty line. The surviving family of the private-industry employee in our example receives benefits only until the youngest child turns age 18. While they receive benefits, the cash annuity is between about 290 to 350 percent of the federal poverty line.

SBP total discounted survivor benefits are greater than those provided by FERS and about the same as those provided to survivors of the private-industry employee (Figure 3.6). Survivors of the FERS-eligible employee have total benefits of about $0.8 million; the private-industry employee survivors and SBP survivors have total benefits of about $1.1 million.

Although the relative generosity of total benefits depends on the age of the surviving children and the time horizon chosen, our overall conclusion that military survivor benefits are in line with or more generous than those provided in the other examples remains robust. In the example described above, we assumed that the surviving children are ages 1 and 3. If we instead assume that the surviving children are ages 8 and 10, then aggregate benefits for survivors of the enlisted member ($1.0 million) would exceed those for survivors of the FERS-eligible employee and private-industry employee (both $0.8 million). This change in relative generosity is a result of workers' compensation benefits for children available under FERS and CA workers' comp, which end when the youngest child turns age 18. As a result, we find that survivor benefits for the enlisted member are in line with or more generous when the surviving children are assumed to be young and are more generous when the surviving children are assumed to be older.

Using a shorter time horizon (e.g., 15 years versus 30 years) will increase the relative generosity of survivor benefits for the private-industry employee compared with those for the FERS-eligible employee and enlisted member because the CA workers' comp installment payments are paid in the years right after the death occurs, as depicted in Figures 3.7. A 15-year time horizon for the family with two surviving children results in private-industry survivor benefits being slightly larger than those provided by SBP ($1.05 million versus $1.01 million). These benefits are both greater than those provided by FERS ($0.70 million) under a 15-year time horizon.

Using a time horizon greater than 30 years will not change total discounted benefits for survivors of the private-industry employee, since benefits end 16 years after the employee dies. However, lengthening the survival period increases total benefits for military and FERS survivors. For example, under a 70-year time horizon, total discounted benefits under SBP are $1.14 million, compared with $1.09 million using a 30-year survival period. Total benefits under FERS are $0.89 million under a 70-year time horizon, compared with $0.82 under a 30-year time horizon. Although benefits increase for military and FERS survivors under the longer survival period, military and private-industry benefits remain similar, and both are greater than those provided by FERS.

Annuitant Death Examples

These examples compare the benefits for survivors of a military retiree who had a secondary career in federal civilian service with those for survivors of federal employees retired under FERS and for survivors of employees who retired from private industry. The examples are constructed separately for a retired officer and a retired enlisted member. We assume that the military retiree chose to work for the federal government following military service and is covered by FERS as a federal employee. The private-industry retiree is covered by Social Security and had access to an employer-sponsored defined contribution plan but not a defined benefit plan. This example is meant to typify what a survivor of a private-industry retiree might have access to in terms of income security.

In both sets of examples, we assume that a married individual had a total of 40 years of service or employment. For the officer-plus-FERS example, the individual served as an officer for the first 20 years and worked as a federal civilian employee under FERS for another 20 years. The DoD, Office of the Actuary (2017c), report shows that the modal years of service when members retire is 20 years of service. We assume that the individual was born on January 1, 1947, and died at age 70 on January 1, 2017.

We assume that the service member and FERS retiree chose the default survivor benefit option. As a result, the survivor of the service member receives benefits from SBP, a survivor annuity under FERS, and Social Security survivor benefits, and the survivor of the FERS-eligible employee receives an annuity through FERS and Social Security. The survivor of the private-industry employee receives Social Security survivor benefits only. In terms of lump-sum payments, the survivor of the officer is estimated to receive FEGLI, the $255 Social Security lump sum, and a refund of unpaid DoD retired pay. The survivor of the FERS-eligible employee receives cash lump-sum payments from FEGLI and Social Security, while the survivor of the private-industry employee receives the lump sum from Social Security only.

In examples in which the deceased employee had an employer-sponsored defined contribution plan, including retired FERS-eligible employees with a TSP account, service members under BRS, and the private-industry employee, we assume that the survivor would be subject to required minimum distributions beginning in the year of death. The required minimum distributions were based on Charles Schwab's online estimator;[25] we assume that the surviving spouse is age 70.5 in the year of death, and the account balance is the amount predicted in the example on the date of death. We assume that defined contribution account balances have an annual real rate of return of 5 percent. For examples with the retired FERS-eligible employee, we note that survivors may be eligible to continue Federal Employee Health Benefit insurance coverage after the death, and this benefit is not included in the comparison, nor is the value of the health benefit available to military retirees.

Table 3.9 summarizes the assumptions and survivor benefits available for each example, by type of employee. Detailed descriptions of the benefits are described in Appendix C. We make separate comparisons by whether the deceased was an officer or an enlisted member, and we construct federal civilian and private-industry counterparts for each. The type of survivor benefits available are the same regardless of whether a retiree is an officer or enlisted member or whether the examples of retired civilians are created to be comparable to an officer or enlisted. The main difference is the assumed pay profiles, with pay being greater for officers.

To compare the package of survivor benefits for an officer retiree across the different examples, we present annual estimates of total benefits for a 20-year span after death (Figures 3.8 to

Table 3.9
Annuitant Death Summary of Assumptions and Benefits

	Military Plus Federal	FERS	Private Industry
Date of birth	1/1/1947	1/1/1947	1/1/1947
Date of employment	Military: 1/1/1970–12/31/1989 Federal: 1/1/1990–12/31/2009	1/1/1970–12/31/2009	1/1/1970–12/31/2009
Years of service	Military: 20 Federal: 20	40	40
Date of death	1/1/2017	1/1/2017	1/1/2017
Cash annuity	SBP, FERS, Social Security	FERS, Social Security	Social Security
Cash lump sum	FEGLI, Social Security, unpaid DoD retired pay	FEGLI, Social Security	Social Security
Other resources	*TRICARE* For BRS: TSPs (assume the maximum contribution rate and that required minimum distributions apply)	TSPs (assume that required minimum distributions apply), *federal employee health benefits*	Defined contribution plan (assume that required minimum distributions apply)

NOTE: Italicized benefits are not included in the figures.

---

[25] Required minimum distributions were estimated using Schwab's online individual retirement account calculator; see Charles Schwab, undated.

3.11) and total cumulative benefits (Figure 3.12). Even though benefit amounts differ across the examples, the surviving spouse would receive income well above the federal poverty line, in all cases.

Figures 3.8 and 3.9 compare survivor benefits under regular military retirement with those under BRS in 2017 dollars. Benefits under BRS are greater than those under regular

Figure 3.8
Officer Plus FERS, Regular Retirement System (2017 Dollars)

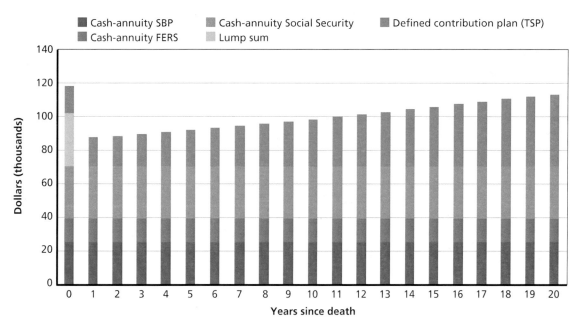

RAND *RR2236-3.8*

Figure 3.9
Officer Plus FERS, BRS (2017 Dollars)

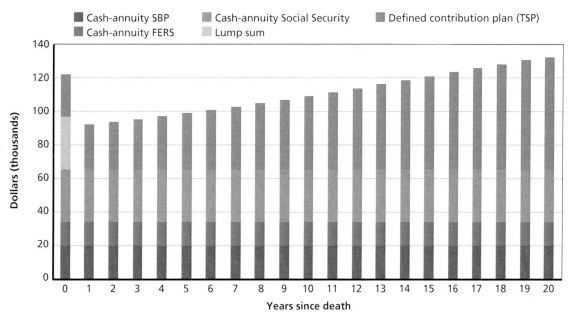

RAND *RR2236-3.9*

retirement in all years. This is because the required minimum distributions from the TSP account more than offset the smaller SBP annuity under BRS. The example assumes that employee contributions into TSP were set to 5 percent to maximize government-matching contributions (5 percent). Annual benefits range between about 725 and 980 percent of the federal poverty line under regular military retirement and between 590 and 870 percent of the federal poverty line under BRS. Figures 3.10 and 3.11 show that survivor benefits in 2017 dollars under FERS are comparable but less generous than those available under SBP and that the surviving spouse of a private-industry employee would have the lowest benefits compared with the other three examples. Survivor benefits under FERS range between about 765 and 1,100 percent of the federal poverty line, while the surviving spouse of the private-industry employee receives benefits ranging between 450 and 660 percent of the federal poverty line.

Cumulative discounted benefits depicted in Figure 3.12 show that the survivor of an officer retiree would receive $1.23–$1.35 million in benefits 20 years after the death, while the survivor of a retired FERS-eligible employee would receive $1.05 million and the survivor of the retired private-industry employee would receive $0.80 million.

Parallel comparisons for an enlisted retiree are in Figures 3.13 to 3.16, with total cumulative discounted benefits in Figure 3.17. Again, the surviving spouse in each example would receive income well above the federal poverty line.

Figures 3.13 and 3.14 look at survivor benefits in 2017 dollars under regular retirement and those under BRS, respectively. Survivor benefits equal between 440 and 560 percent of the federal poverty line under regular retirement and between 460 and 630 percent of the federal poverty line under BRS. Benefits under BRS are greater than under regular retirement in all years; required minimum distributions from the TSP account more than offset reductions in the SBP annuity under BRS. Figure 3.15 shows that survivor benefits in 2017 dollars under FERS are comparable to those under SBP with BRS and more generous than those under

Figure 3.10
FERS, Officer Equivalent (2017 Dollars)

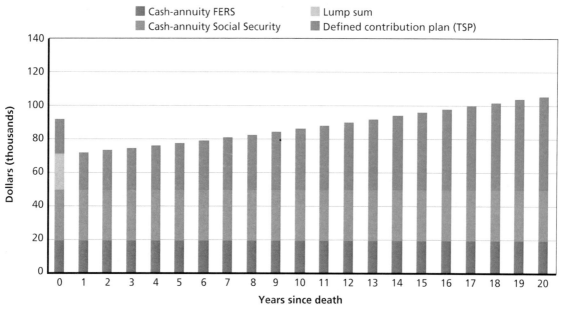

RAND RR2236-3.10

Figure 3.11
Private Industry, Officer Equivalent (2017 Dollars)

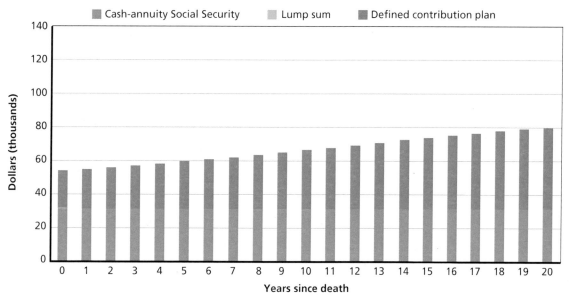

RAND RR2236-3.11

Figure 3.12
Officer Annuitant Comparison of Survivor Benefits 20 Years After Death

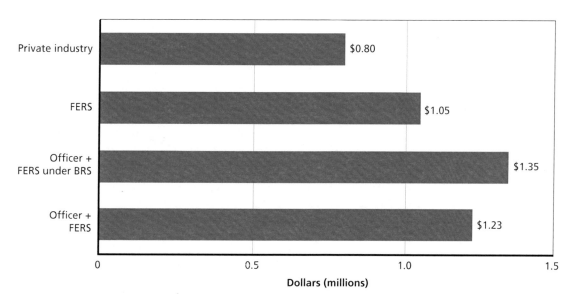

NOTE: Benefits are discounted using an annual discount rate of 6 percent.
RAND RR2236-3.12

Figure 3.13
Enlisted Plus FERS, Regular Retirement System (2017 Dollars)

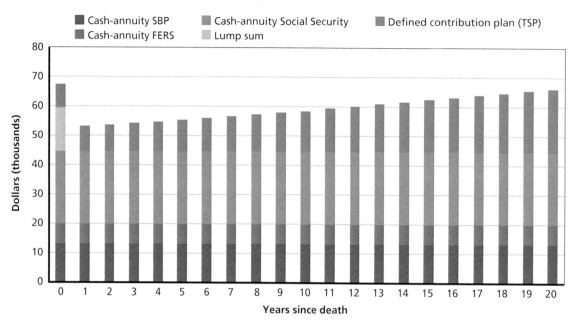

RAND RR2236-3.13

Figure 3.14
Enlisted Plus FERS, BRS (2017 Dollars)

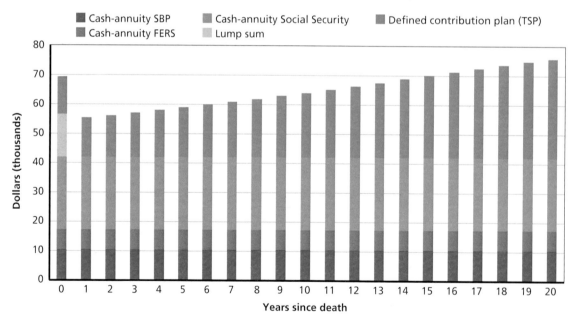

RAND RR2236-3.14

Figure 3.15
FERS Enlisted Equivalent (2017 Dollars)

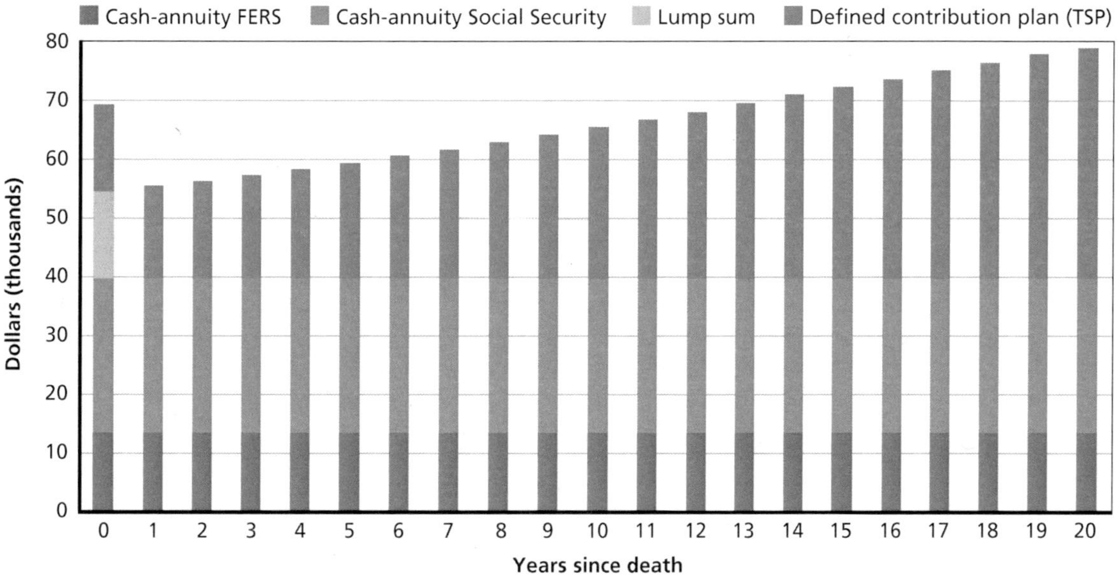

RAND *RR2236-3.15*

SBP with regular retirement. FERS survivor benefits provide income in the range of 460 to 650 percent of the federal poverty line each year. Figure 3.16 shows that the surviving spouse of a retired private-industry employee would have the lowest amount of benefits (in 2017 dollars), compared with the other three examples. Annual survivor benefits for the private-industry annuitant are equal to 310 to 410 percent of the federal poverty line. Cumulative discounted benefits depicted in Figure 3.17 reveal that total survivor benefits under FERS, regular military retirement, and military retirement under BRS are similar, ranging from $0.73 to $0.80 million. The surviving spouse of the retired private-industry employee would receive about $0.52 million.

The result that military SBPs under regular retirement or BRS are in line with those provided by FERS and more generous than those for the private-industry employee survivor remains even if we choose a smaller discount factor or reduce the assumed employer and employee contributions to defined contribution accounts. For example, if we assume that the survivor lives for ten years instead of 20 years, the present discounted value of total survivor benefits over the ten-year period is about $0.5 million for the survivor of the enlisted member (under regular retirement and BRS) and for the survivor of the enlisted equivalent FERS annuitant. These are all greater than that for the survivor of the enlisted equivalent private-industry annuitant ($0.3 million). Similarly, using a ten-year survival period, total benefits for the survivor of the officer are $0.80 to $0.85 million (under regular retirement and BRS), which is greater than that for the officer-equivalent FERS annuitant (about $0.5 million) and private-industry annuitant (about $0.7 million).

As an extreme case, we assume that the service member and FERS-eligible employee would not make any employee contributions to their TSPs. Thus, the only contributions made to TSPs come from the 1 percent employer contribution. Under this scenario, total benefits are lower than our baseline case, but we again find that total military survivor benefits are

Figure 3.16
Private-Industry Enlisted Equivalent (2017 Dollars)

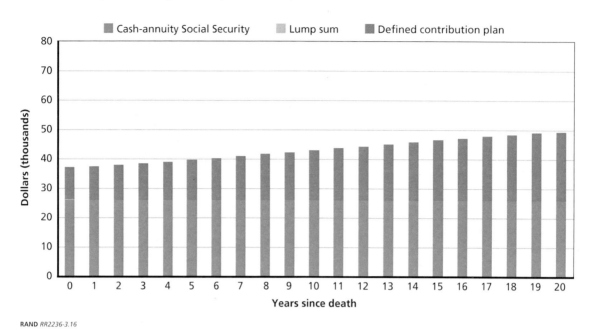

Figure 3.17
Enlisted Annuitant Comparison of Survivor Benefits 20 Years After Death

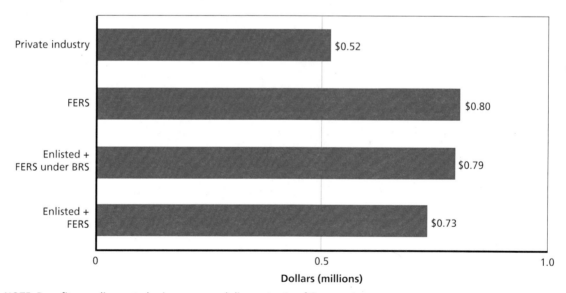

NOTE: Benefits are discounted using an annual discount rate of 6 percent.

in line with or greater than benefits provided to survivors of the FERS annuitant or private-industry annuitant. Total discounted benefits range from $0.52 million for a survivor of an enlisted equivalent private-industry annuitant to $0.56–$0.59 million for a survivor of an enlisted annuitant. The total survivor benefits for the enlisted equivalent FERS annuitant is $0.54 million. For the officer example, total discounted benefits provided by the military are $0.90–$0.94 million, which are greater than benefits provided by FERS ($0.68 million) and by private industry ($0.80 million).

Conclusions

SBP is available through the military's defined benefit retirement plans. Defined benefit plans offered by state and local governments often offer survivor benefits, and private-industry defined benefit plans are required by law to offer survivor benefits. However, defined benefit plans have become less prevalent. The fraction of workers participating in employer-sponsored defined benefit plans has decreased over time, and a large share of employees participating in these plans are in plans no longer available to new employees. Today, the main sources of survivor benefits include employer-sponsored defined contribution plans, life insurance, workers' compensation (in the case of work-related deaths), and Social Security.

To compare SBP with survivor benefit programs, we conducted two types of analysis. We compared survivor benefit annuity generosity among SBP, federal civilian programs, and selected private and public defined benefit plans. This comparison demonstrated that the SBP annuity, as a percentage of FAS, was more generous than or in line with what other programs offered.

We also constructed examples to compare the package of benefits available to survivors receiving SBP with those for survivors of workers under FERS and in private industry. We considered the survivors of workers who died on the job and compared them with the survivors of service members who died on duty. We also considered the survivors of military retirees and compared them with survivors of retired FERS-eligible and private-industry employees.

The current-employee death examples show that benefit generosity for those outside the military hinges on the generosity of the workers' compensation program. The examples indicated that SBP is more generous than benefits offered to a survivor of a FERS-eligible employee who dies from a service-connected death. When a surviving spouse has no children, cumulative benefits under FERS and SBP are similar and are greater than those offered to a surviving spouse of a private-industry employee. When surviving spouses have children, cumulative benefits for the surviving family of the enlisted member and private-industry employee are greater than those offered under FERS.

In the examples comparing survivor benefits among retirees, we find that SBP is generally in line with or more generous than FERS or private-industry survivor benefits. In the officer-retiree examples, the SBP benefits under both regular retirement and BRS are more generous than benefits for survivors of retired FERS-eligible employees and private-industry employees. In the enlisted retiree examples, the SBP benefits under BRS are similar to those for the FERS retiree and higher than the SBP benefits under regular retirement, which in turn are higher than survivor benefits for the private-industry employee.

## CHAPTER FOUR

Evaluating the Effectiveness of SBP

We present our analysis of the effectiveness of SBP in terms of providing survivors with intended benefits. The term *intended benefits* is used in the FY 2017 NDAA (Pub. L. 114-328) guidance for this review, and we interpret it to mean whether SPB is providing benefits so that survivors are as financially well off as the survivors of other types of employees—i.e., nonmilitary. This seems reasonable in light of the deliberations of the 1970 Special Subcommittee on Survivor Benefits, House Armed Services Committee, which noted that the creation of a military survivor benefit would bring military compensation in line with the compensation packages of public and private employers. Other interpretations could be used, such as whether survivors are as well off financially as before their spouses died. However, given that the FY 2017 NDAA directs the review to compare SBP with benefits available to government and private-sector employees, we focus on comparisons of military survivors and survivors of other types of employees. Thus, our approach for measuring effectiveness involves comparing the financial status of widows receiving survivor benefits from the military with that of widows receiving survivor benefits from other sources, as well as widows not receiving survivor benefits. We examine the type and amount of income received, including survivor benefits, their contribution to total income, and whether the survivor is below the poverty line and participates in government public assistance or transfer programs. The chapter differs from Chapter Three by looking at empirical data and extending the context to view survivor benefits as a component of total income. The results we show differ depending on whether the widow is receiving Social Security, so we compare widows given that they do, or do not, receive Social Security, and in each of those groups, we compare widows by their main source of survivor benefits.

Ideally, in comparing the status of widows receiving SBP with others, we would like to have detailed data on the widows and on their deceased spouses, such as education and history of labor-force participation. Unfortunately, the available data limit the conclusions we can draw about SBP, as any systematic difference we see in the status of widows receiving SBP from others may be attributable to unobserved characteristics. Our data show that, generally, SBP widows compare well, but there is a category where this is not the case. This may not indicate a shortcoming of SBP but could derive from prior differences—for instance, lower earnings of the now-deceased spouses of widows receiving SBP compared with widows receiving survivor benefits from other sources—or from differences in the amount of survivor benefit coverage selected. Our data do not include such information, yet we recognize that more-detailed analysis is needed to better understand this and determine whether remedies to the SBP program are warranted.

Overall, our findings indicate that survivor benefits from any source (e.g., the military, companies or unions, and other sources aside from Social Security) are relatively uncommon among widows. Less than one in five reported receiving survivor benefits. We also find that, conditional on the receipt of survivor benefits, they constitute a relatively large source of income for survivors, especially if the widow is not receiving Social Security income (which is the case for widows who are younger than 60, not disabled, and not caring for the deceased's children).

Among widows who receive survivor benefits, we find that the average amount received from the military is similar (among widows who do not receive Social Security) or larger (among widows who do receive Social Security) than the average amount received from companies or unions. The contribution to total income of the benefits received from the military is also similar or larger than the contribution of the benefits received from companies or unions. Most widows who receive survivor benefits from the military or from companies or unions are not below the federal poverty line and are unlikely to receive income assistance from the government. Compared with other sources of survivor benefits, benefits paid by the military are, on average, similar to those paid by VA and smaller than those paid by the federal government and by state and local governments. While our comparisons adjust for differences in observed characteristics of widows, the lack of data on the decedents and correlations in decedent characteristics and main source of survivor benefits could affect our findings.

In this chapter, we describe the data, the information they include, and their limitations. We then describe the percentage of widows with access to Social Security and other survivor benefits. We compare the characteristics of widows receiving survivor benefits, by source, and separately include widows who do not receive them. We then develop inverse probability weights to ensure that nonmilitary widows are similar to military widows in terms of age, race, education, and other observable characteristics. We apply the weights and compare the amount of survivor benefits and total income of widows who receive survivor benefits from different sources and of widows who do not receive survivor benefits. This is followed by a discussion of the relative contribution of survivor benefits to the total income of widows, information about the poverty status of widows, and their participation in public assistance programs.

Data Sources and Variables Measured

We use the Annual Social and Economic Supplement (ASEC) of the Current Population Survey (CPS),[1] pool 20 years of data (from 1996 to 2015), and adjust income measures to 2015 dollars. The sample is limited to widows who are not remarried and age 40 or older. Widows under age 40 are less than 2 percent of all widows in the data, and some of them are very young (e.g., in their 20s). We exclude them for two reasons. They are less likely to serve as a good comparison for widows of military retirees, and, given their young ages, they should be studied separately; however, the small sample size prevents us from doing that analysis. When we refer to widows below, we are referring to those age 40 and older. The final data set contains 102,882 observations.[2]

---

[1]   We accessed the data using the Integrated Public Use Microdata Series at the University of Minnesota (Flood et al., 2017).

[2]   This is the number of unweighted observations. In all tables and figures discussed in this table, we use the person-level weights provided by the Integrated Public Use Microdata Series (Flood et al., 2017) or the weights we constructed to increase comparability of widows receiving survivor benefits from different sources.

The measure of income captured in the CPS ASEC, known as *money income*, is defined as the pretax income that is received by individuals from regular sources in the previous year. It includes wages and salaries, self-employment income, property income, government transfer payments (i.e., Social Security, unemployment and workers' compensation, and public assistance), retirement income (i.e., private and government),[3] interpersonal transfers (e.g., alimony and child support), and other recurrent income. It does not include nonearnings; lump-sum payments; in-kind income; and transfer payments, such as employer-provided food, Medicare, Medicaid, the Earned Income Tax Credit, food stamps, heating and rental subsidy, and public housing. It also does not include employer contributions to retirement or pension plans. In the following, *total income* refers to total money income as measured in the CPS ASEC—total cash income from recurring sources.[4]

One of the regular sources is survivor benefits other than Social Security payments. Respondents can report survivor benefits received regularly from up to two sources. We recorded the amount of survivor benefits received from each of the following sources: military survivor pensions, companies or unions, federal government pensions, state or local government survivor pensions, regular payments from annuities or paid-up life insurance, and other sources.[5] When we refer to *survivor benefits*, we refer to payments other than Social Security, unless noted.

The CPS ASEC also asks respondents to report the total amount of regular payments received from VA. Respondents report whether they receive those payments for any of the following reasons: survivor benefits,[6] educational assistance, veterans' pensions, disability compensation, or another type of veterans' payments. Less than 2 percent of widows who reported receiving payments because of survivor benefits also reported a second reason for receiving regular payments from VA. Therefore, in our analysis, in the cases of widows who reported receiving payments from VA because of survivor benefits, we recorded the total amount of VA payments received as the amount of the survivor benefits.

There are some limitations of the CPS ASEC. First, we cannot directly identify widows of deceased military retirees, or more generally, widows of deceased veterans. We can identify only whether a widow is receiving survivor benefits from the military or VA. Thus, we are not able to identify widows of deceased military retirees who opted out of SBP. These widows are pooled with other widows who are not receiving survivor benefits or with widows who are receiving survivor benefits from other sources, depending on the situation. Also, we cannot establish the relationship of the person receiving the survivor benefit from the military or VA with the deceased veteran. We expect that, in most cases, it would be the surviving spouse, but it could also be, for example, a surviving mother with low income.

---

[3] Although the CPS ASEC asks about regular payments from IRA, Keogh Plan, or 401(k) accounts, there is evidence that income from these sources is underreported. Surprisingly, more regular income from defined benefit pension plans also appears to be underreported (Bee and Mitchell, 2017).

[4] See Rothbaum and Income Statistics Branch (2015) for more thorough discussion of the definition of *money income* in the CPS ASEC and how it compares with other definitions of *income*.

[5] Benefits from other sources are income received from the U.S. railroad retirement survivor pensions, workers' compensation pensions, black-lung survivor pensions, regular payments from estates or trusts, and other unidentified sources.

[6] These payments might include DIC or a death pension paid to a spouse or to the parents of a deceased veteran (if their incomes fall below a threshold). Given the age cutoff in our sample, these payments would not include children of a deceased veteran. For survivors to be eligible, the deceased veteran must have died from disease or injury incurred or aggravated while on active duty or during military training or from a disability compensated by VA.

The second limitation is that we do not know the before-death income of the deceased spouse. Thus, we cannot compare the income of the household before and after the spouse dies. Our analysis is restricted to the income of the widows and the extent to which survivor benefits received, by source, contribute to it.

The third limitation, related to the previous one, is that we observe only characteristics of the widow (e.g., age, race, and education) but not of the deceased spouse. When we develop inverse probability weights and apply them to ensure that we are comparing similar cases, we can only make those adjustments based on the widow's characteristics.

Finally, although the CPS ASEC is the source of the nation's official household income and poverty statistics, there are still concerns about the accuracy of the income reported, especially at older ages. Comparing the 2012 CPS ASEC with administrative records, Bee and Mitchell (2017) found underreporting of retirement income from defined benefit pensions (including survivor and disability payments) and retirement account withdrawals.[7] The authors found that this underreporting occurs mostly at the extensive margin. People who receive retirement income fail to report any of it 46 percent of the time. In contrast, when reported, they do it relatively accurately. The authors also found that survivor income is not reported less accurately than other types of retirement income are. We do not have access to administrative income records and therefore cannot assess the level of misreporting of SBP. However, although our analysis is likely to miss SBP recipients because of underreporting, Bee and Mitchell (2017) also found that misreporting is only weakly related to demographic characteristics. Therefore, we expect the group of widows reporting receipt of SBP in the CPS ASEC to be roughly representative of the population of recipients.

The average amount of survivor benefits received from the military is about $12,000 annually in the CPS ASEC, which matches relatively well with the average monthly annuity of $1,140 in FY 2016, which was reported in Table 2.1 and based on administrative data from DoD's Office of the Actuary (2017c). Therefore, we find evidence that, as suggested by Bee and Mitchell (2017), conditional on reporting, the CPS ASEC accurately measures SBP benefits. Nevertheless, widows can still underreport other sources of retirement income. Therefore, the analyses we present are likely to underreport the total income of widows and overreport the share of survivor benefits to total income. However, since underreporting retirement income is only weakly correlated with demographic characteristics, we expect that the degree of underreporting is similar across widows who report survivor benefits from different sources. Thus, the analyses in this chapter still provide relevant information regarding how SBP compares with other sources of survivor benefits in terms of size and contribution to total income.

Reported Survivor Benefits and Social Security Income

In the data, about 80 percent of widows reported having Social Security income. This might include income from their own retirement, disability, or widowhood or income received on behalf of surviving, dependent, or disabled children. The fact that most widows report Social

---

[7] Bee and Mitchell (2017) reported that, in 2012, the CPS ASEC showed that the median household income was $33,800 for householders age 65 and older, and the poverty rate was 9.1 percent for persons age 65 and older. However, when linked administrative records were used, the median household income was $44,400 (30 percent higher), and the poverty rate was just 6.9 percent.

Security income reflects the age profile of the typical widow.[8] The typical widow in the sample is 76 years old. Among widows age 70 or older, 90 percent receive monthly payments from Social Security, and these payments compose more than 70 percent of total annual income (see Figures 4.1 to 4.3).[9]

Figure 4.2 and Figure 4.3 indicate that survivor benefits other than Social Security are far less common among widows. The typical widow of age 76 has only an 18.3 percent probability of receiving any type of regular payments associated with survivor benefits. Taking the average across all widows, including those with zero survivor benefits, such benefits account for only about 5 percent of the total income. Even if we consider a false-negative rate of 46 percent (meaning that almost half of individuals having survivor income fail to report it), as suggested in Bee and Mitchell (2017), we would find that only a third of widows receive survivor benefits.

Figure 4.4 shows that, among widows who reported receiving survivor benefits, the most common source, at 8.7 percent, is companies or unions. About 1.2 percent of widows receive survivor benefits from the military, and 2.1 percent receive survivor benefits from VA (3.3 percent receive benefits from either VA or the military).

Given that Social Security payments are the main source of income for widows, in the rest of the chapter, we study the financial status of widows by separating them into two groups: those who receive payments from Social Security and those who do not. Furthermore, we classify widows by their receipt and source of survivor benefits not provided by Social Security.

Figure 4.1
Distribution of Widows, by Age

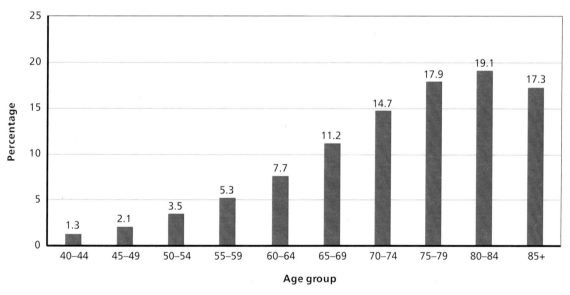

SOURCE: Data from CPS ASEC, 1996–2015 (Flood et al., 2017).
NOTES: Sample includes widows of age 40 and older. The total number of observations is 102,882.
RAND RR2236-4.1

---

[8] As discussed in Chapter Two, widows may receive Social Security at age 60 or older or at age 50 or older if they are disabled. Widows may also receive Social Security if they are caring for the deceased's child who is under age 16 or disabled.

[9] The 70 percent figure includes widows receiving no Social Security payments. The percentage would be slightly higher if the computation were limited to widows receiving some Social Security payments.

Figure 4.2
Receipt of Payments from Social Security and Other Survivor Benefits

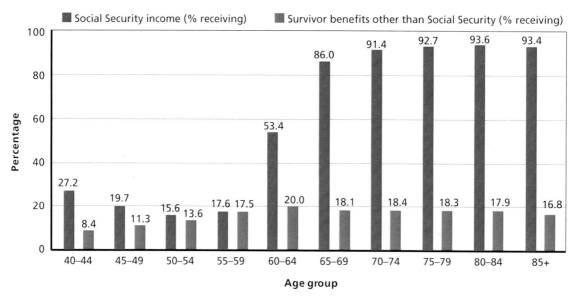

SOURCE: Data from CPS ASEC, 1996–2015 (Flood et al., 2017).
NOTES: Sample includes widows (who are not remarried) age 40 and older. All calculations are weighted using person-level weights for the analysis of the CPS ASEC. The total number of observations is 102,882.
Refer to Figure 4.1 for the fraction of observations in each age group.
RAND *RR2236-4.2*

Figure 4.3
Average Contribution of Payments from Social Security and Other Survivor Benefits to Total Income

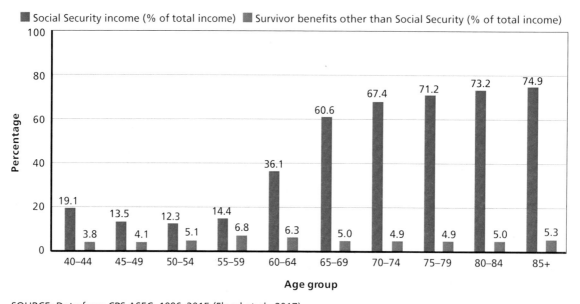

SOURCE: Data from CPS ASEC, 1996–2015 (Flood et al., 2017).
NOTES: Sample includes widows (who are not remarried) age 40 and older. All calculations are weighted using person-level weights for the analysis of the CPS ASEC. The total number of observations is 102,882. Refer to Figure 4.1 for the fraction of observations in each age group.
RAND *RR2236-4.3*

Figure 4.4
Sources of Survivor Benefits (Other Than Social Security)

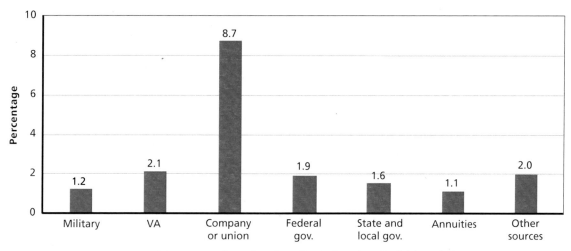

Main source of survivor benefits (other than Social Security)

SOURCE: Data from CPS ASEC, 1996–2015 (Flood et al., 2017).
NOTES: Sample includes widows (who are not remarried) age 40 and older. All calculations are weighted using person-level weights for the analysis of the CPS ASEC. Annuities include regular payments from annuities or paid-up life insurance. Other sources are U.S. railroad retirement survivor pension, workers' compensation pension, black-lung survivor pension, regular payments from estates or trusts, and other unspecified sources. The total number of observation is 102,882.
RAND *RR2236-4.4*

Most widows (94.6 percent) with survivor benefits receive them from a single type of source. However, for those who reported receiving benefits from more than one type of source, we classify them according to the following two-step procedure:

1. We pool in one group widows who receive any survivor benefits from the military or VA, and we pool in a second group widows who receive survivor benefits from other sources but not from the military or VA.
2. In each of these two groups, we classify widows according to the source that provided them with largest amount of benefits. We define this as her main source of benefits.
    a. For example, if a widow receives survivor benefits from the military and VA, we determine the military as her main source if the survivor benefits received from the military are larger than those received from VA (note that this classification is based on the amount effectively received by the survivor, which may include the DIC offset).
    b. Similarly, if a widow receives survivor benefits from employers and from paid-up life insurance, we determine that the employer is her main source of survivor benefits if they are larger than the regular payments received from life insurance.

The categories for the main source of survivor benefits include military, VA, company or union, federal government, state or local government, annuities (which include regular payments from annuities or paid-up life insurance), and other sources.[10] There is also a category for no survivor benefits. We use these categories in Tables 4.1 through 4.9.

Characteristics of Recipients of Social Security and Survivor Benefits

Using the classification described above, we compare widows' characteristics by their receipt of Social Security payments and survivor benefits. These comparisons are presented in Tables 4.1 and 4.2. Table 4.1 indicates that, among widows who do not receive Social Security income, those who receive survivor benefits from the federal government are older, on average, than those who receive survivor benefits from other sources or who do not receive survivor benefits. This is because older widows of federal employees covered by CSRS would not qualify for Social Security if they had not contributed themselves.

The comparisons we report do not control for the characteristics of decedent spouses, because such data were not available. Thus, the differences seen in Tables 4.1 and 4.2 between widows who receive SBP and others may not be due to SBP but due to unobserved factors, such as the deceased spouse's earnings or amount of SBP coverage selected.

Table 4.1 shows that, among widows who do not receive Social Security income, those who receive survivor benefits have higher average incomes than those who do not receive survivor benefits. Also, widows whose main source of survivor benefits is the military have lower average total income than do widows whose main sources are the federal government, state and local governments, and regular payments from annuities or paid-up life insurance. In contrast, they have higher average total income than do widows whose survivor benefits come primarily from VA. However, VA benefits are tax-exempt; therefore, the difference is smaller in after-tax dollars.

Table 4.2 shows that, among widows who receive Social Security, those who receive survivor benefits also have higher total average income than those who do not receive survivor benefits. Table 4.2 also shows that the average amount received from the military is larger than the average amount received from VA and from companies or unions, and it is comparable to the amount received from the federal government, state and local governments, and regular annuities or paid-up life insurance.

Table 4.1 and Table 4.2 indicate that widows who receive survivor benefits from the military are less likely to be black and Hispanic than widows who do not receive survivor benefits (and also than widows who receive survivor benefits from VA). Another difference is educational attainment. Widows receiving survivor benefits from the military are more educated than those who do not receive survivor benefits or who receive them from VA. For widows with Social Security income (Table 4.2), those receiving survivor benefits from the military are also more educated than widows receiving survivor benefits from companies or unions or from other sources.

There are also important differences in terms of employment status, particularly for widows who do not have Social Security income. For these widows, those receiving survivor benefits from the military are less likely to be in the labor force than those who do not receive survivor benefits or receive them from companies or unions or state and local governments.

---

[10] As noted, other sources of survivor benefits are U.S. railroad retirement survivor pension, workers' compensation pension, black-lung survivor pension, regular payments from estates or trusts, and other unspecified sources.

Table 4.1
Widows' Characteristics by Main Source of Survivor Benefits, Conditional on Not Receiving Social Security Payments

	No Survivor Benefits	Main Source of Military or VA Survivor Benefits		Other Main Source of Survivor Benefits				
		Military	VA	Company or Union	Federal Government	State and Local Government	Annuities[a]	Other Sources[b]
Percentage of all widows	17.1%	0.2%	0.4%	1.0%	0.4%	0.3%	0.2%	0.6%
Total money income (pretax)	$27,788*	$41,708	$28,470*	$42,281	$52,763*	$56,299*	$56,458*	$40,580
Age	61.8	61.7	60.7	61.1	67.2*	61.0	58.3*	65.9*
Race								
White	76.5%*	85.4%	79.6%	87.1%	84.9%	87.6%	89.6%	91.9%*
Black	15.5%*	9.9%	16.1%*	10.0%	11.0%	8.8%	7.3%	5.9%
Asian only	4.0%	2.4%	0.9%	1.0%	0.6%	1.5%	1.5%	0.8%
Other race	4.1%	2.3%	3.3%	1.9%	3.5%	2.1%	1.6%	1.4%
Hispanic origin	10.0%*	2.1%	5.1%*	4.5%*	3.0%	3.1%	3.8%	3.3%
Education								
Less than high school	24.4%*	15.3%	34.5%*	14.1%	12.6%	8.9%	9.4%	22.2%*
High school	34.9%	31.0%	33.7%	38.7%	28.9%	34.9%	35.7%	39.9%*
Some college	14.8%*	22.4%	10.9%*	18.5%	23.5%	18.6%	17.8%	14.4%*
Associate's degree	7.3%	8.3%	8.1%	8.1%	5.7%	10.0%	13.9%	7.1%
Bachelor's degree or more	18.5%	23.0%	12.9%*	20.6%	29.3%	27.7%	23.3%	16.4%
Household size								
# members	2.22*	1.61	1.89*	1.73	1.52	1.57	1.64	1.70
# members age 5 or younger	0.086*	0.03	0.05	0.04	0.02	0.04	0.03	0.03
Employment status								
Not in labor force	45.6%*	58.8%	66.9%	45.4%*	63.9%	46.7%*	48.5%	64.9%
Unemployed	2.6%	3.4%	2.0%	3.4%	0.6%	2.6%	2.6%	2.3%
Self-employed	4.4%*	1.9%	3.5%	3.1%	3.4%	2.2%	5.4%	3.7%

Table 4.1—Continued

| | No Survivor Benefits | Main Source of Military or VA Survivor Benefits | | Other Main Source of Survivor Benefits | | | | |
		Military	VA	Company or Union	Federal Government	State and Local Government	Annuities[a]	Other Sources[b]
Wage or salary worker[c]	37.7%*	23.9%	20.2%	34.7%*	16.8%	31.4%	33.7%	21.7%
Government employee[d]	9.6%	12.0%	7.4%	13.5%	15.3%	17.2%	9.8%	7.4%
Work disability	17.9%*	30.3%	34.0%	17.2%*	23.0%	19.7%*	17.2%*	27.7%

SOURCE: Data from CPS ASEC, 1996–2015 (Flood et al., 2017).
NOTES: Sample includes widows age 40 and older who are not receiving income from Social Security. All calculations are weighted using person-level weights for the analysis of the CPS ASEC.

* $p < 0.05$ (there is a statistically significant difference at the 95% confidence level in comparison to the value in the military survivor benefits column).

[a] Main survivor pension is from regular payments from annuities or paid-up life insurance.

[b] Main survivor pension is from the combination of other sources: U.S. railroad retirement survivor pension, workers' compensation pension, black-lung survivor pension, regular payments from estates or trusts, and other unspecified sources.

[c] Includes family workers.

[d] Includes armed forces, federal employment, state employment, and local government employment.

Table 4.2
Widows' Characteristics by Main Source of Survivor Benefits, Conditional on Receiving Social Security Payments

| | No Survivor Benefits | Main Source of Military or VA Survivor Benefits | | Other Main Source of Survivor Benefits | | | | |
		Military	VA	Company or Union	Federal Government	State and Local Government	Annuities[a]	Other Sources[b]
Percentage of all widows	65.3%	1.0%	1.7%	7.3%	1.4%	1.2%	0.8%	1.3%
Total money income (pretax)	$22,020*	$39,781	$30,622*	$33,002*	$39,830	$40,473	$40,104	$44,448*
Age	76.5	76.4	75.8	76.4	76.6	75.6*	76.5	77.0
Race								
White	89.2%	90.9%	88.5%	95.1%*	91.2%	95.6%*	96.5%*	93.7%*
Black	8.4%*	3.9%	9%*	3.7%	6.2%*	3.2%	2.5%	4.7%
Asian only	1.1%*	2.8%	1.1%*	0.6%*	1%*	0.5%*	0.3%*	0.5%*
Other race	1.3%	2.3%	1.4%	0.5%*	1.6%	0.6%*	0.6%*	1.1%*
Hispanic origin	4.2%*	1.4%	2.5%*	2.0%	2.7%*	2.1%	1.8%	1.8%

Table 4.2—Continued

| | No Survivor Benefits | Main Source of Military or VA Survivor Benefits | | Other Main Source of Survivor Benefits | | | | |
		Military	VA	Company or Union	Federal Government	State and Local Government	Annuities[a]	Other Sources[b]
Education								
Less than high school	31.1%*	18.0%	31.4%*	23%*	16.3%	18.3%	15.0%	24.6%*
High school	39.8%*	35.5%	33.4%	44.6%*	44.1%*	40.2%	37.4%	36.8%
Some college	13.2%*	19.9%	15.5%*	15.2%*	17.2%	19.3%	19.8%	15.9%*
Associate's degree	5.1%*	9.6%	7.6%	5.7%*	6.7%	6.2%*	8.1%	7.1%
Bachelor's degree or more	10.8%*	17.0%	12%*	11.5%*	15.7%	16.0%	19.8%	15.5%
Household size								
# members	1.54*	1.43	1.46	1.36	1.38	1.39	1.29*	1.35
# members age 5 or younger	0.021*	0.01	0.02	0.01	0.01	0.01	0.01	0.02
Employment status								
Not in labor force	91.3%	90.4%	95.2%*	92.0%	89.9%	92.1%	92.6%	94%*
Unemployed	0.5%	0.4%	0.2%	0.3%	0.5%	0.6%	0%*	0.3%
Self-employed	1.3%	1.7%	1.3%	1.4%	2.3%	1.6%	1.5%	1.9%
Wage or salary worker[c]	5.7%	5.8%	2.7%*	5.0%	5.6%	4.4%	4.2%	3.2%*
Government employee[d]	1.2%	1.6%	0.5%*	1.3%	1.7%	1.4%	1.6%	0.5%*
Work disability	29.8%	29.1%	40.0%	29.4%	28.4%	30.6%	29.5%	35.8%

SOURCE: Data from CPS ASEC, 1996–2015 (Flood et al., 2017).

NOTES: Sample includes widows age 40 and older who are not receiving income from Social Security. All calculations are weighted using person-level weights for the analysis of the CPS ASEC.

* $p < 0.05$ (there is a statistical significant difference at the 95% confidence level in comparison to the value in the military survivor benefits column).

[a] Main survivor pension is from regular payments from annuities or paid-up life insurance.

[b] Main survivor pension is from the combination of other sources: U.S. railroad retirement survivor pension, workers' compensation pension, black-lung survivor pension, regular payments from estates or trusts, and other unspecified sources.

[c] Includes family workers.

[d] Includes armed forces, federal employment, state employment, and local government employment.

The difference is starker when the main source of benefits is VA (Table 4.1). Although the data do not reveal the reason for this, a possibility is that a larger percentage of widows receiving survivor benefits from the military or VA also reported having a disability that prevents them from working but do not have enough years of earnings subject to Social Security taxes to qualify for Social Security disability.

The decision to work (especially at younger ages) is not independent of the receipt of nonlabor income, including survivor benefits. For example, some widows might choose not to work or to work only part time because they are entitled to survivor benefits, resulting in a lower total income than if they had chosen to work or to work full time. Therefore, when comparing widows without and with survivor benefits, it is important to keep in mind that their labor income and therefore total income can be affected by the receipt and amount of survivor benefits.

Adjusted Comparisons of Income

A goal of the chapter is to compare the financial status of survivors—widows—receiving benefits from the military or VA with the financial status of other survivors. We want to adjust these samples so they have similar characteristics, to avoid confounding the effect of access to survivor benefits with differences in other characteristics, such as race or education.

The findings from Table 4.1 and Table 4.2 suggest that widows receiving survivor benefits from the military are different in some ways from widows who do not receive survivor benefits or who receive survivor benefits from other sources. Therefore, we rely on a statistical method to improve the comparability of these groups—namely, inverse probability weighting (IPW). After applying these weights, widows not receiving survivor benefits or receiving survivor benefits from sources other than the military will be, on average, comparable on selected characteristics to widows receiving benefits from the military. The characteristics that we use to create the weights are age (in age categories), race, Hispanic origin, education, household size, and having a work disability. We exclude characteristics regarding employment status because it can be affected by the receipt and generosity of survivor benefits; therefore, we want to allow it to vary across groups. Appendix E provides more details on the IPW approach.

Tables 4.3–4.6 present the adjusted income comparisons. Tables 4.3 and 4.4, which are for widows not receiving Social Security, are paired to show average income by source and the percentage of widows receiving each type of income. Tables 4.5 and 4.6 are paired to do the same for widows who do receive Social Security. The tables are adjusted by the weights discussed above.

When we compare the total income reported in Table 4.3 with that in Table 4.1, we observe that, in the adjusted analysis, differences in the average incomes of widows across subgroups are more muted. For example, the average incomes of widows without survivor benefits, widows getting survivor benefits mainly from VA, and widows getting survivor benefits from other sources are larger, whereas the average income of widows getting their survivor benefits mainly from companies or unions, federal employers, and state or local government employers has decreased. The adjusted numbers in Table 4.3 still show that widows with access to survivor benefits from the military are in a better financial situation, measured by total income, than widows without access to survivor benefits. However, the average total income of widows receiving survivor benefits mainly from the military is no longer statistically different from the

Table 4.3
Average Income for Widows Who Do Not Receive Payments from Social Security (Analysis Adjusted by IPW)

	No Survivor Benefits	Main Source of Military or VA Survivor Benefits		Other Main Source of Survivor Benefits				
		Military	VA	Company or Union	Federal Government	State and Local Government	Annuities[a]	Other Sources[b]
Total money income	30,747* (29,900– 31,594)	41,708 (35,266– 48,150)	35,510 (31,109– 39,910)	42,300 (39,025– 45,573)	49,573* (44,694– 54,452)	47,774 (41,020– 54,526)	49,617 (39,448– 59,786)	47,752 (41,989– 53,513)
Wages	21,976 (21,225– 22,727)	18,208 (12,677– 23,738)	14,528 (11,095– 17,962)	19,977 (17,419– 22,535)	17,815 (13,987– 21,643)	20,048 (15,547– 24,549)	16,735 (11,822– 21,649)	18,286 (14,025– 22,547)
Social Security	N/A	N/A	N/A	N/A	N/A	N/A	N/A	N/A
Retirement income[c]	2,403 (2,166– 2,640)	2,205 (1,091– 3,320)	2,624 (1,118– 4,130)	2,816 (2,072– 3,559)	3,705 (2,114– 5,296)	4,269* (2,640– 5,897)	1,757 (674– 2,840)	2,056 (1,134–2,977)
Survivor benefits from main source	N/A	11,917 (10,533– 13,301)	12,588 (11,176– 14,000)	13,068 (11,662– 14,475)	20,029* (18,227– 21,831)	17,536* (15,156– 19,916)	22,615* (17,343– 27,887)	19,029* (16,181– 21,877)
Survivor benefits from other sources	N/A	3,507 (1,339– 5,674)	2,872 (1,159– 4,584)	149* (59–239)	265* (85–444)	212* (38–386)	1,271 (–81–2,622)	355* (88–622)
Total survivor benefits	N/A	15,424 (12,879– 17,969)	15,460 (13,186– 17,733)	13,217 (11,796– 14,639)	20,294* (18,495– 22,092)	17,748 (15,353– 20,143)	23,886* (18,155– 29,617)	19,384* (16,439– 22,330)
Other income[d]	6,368 (5,985– 6,751)	5,871 (3,505– 8,238)	2,898* (1,881– 3,915)	6,290 (5,086 –7,494)	7,759 (5,738 –9,780)	5,710 (3,655 –7,764)	7,240 (4,263– 10,216)	8,026 (5,625– 10,426)

SOURCE: Data from CPS ASEC, 1996–2015 (Flood et al., 2017).

NOTES: Sample includes widows age 40 and older who are not receiving income from Social Security. All calculations are weighted using person-level weights for the analysis of the CPS ASEC, adjusted for differences in observed characteristics with the IPW methodology. All figures reflect pretax income adjusted for inflation to 2015 dollars. Numbers in parentheses represent 95% confidence intervals. N/A = not applicable.

* $p < 0.05$ (there is a statistically significant difference at the 95% confidence level in comparison to the value in the column on military survivor benefits, based on 300 bootstrap replications).

[a] Main survivor pension is from regular payments from annuities or paid-up life insurance.

[b] Main survivor pension is from the combination of other sources: U.S. railroad retirement survivor pension, workers' compensation pension, black-lung survivor pension, regular payments from estates or trusts, and other unspecified sources.

[c] The following types of retirement income are included: company or union pension, including profit sharing; annuities; U.S. military retirement; federal government employee pensions; state or local government employee pensions; U.S. railroad retirement; regular payments from annuities or paid-up insurance policies; and other sources, such as IRA or Keough accounts.

[d] Other income summarizes income received from business, farming, welfare assistance, Supplemental Security Income, interest, unemployment, worker compensation, disability benefits, rent, educational assistance, child support, alimony, assistance from friends or relatives, and other sources not specified.

average total income of widows receiving survivor benefits from other sources (except for those receiving survivor benefits from the federal government).

Table 4.3 also shows that, among widows without Social Security income, the average survivor benefits from the military are similar to the average survivor benefits from VA and private employment (i.e., companies or unions), although they are smaller than the average survivor benefits from the federal government, state and local governments, annuities, and other sources. Our examples in Chapter Three suggested that military survivor benefits compare favorably with federal survivor benefits. Thus, it is likely that the higher benefits of these widows, compared with widows for whom the main source of survivor benefits is the military, are not attributable to more-generous federal survivor benefits but are instead attributable to differences in decedent and unobserved widow characteristics. Unfortunately, the data do not allow us to investigate whether the larger benefits are explained by higher earnings of the deceased spouse. Furthermore, 90 percent of survivors receiving federal civilian benefits were covered by CSRS as of September 30, 2014 (U.S. Office of Personnel Management, 2016, p. 19). This suggests that the survivor benefits from the federal government are mainly coming from federal CSRS, which is phasing out and being replaced by the less generous FERS survivor program. As a result, the difference between federal government survivor benefits and military survivor benefits may decrease in the future.

Another finding is that widows receiving survivor benefits mainly from the military or the VA reported, on average, a larger amount of survivor benefits received from secondary sources in comparison to widows receiving survivor benefits mainly from companies or unions; from federal, state, and local government employment; or from other sources. Table 4.4 indicates that the larger average amounts are explained by a larger probability of receipt of additional survivor benefits. About 18.8 percent of widows receiving benefits from the military (who do not have Social Security income) also receive survivor benefits from a second source. Table 4.4 shows that the most common source is federal employment (7.6 percent), followed by VA (4.3 percent).[11] Widows receiving benefits mainly from VA also reported at least a second source of survivor benefits in 18.3 percent of the cases. In comparison, widows receiving survivor benefits mainly from companies or unions reported a second source in only 2.2 percent of cases. The percentages having at least a second source of survivor benefits are also small for widows whose benefits come mainly from federal employment (4.7 percent), from state and local government (2.4 percent), from annuities (10.2 percent), and from other sources (4.8 percent).

Table 4.5 and Table 4.6 show the adjusted average income and sources of income of widows with Social Security income. Like Table 4.3, Table 4.5 shows that widows who receive survivor benefits from the military have higher total average income than widows who do not receive survivor benefits. These widows also have larger average total income than widows who receive survivor benefits mainly from VA or from companies or unions and similar total income to widows who receive their survivor benefits mainly from federal employment, state and local governments, or annuities.

Table 4.5 also shows that survivor benefits received from the military are, on average, similar to those received mainly from annuities; larger than those received mainly from VA

---

[11] Note that the reported survivor benefits received from the military are net of any potential offset from the receipt of DIC from VA.

Table 4.4
Share of Widows Receiving Income from Selected Sources (Conditional on Not Receiving Social Security; Analysis Adjusted by IPW)

| | No Survivor Benefits | Military or VA Survivor Benefits | | Other Sources of Survivor Benefits | | | | |
| | | Main Source | | Main Source | | | | |
		Military	VA	Company or Union	Federal Government	State and Local Government	Annorities[a]	Other Sources[b]
Total money income	87.3%*	100.0%	100.0%	100.0%	100.0%	100.0%	100.0%	100.0%
Wages	53.7%*	43.9%	39.7%	49.5%	46.5%	45.5%	47.4%	45.1%
Social Security	0.0%	0.0%	0.0%	0.0%	0.0%	0.0%	0.0%	0.0%
Retirement income[c]	10.9%	10.7%	10.9%	14.5%	13.5%	17.5%	9.9%	10.0%
Income from survivor benefits								
From the military	N/A	100.0%	3.4%*	N/A	N/A	N/A	N/A	N/A
From the VA	N/A	4.3%	100.0%*	N/A	N/A	N/A	N/A	N/A
From company or union	N/A	3.1%	5.9%	100.0%*	2.7%	0.8%	4.7%	2.4%
From federal employer	N/A	7.6%	3.6%	0.4%*	100.0%*	0.2%*	0%*	0.5%*
From state and local government employer	N/A	1.1%	1.3%	0.7%	1.4%	100.0%*	2.1%	0.1%
From annuities	N/A	0.5%	2.5%	0.6%	0.4%	0.2%	100.0%*	1.9%
From other sources	N/A	2.1%	1.7%	0.5%	0.2%	1.2%	3.4%	100.0%*
Other income[d]	87.3%*	100.0%	100.0%	100.0%	100.0%	100.0%	100.0%	100.0%

SOURCE: Data from CPS ASEC, 1996–2015 (Flood et al., 2017).

NOTES: Sample includes widows age 40 and older who are not receiving income from Social Security. All calculations are weighted using person-level weights for the analysis of the CPS ASEC, adjusted for differences in observed characteristics with the IPW methodology. All figures reflect pretax income adjusted for inflation to 2015 dollars. N/A = not applicable.

* $p < 0.05$ (there is a statistical significant difference at the 95% confidence level in comparison to the value in the column on military survivor benefits, based on 300 bootstrap replications).

[a] Main survivor pension is from regular payments from annuities or paid-up life insurance.

[b] Main survivor pension is from the combination of other sources: U.S. railroad retirement survivor pension, workers' compensation pension, black-lung survivor pension, regular payments from estates or trusts, and other unspecified sources.

[c] The following types of retirement income are included: company or union pension, including profit sharing; annuities; U.S. military retirement; federal government employee pensions; state or local government employee pensions; U.S. railroad retirement; regular payments from annuities or paid-up insurance policies; and other sources, such as IRA or Keough accounts.

[d] Other income summarizes income received from business, farming, welfare assistance, Supplemental Security Income, interest, unemployment, worker compensation, disability benefits, rent, educational assistance, child support, alimony, assistance from friends or relatives, and other sources not specified.

Table 4.5
Average Income for Widows Who Receive Payments from Social Security (Analysis Adjusted by IPW)

	No Survivor Benefits	Military or VA Survivor Benefits Main Source		Other Sources of Survivor Benefits Main Source				
		Military	VA	Company or Union	Federal Government	State and Local Government	Annuities[a]	Other Sources[b]
Total money income	24,443* (24,193– 24,693)	39,781 (37,075– 42,487)	34,028* (32,656– 35,400)	35,180* (34,130– 36,230)	40,444 (38,627– 42,261)	41,134 (38,826– 43,441)	40,288 (37,485– 43,091)	47,238* (43,775– 50,701)
Wages	2,139 (2,021– 2,257)	2,961 (1,955– 3,967)	829* (575– 1,083)	1,641* (1,253– 2,028)	1,742* (1,230– 2,254)	1,468* (1,008– 1,927)	1,293* (585– 2,001)	1,424* (894– 1,953)
Social Security	14,527* (14,461– 14,593)	13,827 (13,348– 14,307)	13,152* (12,740– 13,564)	15,519* (15,333– 15,705)	11,537* (11,085– 11,989)	13,708 (13,245– 14,170)	14,635* (14,005– 15,265)	14,974* (14,377– 15,570)
Retirement income[c]	3,224* (3,123– 3,326)	2,496 (1,946– 3,045)	2,663 (2,149– 3,177)	2,878 (2,394– 3,362)	3,239 (2,719– 3,759)	3,317* (2,711– 3,923)	2,922 (2,327– 3,517)	2,480 (1,886– 3,075)
Survivor benefits from main source	N/A	12,027 (11,262– 12,791)	11,103* (10,586– 11,619)	8,836* (8,477– 9,194)	17,233* (16,229– 18,237)	15,379* (14,224– 16,533)	13,120 (11,293– 14,947)	15,579* (14,128– 17,031)
Survivor benefits from other sources	N/A	1,685 (1,289– 2,080)	1,541 (1,106– 1,975)	78* (50– 107)	242* (151– 332)	464* (261– 667)	352* (208– 496)	826* (295– 1,357)
Total survivor benefits	N/A	13,711 (12,867– 14,555)	12,643 (11,948– 13,338)	8,914* (8,551– 9,277)	17475* (16,466– 18,484)	15,843* (14,632– 17,054)	13,472 (11,624– 15,320)	16,406* (14,691– 18,120)
Other income[d]	4,553* (4,388– 4,717)	6,786 (4,897– 8,675)	4,740* (3,971– 5,509)	6,228 (5,667– 6,789)	6,451 (5,486– 7,417)	6,799 (5,313– 8,284)	7,966 (6,382– 9,550)	11,955* (9,704– 14,207)

SOURCE: Data from CPS ASEC, 1996–2015 (Flood et al., 2017).

NOTES: Sample includes widows age 40 and older who are not receiving income from Social Security. All calculations are weighted using person-level weights for the analysis of the CPS ASEC, adjusted for differences in observed characteristics with the IPW methodology. All figures reflect pretax income adjusted for inflation to 2015 dollars. Numbers in parentheses represent 95% confidence intervals. N/A = not applicable.

* $p < 0.05$ (there is a statistical significant difference at the 95% confidence level in comparison to the value in the column on military survivor benefits, based on 300 bootstrap replications).

[a] Main survivor pension is from regular payments from annuities or paid-up life insurance.

[b] Main survivor pension is from the combination of other sources: U.S. railroad retirement survivor pension, workers' compensation pension, black-lung survivor pension, regular payments from estates or trusts, and other unspecified sources.

[c] The following types of retirement income are included: company or union pension, including profit sharing; annuities; U.S. military retirement; federal government employee pensions; state or local government employee pensions; U.S. railroad retirement; regular payments from annuities or paid-up insurance policies; and other sources, such as IRA or Keough accounts.

[d] Other income summarizes income received from business, farming, welfare assistance, Supplemental Security Income, interest, unemployment, worker compensation, disability benefits, rent, educational assistance, child support, alimony, assistance from friends or relatives, and other sources not specified.

Table 4.6
Share of Widows Receiving Income from Selected Sources (Conditional on Receiving Social Security; Analysis Adjusted by IPW)

| | | Military or VA Survivor Benefits | | Other Sources of Survivor Benefits | | | | |
| | | Main Source | | Main Source | | | | |
	No Survivor Benefits	Military	VA	Company or Union	Federal Government	State and Local Government	Annuities[a]	Other Sources[b]
Total money income	100.0%	100.0%	100.0%	100.0%	100.0%	100.0%	100.0%	100.0%
Wages	10.6%	10.8%	5.7%*	9.0%	10.3%	9.3%	8.0%	6.6%*
Social Security	100.0%	100.0%	100.0%	100.0%	100.0%	100.0%	100.0%	100.0%
Retirement income[c]	27.4%*	20.7%	22.2%	23.4%	26.5%*	25.8%*	28.9%*	21.4%
Income from survivor benefits								
From the military	N/A	100.0%	3.3%*	N/A	N/A	N/A	N/A	N/A
From the VA	N/A	3.0%	100.0%*	N/A	N/A	N/A	N/A	N/A
From company or union	N/A	5.4%	5.1%	100.0%*	2.5%*	2.8%*	3.9%	5.0%
From federal employer	N/A	5.2%	2.9%*	0.2%*	100.0%*	0.7%*	0.3%*	0.4%*
From state and local government employer	N/A	1.0%	2.1%	0.2%*	0.9%	100.0%*	0%*	1.0%
From annuities	N/A	1.8%	1.9%	0.5%*	0.6%*	1.0%	100%*	1.9%
From other sources	N/A	0.3%	1.8%*	0.6%	0.3%	1.7%*	2.1%*	100.0%*
Other income[d]	100.0%	100.0%	100.0%	100.0%	100.0%	100.0%	100.0%	100.0%

SOURCE: Data from CPS ASEC, 1996–2015 (Flood et al., 2017). NOTES: Sample includes widows age 40 and older who are not receiving income from Social Security. All calculations are weighted using person-level weights for the analysis of the CPS ASEC, adjusted for differences in observed characteristics with the IPW methodology. All figures reflect pretax income adjusted for inflation to 2015 dollars. N/A = not applicable.

* $p < 0.05$ (there is a statistical significant difference at the 95% confidence level in comparison to the value in the column on military survivor benefits, based on 300 bootstrap replications).

[a] Main survivor pension is from regular payments from annuities or paid-up life insurance.

[b] Main survivor pension is from the combination of other sources: U.S. railroad retirement survivor pension, workers' compensation pension, black-lung survivor pension, regular payments from estates or trusts, and other unspecified sources.

[c] The following types of retirement income are included: company or union pension, including profit sharing; annuities; U.S. military retirement; federal government employee pensions; state or local government employee pensions; U.S. railroad retirement; regular payments from annuities or paid-up insurance policies; and other sources, such as IRA or Keough accounts.

[d] Other income summarizes income received from business, farming, welfare assistance, Supplemental Security Income, interest, unemployment, worker compensation, disability benefits, rent, educational assistance, child support, alimony, assistance from friends or relatives, and other sources not specified.

and from companies and unions; and smaller than those received from federal employment, state or local government employment, and from other sources.[12]

As was the case for widows without Social Security, widows receiving survivor benefits mainly from the military or VA also reported, on average, larger amounts of survivor benefits from secondary sources than did women receiving survivor benefits from other sources. These larger average amounts are explained by a higher probability of receipt of additional benefits, as shown in Table 4.6. About 16.2 percent of widows receiving benefits from the military (who have Social Security income) also receive survivor benefits from a second source, with the most-common sources being companies or unions (5.4 percent) and federal employment (5.2 percent), followed by VA (3.0 percent). Widows receiving benefits mainly from VA also reported at least a second source of survivor benefits in 16.2 percent of the cases. The percentages of having at least a second source of survivor benefits are small for widows whose benefits mainly come from companies or unions (1.5 percent), federal employment (4.3 percent), state and local government (6.1 percent), annuities (6.3 percent), and other sources (8.3 percent).

Contribution of Survivor Benefits to Total Income

Another goal of this chapter is to analyze the extent to which survivor benefits contribute to total income. We continue to use the IPW approach in our analysis.

Figure 4.5 shows that the contribution of survivor benefits to total income is larger among widows who do not have Social Security income, averaging about 50 percent of their total income. In comparison, among widows with Social Security income, survivor benefits are on average 30 percent of their total income.[13]

Figure 4.5 also shows that, among widows without Social Security income, survivor benefits are statistically a larger portion of total income for widows whose main source is VA. In comparison, among widows with Social Security income, survivor benefits are a lower proportion of income for widows receiving benefits from companies or unions or from annuities and are a higher proportion of income for widows receiving benefits from federal employment and state and local governments.

In addition to the average contribution to total income, we calculated the percentage of widows for whom survivor benefits represent a low percentage (0–20 percent), relatively low percentage (20–40 percent), medium percentage (40–60 percent), relatively high percentage (60–80 percent), or high percentage (80–100 percent) of total income. The results are shown in Table 4.7, separately for widows with and without Social Security income.

Among widows without Social Security income, a nontrivial percentage of them rely heavily on survivor benefits for their total income. For example, for 27.3 percent of these widows who also receive survivor benefits from the military, survivor benefits are 80 to 100 percent

---

[12] VA benefits are tax-exempt. Considering a marginal tax rate of 15 percent, the average survivor benefits received from the military or VA would not be statistically different from those received from the military when measured in after-tax dollars. Another important consideration is that the reported survivor benefits from the military are net of the offsets from DIC and Social Security.

[13] The calculations in Figure 4.5 consider only the amount of survivor benefits received from the main source (and exclude survivor benefits received from other sources). The estimations were done by first calculating the contribution of the survivor benefits to total income for each widow and then averaging those contributions across all widows in the same category (using the IPW methodology).

Figure 4.5
Average Contribution of Survivor Benefits to Total Income (Analysis Adjusted by IPW)

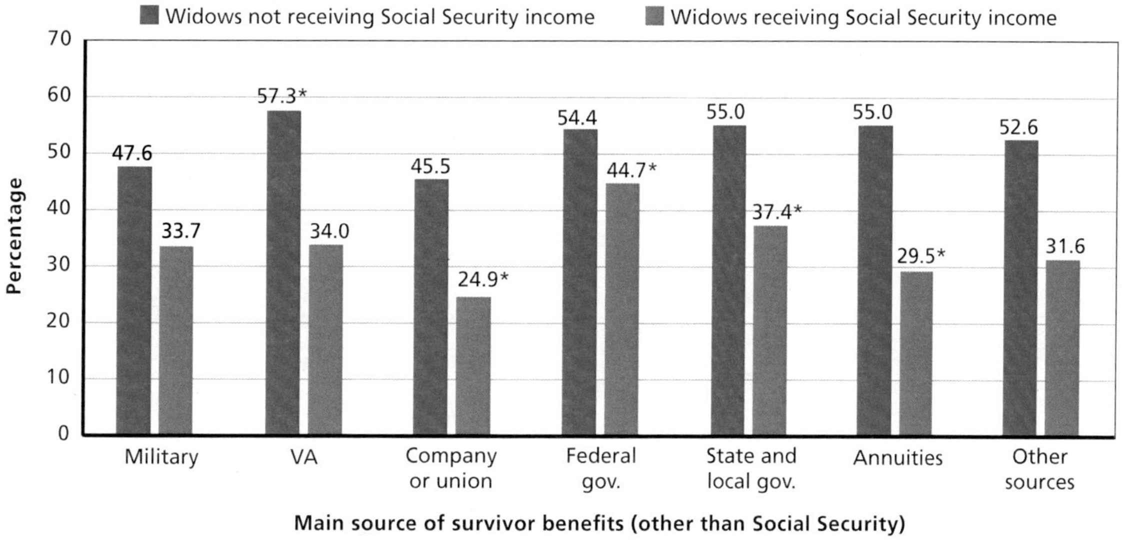

SOURCE: Data from CPS ASEC, 1996–2015 (Flood et al., 2017).
NOTES: Sample includes widows age 40 and older. All calculations are weighted using person-level weights for the analysis of the CPS ASEC, adjusted for differences in observed characteristics with the IPW methodology. Annuities are regular payments from annuities or paid-up life insurance. Other sources are U.S. railroad retirement survivor pension, workers' compensation pension, black-lung survivor pension, regular payments from estates or trusts, and other unspecified sources.
$*$ $p < 0.05$ (there is a statistical significant difference at the 95% confidence level in comparison to the value for military survivor benefits, based on 300 bootstrap replications).
RAND RR2236-4.5

of their total income. For other widows without Social Security income and receiving survivor benefits from other sources, the numbers are similar. That is, for 25 to 35 percent of these widows, survivor benefits are 80 to 100 percent of their total income.

We note that 39.7 percent of widows without Social Security income and for whom VA is the main source of survivor benefits are very dependent on these benefits (80 to 100 percent of total income). This is much higher than the 27.3 percentage of widows for whom military benefits are the main source.

Widows with Social Security income are less likely to have a high dependency on survivor benefits for their total income (see Table 4.7). Although survivor benefits are still an important fraction of their total income, that fraction is above 80 percent for only a small percentage of widows. For example, Table 4.7 indicates that these benefits represent 80 percent or more of total income for only 1.3 percent of widows with Social Security income and receiving survivor benefits from the military.

As discussed, widows' labor-supply decisions can be affected by having access to survivor benefits and the amount of those benefits. This would affect their labor income and therefore the denominator in the calculations above. An alternative analysis is to ask to what extent survivor benefits are enough by themselves to lift widows out of poverty. In addition to providing more insights into the adequacy of SBP, this analysis has the advantage that the denominator is fixed and is given by the official poverty threshold used by the Census Bureau to evaluate the poverty status of each family.

Table 4.7
Distribution of Widows by the Contribution of Survivor Benefits to Total Income (Analysis Adjusted by IPW)

| | Military or VA Survivor Benefits | | Other Sources of Survivor Benefits | | | | |
| | Main Source | | Main Source | | | | |
	Military	VA	Company or Union	Federal Government	State and Local Government	Annuities[a]	Other Sources[b]
Widows without Social Security income							
Survivor benefits are 0–20% of total income	27.0%	19.7%	37.3%*	15.4%*	24.8%	27.4%	30.4%
Survivor benefits are 20–40% of total income	25.8%	25.0%	18.2%*	26.0%	18.6%	11.8%*	15.6%*
Survivor benefits are 40–60% of total income	16.3%	10.2%	10.1%	16.8%	13.2%	14.8%	10.3%
Survivor benefits are 60–80% of total income	3.6%	5.4%	6.6%	15.1%*	6.5%	12.8%*	7.0%
Survivor benefits are 80–100% of total income	27.3%	39.7%*	27.8%	26.8%	36.9%	33.2%	36.6%*
Widows with Social Security income							
Survivor benefits are 0–20% of total income	27.2%	30.0%	47.7%*	14.6%*	25.6%	44.7%*	35.6%*
Survivor benefits are 20–40% of total income	39.5%	29.4%*	33.2%*	29.2%*	30.4%*	23.9%*	31.2%*
Survivor benefits are 40–60% of total income	22.4%	31.8%*	13.9%*	28.6%*	27.2%*	19.7%	21.4%
Survivor benefits are 60–80% of total income	9.6%	8.1%	4.3%*	22.3%*	14.1%*	8.7%	9.1%
Survivor benefits are 80–100% of total income	1.3%	0.7%	0.9%	5.4%*	2.7%	2.9%	2.6%

SOURCE: Data from CPS ASEC, 1996–2015 (Flood et al., 2017).

NOTES: Sample includes widows age 40 and older. All calculations are weighted using person-level weights for the analysis of the CPS ASEC, adjusted for differences in observed characteristics with the IPW methodology.

* $p < 0.05$ (there is a statistical significant difference at the 95% confidence level in comparison to the value in the column on military survivor benefits, based on 300 bootstrap replications).

[a] Main survivor pension is from regular payments from annuities or paid-up life insurance.

[b] Main survivor pension is from the combination of other sources, which may include U.S. railroad retirement survivor pension, workers' compensation pension, black-lung survivor pension, regular payments from estates or trusts, and other unspecified sources.

Figure 4.6 indicates the percentage of widows receiving survivor benefits that are larger in amount (counting only widows' main-source survivor benefits) than the poverty-level threshold applicable to their families. We do not observe notable differences depending on whether the widows receive Social Security income, but we do observe differences depending on the source of the benefits. The amount of survivor benefits received from the military alone is enough to lift widows out of poverty in about 37–39 percent of the cases. This fraction is higher for widows receiving their survivor benefits mainly from VA, despite the average amount of survivor benefits received from the military and from VA being similar (using the IPW methodology). This difference is explained by the distribution of the benefits paid out, as shown in Table 4.8. In particular, VA is more likely to pay benefits in the range of $10,000 to $20,000, which is the range of income needed to lift a family out of poverty. In addition, the VA benefits are tax-exempt.

Figure 4.6 also indicates that military survivor benefits alone are enough for lifting widows out of poverty in more cases than benefits obtained from companies or unions. In the latter case, only between 21 percent (if receiving social security) and 31 percent (if not receiving social security) of the benefits paid out are alone enough to lift the recipients out of poverty.

In contrast, survivor benefits received from federal civilian employment are more likely to be enough (standing alone) to lift their recipients out of poverty than survivor benefits from the military or VA. This finding is not unsurprising given that Table 4.3 and Table 4.5

Figure 4.6
Percentage of Widows Receiving Survivor Benefits Larger Than the Poverty Level (Analysis Adjusted by IPW)

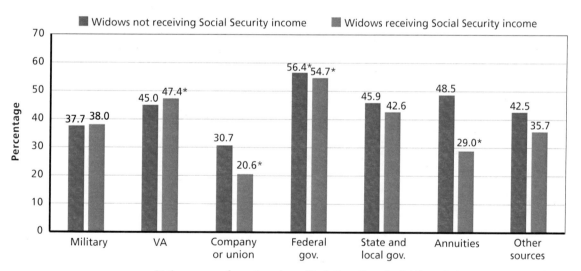

SOURCE: Data from CPS ASEC, 1996–2015 (Flood et al., 2017).
NOTES: Sample includes widows age 40 and older. All calculations are weighted using person-level weights for the analysis of the CPS ASEC, adjusted for differences in observed characteristics with the IPW methodology. Annuities are regular payments from annuities or paid-up life insurance. Other sources are U.S. railroad retirement survivor pension, workers' compensation pension, black-lung survivor pension, regular payments from estates or trusts, and other unspecified sources.
* $p < 0.05$ (there is a statistical significant difference at the 95% confidence level in comparison to the value for military survivor benefits, based on 300 bootstrap replications).
RAND RR2236-4.6

Table 4.8
Distribution of Widows by the Size of Survivor Benefits Received (Analysis Adjusted by IPW)

| | Military or VA Survivor Benefits | | Other Sources of Survivor Benefits | | | | |
| | Main Source | | Main Source | | | | |
	Military	VA	Company or Union	Federal Government	State and Local Government	Annarities[a]	Other Sources[b]
Widows without Social Security income							
Survivor benefits are less than or equal to $5,000	18.7%	14.3%	33.5%*	7.7%*	20.5%	15.0%	26.5%
Survivor benefits are greater than $5,000 but equal to or less than $10,000	25.9%	27.6%	23.7%	20.6%	18.4%	24.8%	18.3%
Survivor benefits are greater than $10,000 but equal to or less than $20,000	45.6%	52.6%	24.6%*	30.3%*	30.3%*	31.4%*	28.3%*
Survivor benefits are greater than $20,000 but equal to or less than $40,000	8.8%	3.9%	14.3%	34%*	22.9%*	19.2%*	14.8%*
Survivor benefits are greater than $40,000	1.0%	1.6%	3.9%*	7.3%*	7.9%*	9.5%*	12.0%*
Widows with Social Security income							
Survivor benefits are less than or equal to $5,000	20.7%	29%*	44%*	9.6%*	21.1%	40.1%*	31.8%*
Survivor benefits are greater than $5,000 but equal to or less than $10,000	27.6%	14.5%*	28.5%	22.6%*	24.8%	23.7%	24.1%
Survivor benefits are greater than $10,000 but equal to or less than $20,000	40.3%	50.3%*	19.1%*	40.4%	30.2%*	20.2%*	21.2%*
Survivor benefits are greater than $20,000 but equal to or less than $40,000	9.7%	5.6%*	6.5%*	22.0%*	18.5%*	9.4%	13.9%*
Survivor benefits are greater than $40,000	1.8%	0.6%*	2.0%	5.3%*	5.5%*	6.5%*	9.0%*

SOURCE: Data from CPS ASEC, 1996–2015 (Flood et al., 2017).

NOTES: Sample includes widows age 40 and older. All calculations are weighted using person-level weights for the analysis of the CPS ASEC, adjusted for differences in observed characteristics with the IPW methodology.

* $p < 0.05$ (there is a statistical significant difference at the 95% confidence level in comparison to the value in the column on military survivor benefits, based on 300 bootstrap replications).

[a] Main survivor pension is from regular payments from annuities or paid-up life insurance.

[b] Main survivor pension is from the combination of other sources, which may include U.S. railroad retirement survivor pension, workers' compensation pension, black-lung survivor pension, regular payments from estates or trusts, and other unspecified sources.

indicate that the average survivor benefits from federal employment is larger than the average benefit received from the military or VA.

Poverty Status and Participation in Public Assistance Programs

Our previous analysis showed that survivor benefits from the military alone are not enough to lift widows out of poverty in the majority of cases. Therefore, in this section we analyze the poverty status of widows receiving benefits from the military, and we compare that status with widows receiving benefits from other sources and with widows who do not receive benefits. We also analyze participation in public assistance programs. We continue to use IPW for adjusted comparisons.

There is a lower percentage of widows receiving survivor benefits from the military who are below the poverty line than widows who do not receive survivor benefits (see Table 4.9). Participation in public assistance programs is also lower.

Among widows without Social Security income, about 15.7 percent of widows whose main source of survivor benefits is the military have income below the poverty line. This compares with 22.5 percent if the main source is VA and 16.5 percent if the main source is a company or union, and there are lower percentages for the other main sources (although, in most cases, the values are not statistically different). By comparison, for widows without both Social Security and survivor benefits, 29.8 percent are below the poverty line.

Among widows with Social Security income, 3.6 percent of widows whose main source of survivor benefits is the military have income below the poverty line. This compares with 7.1 percent if the main source is VA (the difference is statistically different) and 2.7 percent if the main source is a company or union (the difference is not statistically different), and there are lower percentages for the other main sources (the difference is statistically different only in the case of the federal government). For widows with Social Security but without survivor benefits, 13.6 percent are below the poverty line (statistically higher than for widows receiving survivor benefits from the military).

Among widows without Social Security, 7.7 percent of widows whose main source of survivor benefits is the military participate in food stamps, as do 12.5 percent of widows whose main source is VA (the difference is not statistically significant). For widows with Social Security, these percentages are 2.3 percent and 5.0 percent, respectively (the differences are statistically significant). One potential reason contributing to higher poverty incidence and higher participation in assistance programs is that some recipients of VA survivor benefits might be mothers of deceased veterans who qualify for the benefits because of low income. An in-depth analysis of the reasons is not possible with the CPS ASEC data.

Further analysis is also needed to better understand why nearly 16 percent of widows whose main source of survivor benefits is the military are below the poverty line if they do not also receive Social Security. The finding does not necessarily mean that military survivor benefits are ineffective. For example, data limitations prevent us from being able to adjust for the characteristics of the deceased spouse, which could affect this finding.

Table 4.9
Poverty Status and Participation in Public Assistance Programs (Analysis Adjusted by IPW)

| | No Survivor Benefits | Military or VA Survivor Benefits | | Other Sources of Survivor Benefits | | | | |
| | | Main Source | | Main Source | | | | |
		Military	VA	Company or Union	Federal Government	State and Local Government	Annuities[a]	Other Sources[b]
Widows without Social Security income								
Poverty status								
Below poverty line	29.8%*	15.7%	22.5%	16.5%	9.2%	14.8%	6.2%*	14.2%
100–124% of the poverty line	5.3%	4.0%	8.4%	6.3%	3.3%	2.3%	10.6%	5.9%
125–149% of the poverty line	4.7%	4.7%	5.1%	4.7%	4.7%	2.0%	14.3%	7.2%
150% and above of the poverty line	60.3%*	75.6%	64.0%*	72.4%	82.8%	81.0%	69.0%	72.7%
Public assistance								
Welfare[c]	1.2%*	0.0%	0.6%*	0.1%	1.8%	0.2%	0.0%	0.6%*
Food stamps	12.0%	7.7%	12.5%	4.7%	7.8%	6.3%	2.2%*	7.7%
EITC	8.7%*	2.2%	7.1%*	5.0%	3.8%	3.9%	5.6%	6.3%*
Public housing	4.9%*	0.6%	4.2%*	2.1%	1.0%	1.1%	3.7%	3.8%*
Rent subsidy	2.4%	1.4%	1.5%	0.5%	1.9%	0.1%	0.0%	0.7%
Heat subsidy	5.0%	6.8%	7.3%	4.1%	3.7%	4.1%	1.2%*	3.0%
Free or reduced lunch program	2.8%	2.4%	2.5%	3.3%	3.5%	4.2%	1.0%	2.8%
Widows with Social Security income								
Poverty status								
Below poverty line	13.6%*	3.6%	7.1%*	2.7%	1.7%*	2.5%	2.4%	4.0%
100–124% of the poverty line	11.5%*	2.6%	4.1%	3.2%	2.4%	3.0%	4.8%	3.0%
125–149% of the poverty line	13.1%*	3.6%	4.3%	6.9%*	4.6%	5.1%	5.5%	5.7%*
150% and above of the poverty line	61.8%*	90.2%	84.6%*	87.2%*	91.3%	89.4%	87.2%	87.4%

Table 4.9—Continued

| | No Survivor Benefits | Military or VA Survivor Benefits | | Other Sources of Survivor Benefits | | | | |
| | | Main Source | | Main Source | | | | |
		Military	VA	Company or Union	Federal Government	State and Local Government	Annuities[a]	Other Sources[b]
Public assistance								
Welfare[c]	0.3%*	0.0%	0.1%	0.1%*	0.0%	0.2%	0.0%	0.2%
Food stamps	5.7%*	2.3%	5.0%*	2.4%	1.8%	1.6%	2.9%	2.8%
EITC	0.9%	0.7%	1.0%	0.6%	0.3%	0.6%	0.3%	0.5%
Public housing	4.7%*	2.5%	2.6%	2.4%	1.6%	2.5%	1.4%	2.6%
Rent subsidy	1.7%	1.2%	1.6%	0.9%	0.6%	0.2%*	1.1%	0.5%
Heat subsidy	4.5%*	2.0%	3.9%*	2.4%	1.2%	1.9%	2.9%	2.1%
Free or reduced lunch program	1.0%	1.0%	1.1%	0.9%	1.2%	1.0%	1.2%	0.4%

SOURCE: Data from CPS ASEC, 1996–2015 (Flood et al., 2017).

NOTES: Sample includes widows age 40 and older. All calculations are weighted using person-level weights for the analysis of the CPS ASEC, adjusted for differences in observed characteristics with the IPW methodology. EITC = Earned Income Tax Credit.

* $p < 0.05$ (there is a statistical significant difference at the 95% confidence level in comparison to the value in the column on military survivor benefits, based on 300 bootstrap replications).

[a] Main survivor pension is from regular payments from annuities or paid-up life insurance.

[b] Main survivor pension is from the combination of other sources, which may include U.S. railroad retirement survivor pension, workers' compensation pension, black-lung survivor pension, regular payments from estates or trusts, and other unspecified sources.

[c] Includes Aid to Families with Dependent Children, Aid to Dependent Children, General Assistance, and other assistance programs.

Conclusions

Our findings indicate that fewer than one in five widows reported regular income from survivor benefits other than Social Security. We saw earlier (Table 2.1) that two-thirds of military retirees are enrolled in SBP, and, should they die, their widows will receive SBP survivor benefits. Many of these widows will also receive Social Security. Thus, while survivor benefits other than Social Security are relatively uncommon as a source of income for widows in general, a large fraction of military survivors is eligible to receive survivor benefits.

The receipt of any survivor benefits is generally associated with higher total income and a lower percentage below the poverty line, especially for widows without Social Security income. For these widows, survivor benefits are, on average, 50 percent of their total income. And for nearly 30 percent of those widows, survivor benefits are more than 80 percent of their total income.

The average amount of survivor benefits received from the military is similar to or higher than the average survivor benefits received from companies or unions by widows of similar characteristics. Average total income, poverty rates, and participation in public assistance programs are also similar between widows receiving benefits from the military and widows receiving benefits from companies or unions. Thus, overall, survivor benefits from the military compare well with respect to survivors' financial status when they are benchmarked against those provided by the private sector.

We also find that survivor benefits received from federal, state, and local government pensions plans are larger, on average, than survivor benefits received from the military. Widows receiving survivor benefits from federal, state, and local government pension plans also have higher average total income, lower poverty rates, and lower participation in public assistance-programs than widows with similar characteristics who receive benefits from the military. Because our analysis in Chapter Three indicated that military survivor benefits compare favorably with federal and state and local survivor benefits, it seems likely that the higher survivor benefits and total income among government widows in comparison to military widows could be due to differences in wages and other characteristics of deceased spouses. Unfortunately, data limitations do not allow us to adjust for differences in decedent characteristics.

Finally, we find that widows receiving survivor benefits from VA have relatively similar average survivor benefits compared with widows with similar characteristics who receive survivor benefits from the military, especially when measured in after-tax dollars (since the VA benefits are tax-exempt). Nevertheless, widows receiving survivor benefits from VA have lower average total income even after accounting for tax savings, higher rates of poverty, and higher rates of participation in public assistance programs than widows with similar characteristics who receive survivor benefits from the military (or than widows who receive survivor benefits from other sources). Differences in labor force participation contribute to explaining these differences.

In summary, we find that SBP benefits typically make up a third to a half of survivors' incomes, depending on whether Social Security was also received. For widows not receiving Social Security, the percentage with total incomes below the poverty line was typically higher for widows with SBP than for widows whose main source of survivor benefits is federal, state, or local government; annuities; or "other." However, the differences in the percentages are not statistically significant except for one case. Also, as we stated in the introduction to this chapter, this may not indicate a shortcoming of SBP but could derive from prior differences—for instance, lower earnings of the now-deceased spouses of widows receiving SBP compared with widows receiving survivor benefits from other sources—or to differences in the amount of survivor benefit coverage selected. Our data do not include such information, yet we recognize that more-detailed analysis is needed to better understand the differences in outcomes we observe and determine whether remedies to the SBP program are warranted.

## CHAPTER FIVE

Feasibility and Advisability of Providing SBP Commercially

The final requirement of the review of SBP mandated by Congress concerns the feasibility and advisability of providing SBP commercially. To assess feasibility, we consider whether insurance products similar to SBP currently exist in the commercial market and whether those products could incorporate and recognize some of the distinctive features of SBP, such as its interaction with DIC. The features we consider are not all necessarily unique to SBP in the sense that they do not exist in the private sector, but they would be features that a commercial source would need to provide for the insurance product to be similar to SBP.

To assess advisability, we consider whether the price at which commercial providers offer to administer and manage SBP would be lower than the current cost to DoD at a quality of service acceptable to DoD. If the commercial price, plus DoD's cost of contracting, is less than the in-house costs of administering and managing SBP, and if the SBP subsidy were the same either way, then outsourcing SBP would be advisable. We consider factors that could affect cost.

A definitive answer as to the feasibility and advisability of shifting to commercial sources would require data about the current DoD costs, as well as about the likely commercial-provider costs of managing and administering SBP and about the quality and cost of service under DoD versus commercially provided sourcing. Unfortunately, such data are lacking, and collection of such was beyond the time and resource scope of the current study. Further research into DoD's internal costs, at a minimum, is indicated, as well as research into contract mechanisms that could induce insurers to provide a sufficiently high-quality product to service members at a reduced cost to the government. Because of the lack of data, our assessment of feasibility and advisability is primarily conceptual rather than evidence- or data-driven.

We first consider feasibility by discussing the types of commercial insurance products that exist and whether these products resemble SBP. We also discuss some distinctive features of SBP that would have to be handled by the commercial provider. We then turn to conditions under which outsourcing SBP would be advisable and factors that could affect cost and quality. Our assessment focuses on contracting approaches where DoD would contract with a commercial source or sources to handle the administration of SBP and be responsible for funding the SBP liability, and DoD would make a payment to the contractor. We briefly consider an alternative approach whereby DoD pays the subsidy directly to the retiree to purchase an SBP-like product in the private sector.

Feasibility of Providing SBP Commercially

Commercially Available Insurance Policies

In general, there are two types of life insurance policies, whole life policies and term life policies. Within whole life policies, survivor benefits can be paid as a lump sum or an annuity. SBP can be thought of as a hybrid: a whole life policy that pays a whole life annuity to the survivor.

By definition, a whole life policy is in force throughout the life of the insured, provided the premiums are paid. At death, the insured amount is paid to the beneficiary. Whole life premium rates in the commercial market increase with the age at which the policy is taken out. Consider two policies, one taken out at age 25 and the other at age 45. Although the mortality hazard after age 45 is about the same for the 25-year-old and the 45-year-old, the mortality hazard from 25 to 45 is quite low. But at age 45, there are 20 fewer years over which to pay premiums and for the company to earn a rate of return on those premiums.[1]

Premiums paid into whole life policies are invested, and the return on investment and inflow of premiums enable the insurance fund to grow and cover the expected liability of the insured. At some point, an actuarial assessment might determine that the current and projected fund accumulation exceeds the projected liability, and at this point money could be disbursed from the fund. Whole life insurance may be participating or nonparticipating. If it is nonparticipating, the disbursement goes to the fund owners. If it is participating, part of the disbursement goes to the insured. By comparison, the federal government owns the SBP fund, and it is nonparticipating. The Department of the Treasury ensures that beneficiaries are paid, keeps actuarial gains, and covers actuarial losses, all the while holding the premium structure constant.

Term life insurance is an alternative to whole life insurance. We mention term life insurance because its lower premium rates might appear to make it an attractive commercial counterpart to SBP. A term life policy provides insurance against death occurring within a given period—the term—which may be five, 10, 20, or even 30 years. Term life insurance is useful to protect beneficiaries against the loss of income resulting from the insured's death if it were to occur before other income became available. For example, if the insured died at age 55 and Social Security survivor benefits could not be claimed until age 60 at a reduced rate or until age 65 or older at a full rate, term insurance could cover this potential gap in income. Because term insurance is for a fixed-length term, its premium is lower than the whole life premium, which must build in uncertainty over time to death. Therefore, term life insurance is a more affordable option to cover risk for a given period. But, like whole life policies, a purpose of SBP is to provide for survivors regardless of when the insured dies.

Distinctive Features of SBP

SBP has several features that are not necessarily unique to this program but that are distinctive and that commercial providers would need to recognize.

---

[1] Whole life policies may be obtained for a given length of premium payments—e.g., 20 years of premiums. Still, the premium rate would be lower at a younger age because the company would have more years until the expected date of death to earn a return on the premiums.

Premiums

In contrast to whole life policies provided commercially, SBP's premium rate for an insured spouse is a flat 6.5 percent of covered retired pay, and the premium rate never exceeds 6.5 percent of the gross retirement benefit regardless of the beneficiary category. Importantly, the rate does not differ by age at enrollment into SBP or health status at the time of enrollment. To embed these features into a whole life policy, a commercial administrator of SBP would need to design a universal flat premium rate that covered members retiring from the military at different ages and with different health conditions (and disability ratings). Doing so requires recognizing the different longevities associated with retirees' ages and health status and, after the retirees' deaths, the longevity of the surviving spouses (and the covered years of other beneficiary types, such as children or NIP), in effect, averaging across them all.

The flat 6.5 percent premium under SBP also contrasts with typical term life policies where premiums increase with age, or, more precisely, increase with mortality rates, which rise after age 40. If term life policies were used to provide survivor benefits for military survivors, military retirees would face increasingly high premiums as they age. Furthermore, term life policies might not be offered at older ages. This reflects the fact that the probability of death within the term grows toward one when the policy begins at older and older ages. At older ages, a term life policy is in effect a savings account in anticipation of death. It is not surprising that commercial providers generally do not offer term life policies beyond a certain age.[2] The insured would need to put in enough money to cover the increasingly near-certain payout that would be made if death occurred during the term. Both of these factors—rising premiums with age and the possibility of no policies being offered to older individuals—mean that commercially provided term life policies are less likely to feasibly replicate the current SBP, since SBP has neither feature.

Inflation and Mortality and Other Risks

The annuity feature of SBP insures against two risks that also must be covered if SBP were provided commercially. These risks are survivor mortality and inflation. One can think of SBP as a whole life policy on a retiree, and when the retiree dies, the beneficiary receives a lump payment for the insured amount that is immediately converted into an annuity. If the beneficiary is the surviving spouse, the annuity is a whole life annuity—i.e., it pays benefits throughout the spouse's remaining years of life. Although one could envision annuitizing for a fixed term, such as 15 years, that would be contrary to the SBP approach of providing a lifelong annuity for the surviving spouse. Hence, annuitizing a whole life insurance payout requires an assessment of the surviving spouse's mortality—how long will the spouse live, given that the spouse has outlived the insured. Further, the SBP annuity is adjusted for inflation, so the lump sum in the thought experiment must be large enough to cover inflation risk. Covering the mortality and inflation risks is a cost of annuitizing.

In addition to its whole life and annuity features, SBP covers routine insurance risks related to variance in the rate of return on assets, actuarial gains and losses from experience, and assumption changes.

---

[2] For instance, the Military Benefit Association provides term life coverage up to age 75 (see Military Benefit Association, undated).

Survivor Benefits to Active Duty Members

SBP benefits are paid to survivors of service members who die on duty. Yet members do not pay SBP premiums, so the funds for their survivor benefits must come from the other sources of inflow into the SBP fund, which are premiums paid by retirees, DoD SBP accrual charges, interest earned on the fund, and the subsidy. A commercially provided product would need to include the same feature.

Interaction with DIC

As discussed in Chapter Two, DIC is paid to eligible survivors of service members who died in the line of duty or to eligible survivors of veterans who died from a service-related injury or disease. The possibility of receiving DIC implies that the expected liability from SBP is decreased by the expected DIC offset adjusted for SSIA. Commercial sources would need to factor this into the SBP liability estimate, and decreases in the liability should be reflected in decreased premiums. Also, the requirement to refund SBP premiums to the extent that SBP benefits are offset by DIC should largely be a matter of indifference to commercial sources. If the DIC offset were eliminated, the insurer would not be hurt because premiums would have been paid on the SBP policy, providing the funds needed to pay SBP benefits upon the death of the insured. If the DIC offset continued, the insurer, having received SBP premiums, could refund them to the survivor.

Different Maximum Base Rates Under Different Retirement Systems

The military has several different retirement systems, as described in Chapter Two. These systems have different retirement multipliers, which may affect a member's maximum SBP base amount. Under the regular retirement system, the retirement benefit multiplier is 2.5 percent per year of service, and the retirement benefit—hence, the maximum base amount—is 50 percent of high-36 basic pay at 20 years of service, 75 percent at 30 years, and 100 percent at 40 years. Under the CSB/Redux system, the maximum base amount for SBP is based on the same retirement benefit formula as for non-CSB/Redux takers—e.g., 50 percent of high-36 basic pay at 20 years and 75 percent at 30 years.[3] BRS begins on January 1, 2018, and its defined benefit retirement multiplier is 2 percent for each year of service, so that the retirement benefit is 40 percent at 20 years of service, 60 percent at 30 years, and 80 percent at 40 years. Members under BRS will be able to make their SBP election on their full retirement benefit amount even if they chose to take a lump sum.

Thus, the maximum base amount is the same under the regular system and CSB/Redux and is lower under BRS. The lower maximum base amount under BRS implies that the maximum SBP annuity will be lower. But savings in TSP, another component of BRS, compensate for this (see examples in Chapter Three). Also, even though the maximum base amount may differ among the retirement systems, there is no effect on the SBP premium rate. Commercial sources, too, should be able to offer the same premium rate regardless of retirement system.

---

[3] However, there is a difference in the inflation protection of benefits—the annuity for a survivor of a CSB/Redux retiree is subject to a lower COLA than that under SBP: "Benefits associated with members entering on or after August 1, 1986, who elect the $30,000 CSB bonus payment are annually increased by the percentage change in the CPI minus 1 percent (except when the change in the CPI is less than or equal to 1 percent), but at the military member's age 62, or when the member would have been age 62 for a survivor annuity, the benefits are restored to the amount that would have been payable had full CPI protection been in effect. This restoral is in combination with the elimination of the multiplier penalty for retiring with less than 30 years of service. However, after this restoral, partial indexing (CPI minus 1 percent) continues for future retired pay and survivor annuity payments" (DoD, Office of the Actuary, 2017a).

DoD Subsidy to SBP

The DoD subsidy to SBP is fundamental to maintaining low SBP premium rates. Therefore, any decision to provide SBP though commercial sources must consider the relationship between the DoD subsidy, presuming it is continued in some form, and the premium rates offered by commercial sources.

The DoD subsidy is the portion of the SBP liability paid by DoD, as reflected through DoD's SBP accrual charge: "Retired pay is reduced, before taxes, for the member's cost of SBP. Total SBP costs are shared by the government and the retiree, so the reductions in retired pay are only a portion of the total cost of the SBP program."[4] The accrual charge is based on the normal cost percentage (NCP) for SBP applied to the basic pay payroll. There are also NCPs for nondisability benefits and disability benefits.

NCPs are constructed to be a constant percentage of basic pay that must be contributed over the service career of an entering cohort of personnel to pay for its future retirement and survivor benefits. The accrual charges are included in DoD's personnel budget; they are not deducted from service members' pay. In FY 2016, DoD's NCP for full-time service members was 27.2 percent for nondisability benefits, 0.8 percent for disability benefits, and 1.2 percent for survivor benefits. The percentages for part-time members (reservists) were 19.9, 1.0, and 2.0, respectively (DoD, Office of the Actuary, 2017a, Table 5). In FY 2015, the total accrual charges for full- and part-time personnel were $18 billion and $1.9 billion, respectively (DoD, Office of the Actuary, 2017a, Table 1). Applying the NCP for survivors to these amounts indicates SBP-related accrual charges of $0.74 billion for full time and $0.17 for part time, for a total of $0.91 billion. This should be interpreted as an amount that would cover the cohorts in the current active and reserve components.

On net, the SBP fund is designed to be in actuarial balance. For instance, members who retire with more than 20 years of service or at an age older than 40 can be expected to pay fewer SBP premiums because they might die before completing the maximum number of payments. Spouses might receive benefits for more years. In addition, funds are required for SBP benefits for survivors of service members dying on duty. Members who retired with a disability retirement have higher mortality rates, implying that they would make fewer premium payments. Finally, the accrual charge must allow for financial risk related to mortality, fund experience gains and losses, return on assets, and COLA. For instance, not only has mortality tended to decrease over time—people are living longer—but also members with SBP spouse coverage tend to live longer than other retirees do.[5] DoD's Office of the Actuary adjusts for this (see DoD, Office of the Actuary, 2017a, Appendix J) and has separate tables for disability retired and nondisability retired (DoD, Office of the Actuary, 2017a, Appendix I).

DoD's Office of the Actuary (2017b) estimates DoD's SBP subsidy at 44.6 percent for the FY 2016 cohort of retirees (see Chapter Two). Appendix F develops an example to illustrate the

---

[4]   DoD, Office of the Actuary, 2017a. The *outlay* for SBP benefits is the responsibility of the U.S. Department of the Treasury, but, as with the liability for military retirement benefits, the liability for SBP is represented by an SBP accrual charge in the DoD personnel budget.

[5]   Regarding "retired pay adjustment to members with SBP spouse coverage," DoD's Office of the Actuary wrote, "These factors model data that show mortality is better (or less), and non-death loss from paid status is generally higher, for those retired members who elect SBP spouse coverage. Rather than develop additional sets of mortality and loss rates, the respective retiree death and loss rates (Appendix I) are adjusted with these factors. This impacts retirees with SBP spouse coverage. The factors are given by active/reserve, disability/nondisability status, and officer/enlisted status" (DoD, Office of the Actuary, 2017a, Appendix F, Table F-1).

DoD subsidy to SBP and shows that DoD cost-sharing is sizable and has enabled SBP rates to be lower than otherwise and stable. In the absence of the subsidy but in the presence of SBP's features, the premium rates offered by private insurers would no doubt be higher than current SBP premium rates are. Based on history, higher premium rates would decrease participation and diminish the role of SBP in providing financial protection for survivors. SBP's predecessor, the RSFPP, was designed to be actuarially fair to the member and self-funding, yet its participation rate never exceeded 15 percent. In contrast, SBP is subsidized by DoD, allowing premium rates to be lower, and its participation rate is 66 percent overall and nearly 80 percent for recent retiree cohorts. To maintain lower premiums and higher participation if SBP were commercially sourced, the DoD subsidy would need to continue.

Intergovernmental Transfers Versus Outlays

The accrual charges, including the charge related to the SBP subsidy, are included in DoD's personnel budget and paid to the Treasury's military retirement fund. Therefore, the charges and the subsidy are an intergovernmental transfer of funds between DoD and Treasury. A government outlay occurs only when survivor benefits are paid by the Treasury to survivors. Under a commercially sourced SBP, the subsidy would be paid to the commercial provider. This could be accomplished as a two-step procedure: The commercial source would first estimate the SBP liability—presumably for the same populations now covered and with the same eligibility conditions and premium rates—and then estimate how much of the liability would be funded under the existing SBP premium rates. These calculations will depend on assumptions about the rate of return of fund assets, discount rate, rate of inflation, mortality projections, and financial risks (uncertainty in rates of return) and ways of hedging them (e.g., through reinsurance and risk tolerance). DoD would require the estimates to be reviewed and approved by third-party actuaries, who would be approved by DoD. The unfunded part of the liability, after allowing for premiums, would be funded by DoD. In effect, this would continue DoD's subsidy to SBP.

If SBP were commercially provided, the subsidy would be a government outlay and not an intergovernmental transfer as it is today. On the other hand, the payout of benefits to survivors would no longer be a government outlay as it is today. In the long run, when the government no longer pays outs survivor benefits to survivors, the effect on outlays depends on whether the commercial provider is less costly than government provision of SBP, in which case the subsidy might be lower than it is today. But, in the short run, commercialization of SBP may affect outlays, and the time pattern of that effect will depend on how the transition to a commercial provider is done.

If only new cohorts of enrollees and survivors are enrolled into the commercial source as of the date of the contract, DoD could pay an annual amount to the contractor for its share of the accruing liability. This would be a fiscal outlay. At the same time, DoD would retain responsibility for incumbent populations; these are the current SBP enrollees and the beneficiaries. With responsibility for new cohorts shifted to commercial sources, the SBP fund for incumbent populations would be closed. DoD would continue to have an SBP accrual charge, but it would diminish over time as these populations aged out. Likewise, Treasury outlays for these populations would decline over time. At the same time, DoD might have an accrual charge to fund its accruing liability to pay the contractor, and Treasury outlays to the contractor would increase over time as new cohorts continued to enter. If the contractor could operate SBP at lower total cost than does DoD, these accrual charge and outlays would be smaller than they would have been under continued DoD management of SBP. But there would also be contracting costs, and these would need to be assigned to some budget—perhaps to the military retirement fund.

If the responsibility for *both* new cohorts and incumbent SBP populations shifted to commercial sources, the SBP accrual charge would be understood to cover the accruing liability of SBP populations now handled commercially, and outlays would be for the SBP benefits to be disbursed by the commercial provider to existing and new beneficiaries. A decision would need to be made for each cohort of the incumbent enrollees regarding what share of the liability would be DoD's responsibility. For instance, for service members at the 19th year of service (and therefore be eligible to retire in one more year) who enroll in SBP, DoD would already have paid accrual charges for much of their liability. But when they began to enroll in SBP when retiring after 20 or more years of service, the contractor would receive premiums from them for 30 or more years. Actuarial calculations are required to figure out what DoD would owe.

Changes in government outlays that affect computation of the federal deficit and policies that increase outlays in the short term, even if they result in reductions in outlays in the long term, may be viewed as unfavorable by Congress. Insofar as commercial provision of SBP will change the time pattern and possibly the level of government outlays, the feasibility of commercialization depends on whether and how much outlays increase and on Congress's tolerance for changes in outlays.

Discussion

Commercial sources offer a variety of insurance policies and annuities. SBP is a whole life insurance policy that pays a whole life annuity to the survivor, and the SBP premium rate does not depend on the age or health of the insured, benefits are inflation-protected, and benefits are provided to the survivors of members who die on duty even though they pay no premiums. SBP benefits interact with DIC, and the maximum base amount of retired pay differs depending on retirement plan. Furthermore, DoD subsidizes SBP premiums. These features distinguish it from readily available commercial products and would need to be incorporated into a commercially developed product.

Term life insurance policies are widely promoted as an affordable means of income protection, but their coverage extends only for the term chosen. Term life insurance policies could be attractive to retirees who expect to accumulate adequate savings for retirement and to provide income for the surviving spouse. These retirees already have the option not to participate in SBP, and there is little reason to think that they would participate in commercial SBP or that retirees enrolling in SBP would find term policies to be an attractive alternative, especially given that SBP premiums are subsidized and that SBP is whole life for the enrollee and a whole life annuity for the survivor, whereas term life is finite-year coverage with a premium that increases steeply with age.

Although there are no readily available commercial versions of SBP, the expertise and capability underlying the existing variety of commercial products indicate that it is feasible for commercial sources to design a product with SBP's features. The key elements are the construction of inflation-adjusted, flat-rate, single-rate whole life policies that pay an amount sufficient to fund an inflation-adjusted whole life annuity for the life of a surviving spouse and fund the payouts for the other categories of SBP beneficiaries.

In constructing a commercial SBP product, commercial sources should have access to DoD data on retiree and survivor mortality rates and on retiring service members, SBP enrollees, designated beneficiaries, and benefit recipients. In addition to using these data to design an SBP policy and support day-to-day operations, commercial sources might create variants with wider choices than are available from today's SBP. The variants could, for example, allow SBP benefits to be shared by more beneficiaries (e.g., spouse and dependent parents), allow for a wider selection of beneficiaries, provide a cash-out option for a portion of the annuity stream, and offer a wider range of coverage (e.g., more than a maximum of 55 percent of the retiree's retirement benefit).

Another aspect of feasibility is the quality of service that would be provided by commercial sources. As a relevant example, SGLI is a VA program provided by a commercial source, Prudential Insurance. The Better Business Bureau (undated) rates SGLI highly (A+), and a study (Callan, Schmid, and Voogd, 2011) concluded that Prudential ran SGLI in a way that benefited both Prudential and the SGLI policyholders. This suggests that commercial sources for SBP could provide high-quality service.

Advisability of Providing SBP Through Commercial Sources

The advisability of providing SBP through commercial sources will depend on the price at which commercial providers offer to administer and manage the SBP fund at a quality of service acceptable to DoD. If the commercial price, the cost of contracting, and the subsidy DoD would deliver to the commercial provider sum to an amount less than the in-house costs of administering, managing, and subsidizing the SBP fund, then outsourcing SBP is more likely to be advisable. The cost information to make this assessment is not currently available, so, instead, we focus on some of the factors that could affect the cost of SBP provided by commercial sources.

Administration Costs and Funding Efficiency

Administration of SBP involves keeping track of beneficiary designation, collecting premiums, paying benefits, and resolving day-to-day administrative questions. Today, premiums are collected more or less automatically by DFAS as pretax deductions from retired pay or in some cases from DIC. DFAS has files on retirees enrolled in SBP and their designated beneficiaries. There seems to be little gain in having a commercial source collect premiums instead. However, the premiums collected under the current procedures could be sent to the commercial source for investment in the SBP fund it creates. DFAS also pays SBP benefits. Benefit payment could be done by a commercial source, and to enable this, DFAS would share its file of SBP benefit recipients. Another facet of administering SBP is enrollment. This is done in service, before the member retires, and it is to be handled along with other steps in DoD out-processing. The services and the commercial provider would need to establish protocols for the provider's role. Some questions are whether commercial agents would be present on base, whether they would offer financial counseling and market products more broadly, and whether enrollment could instead be done electronically.

A commercial source's administrative cost and funding efficiency are private information that is difficult, if not impossible, to verify. However, contracting competitions are a means of inducing firms to report their cost truthfully, and their potential to succeed depends on having multiple qualified bidders and an absence of collusion among the bidders. With more than 1 million enrollees and roughly 300,000 annuitants, SBP appears large enough to attract multiple bidders. These populations would be available only if the entire SBP program moved to a commercial source, but the populations would be much smaller if only new cohorts of retirees and new survivors of service members who died on duty shifted to commercial providers. Among bidding firms, those that could provide the administration and funding functions more efficiently—at lower total cost, given quality and premium rates—would be willing to accept a lower subsidy from DoD. The firm or firms winning a contract would be those with the lowest required subsidy.

Contracting Costs

DoD's costs of contracting must also be considered. These costs are not negligible and include developing specifications for services required and contract terms regarding quality of service, implementing the bid and proposal process, and the adjudication of complaints or lawsuits if unselected bidders contest the choice of the winner. These costs would be periodical—e.g., contracts might be for a five-year term, followed by another competition. In addition, DoD would want oversight authority to monitor the quality of service provided by the commercial sources, and DoD would need to interact with the contractors to exchange data, maintain files, audit for timeliness and accuracy, and clarify responsibility (e.g., who determines whether a death was in the line of duty).

Profitability and Bankruptcy

The cost of capital is higher to commercial providers than to DoD. For SBP to remain at the same or lower cost to the government, commercial providers may need to be more efficient at administering and managing an SBP while providing an acceptable quality of service.

One avenue may be through more-efficient asset management. A large share of military retirement fund assets is invested in special-issue Treasury obligations that mirror Treasury Inflation-Protected Securities. These assets provide an effective hedge against inflation but tend to provide a low real returns on investment. Private firms might be able to realize a higher real rate of return without incurring undue risk, by not being under the constraint of having to invest solely in Treasury obligations that mirror publicly traded U.S. obligations. Firms in the life and health insurance sector currently hold asset portfolios in which 74 percent is invested in bonds, 11 percent in mortgage loans, and the remainder is spread across stocks and other investments (U.S. Department of the Treasury, 2017). The real difference in return may be small but will accumulate over many years and potentially make a difference of several billion dollars in annual premiums. The potential yield from asset management may provide inducement for firms to enter and stay in the SBP market.

One risk posed by outsourcing SBP is that the commercial provider may go bankrupt, in which case the government would need to step in to protect the interests of service members and their survivors and to fulfill the obligations that the insurer is no longer able to fulfill. This might happen if a there were an unexpectedly large number of claims resulting from a conflict where the United States suffered massive casualties. Members covered under SGLI are automatically entered into the Traumatic Injury Protection program, which provides for members who suffer a serious traumatic injury in service, and the agreement governing the program is such that DoD will pay for any claims cost in excess of premiums collected (VA, 2012, p. III-53). Still, private insurers are required to hold capital to protect against the possibility of bankruptcy, which should be sufficient for less extreme realizations. Holding capital is a cost that a public insurance program, such as SBP, does not have—SPB can borrow from the Treasury at low rates or seek funds from Congress. Thus, commercial providers may be able to earn a better return than DoD does on the premiums paid by policyholders, but the requirement to hold capital to avoid the risk of default decreases the potential gain. Further data and analysis would be required to determine whether commercial providers could perform the insurance function more cheaply than the public sector does.

Transition Costs

The process of migrating SBP to commercial sources would require extensive actuarial calculation to determine DoD's share of the liability, a setup cost that DoD would bear. Similarly, bidding firms would need to estimate their setup costs (designing the SBP product, developing data systems, training agents), and this would factor into the cost stated in their bids. With respect to making SBP more flexible by expanding beneficiary designation options and payment options, this could be pursued by DoD or commercial providers, although commercial providers may have fewer constraints to make changes than DoD has, especially if changes require congressional legislation.

Adjustment in Premiums over Time

Commercial providers might increase premium rates over time. Depending on the size of the increase, more military retirees might opt out of SBP. This would diminish the income security of retirees' survivors, and the composition of SBP participants could change. Healthier retirees might opt for term life insurance, while less healthy retirees might opt for SBP. This self-selection could occur even if the commercial providers were barred from differentiating rates by health status (everyone who wanted to obtain SBP could do so). The higher rates would lead retirees to sort based on their health status. If significant sorting occurred, it would put upward pressure on the unfunded liability, which could require a higher DoD subsidy per enrollee.

Discussion

The advisability of DoD contracting for the administration and funding of SBP thus depends on whether commercial sources' administration cost and required subsidy from DoD, plus DoD's contracting cost, would be less than DoD's in-house administration, subsidy, and accrual costs. In addition, DoD could consider whether the quality of service should be improved, maintained, or perhaps decreased relative to SBP's current quality. If we can determine that the quality of service is currently high and if we know that there could be substantial savings from slightly reducing the quality, it might be appropriate to do so. Cost information is not currently available, but DoD could have a preliminary competition where firms would submit estimates of what their (unsubsidized) premium rates would be. With respect to making SBP more flexible by expanding beneficiary designation options and payment options, this could be pursued either by DoD or by commercial providers and does not necessitate commercial providers, although commercial providers may have more flexibility and possibly could accomplish such changes more readily. Yet another possibility would be to enable a private system that runs in parallel to the current program. Beneficiaries could choose between the two systems (with DoD providing the beneficiary who chooses the private system the same subsidy that he or she would receive in the SBP system). This way, DoD could better assess how well a private system would work and whether there are substantial efficiencies in a private program.

Paying a Subsidy to Retirees Enrolled in Commercialized SBP

Rather than contract with a commercial source, DoD could pay the difference between the SBP premium offered by a commercial source and the SBP premium that the military retiree pays today. Under this approach, SBP would cost the retiree the same as now, so there would be no decrease in enrollment, provided that quality of service were maintained. However, this approach has downsides. First, while it would be ideal to have many commercial firms offer SBP and compete for business, there is a question of whether the market would be large enough for individual firms to make the investment in developing an SBP product and marketing it. If few firms offered SBP, one could not expect premium rates to be at competitive levels. Second, if DoD committed to holding premium rates constant for retirees and thereby committed to paying the difference between the rate charged and that rate, firms would have an incentive to overcharge. This contrasts to the contracting approach described above, where firms have an incentive to submit low-cost bids. Third, having many commercial sources could complicate the detection of poor-quality service and possibly weaken DoD's leverage to induce a firm to improve quality. Finally, because whole life premium rates differ by age, the subsidy that DoD would pay would differ by age. This is implicitly the case today with SBP under DoD management, but these differences would become explicit and might possibly be a source of annoyance to enrollees and DoD.

Conclusions

The discussion in this chapter considered conceptually the issue of feasibility and advisability. We argued that using commercial sources to provide survivor benefits is, broadly speaking, feasible if such products currently exist in the commercial insurance market or could be combined to provide something equivalent to the benefits provided under SBP. Although there are no readily available commercial versions of SBP, the expertise and capability underlying the existing variety of commercial products indicate that it is feasible for commercial sources to design a product with SBP's features. The key elements are the construction of inflation-adjusted, flat-rate, single-rate whole life policies that pay an amount sufficient to fund an inflation-adjusted whole life annuity for the life of a surviving spouse and fund the payouts for the other categories of SBP beneficiaries. The policy would have to be offered to retiring members regardless of age or health status, and the benefits would have to cover the survivors of members who die on duty, even though they paid no premiums.

We also argued that advisability depends on whether, combined, the commercial price, the cost of DoD's SBP subsidy to the commercial provider, and DoD's cost of contracting are less than the in-house costs of administering, managing, and subsidizing the SBP fund. While data are lacking to assess whether this is the case, key factors will include administration costs, contracting costs, transition costs, and return on investment. To get more information on these costs, DoD could have a preliminary competition in which firms would submit estimates of what their (unsubsidized) premium rates would be.

## CHAPTER SIX

Conclusion

In this report, we set out to address four topics specified by Congress. In brief, the topics were to assess the purposes of SBP and its interaction with other federal programs, to compare SBP benefits with those available to government and private-sector employees, to evaluate the effectiveness of SBP in shoring up survivors' income, and to assess the feasibility and advisability of having commercial sources provide SBP.

We reviewed SBP in detail, describing its premium and benefit rates, designation of beneficiaries, legislative history, and other possible sources of monetary support available to survivors of service members, such as life insurance and Social Security. Established in 1972, SBP's main purpose is to provide an annuity for service members' and retirees' survivors. In 2016, nearly all annuitants were survivors of military retirees, and participation was 66 percent of all retirees and 78 percent of the 2016 cohort of retirees. The base amount covered by SBP has also been rising, reaching 98 percent for the 2016 retiree cohort. DoD subsidizes SBP, allowing premiums paid by retirees to be lower than what would be required to cover the full SBP liability. SBP interacts with VA disability compensation and DIC and is one of a number of benefits available to survivors. Other benefits include the DoD death gratuity, life insurance, housing, TRICARE, commissary and exchange use, child care, education assistance, the VA Survivors Pension, the ACMSS, the Minimum Income Widow Annuity, tax forgiveness, and Social Security benefits.

We compared SBP with public and private retirement plans offering survivor benefits and examined data on access to such plans and the level of benefits provided. We found that survivor benefits are often available in defined benefit retirement plans, but because these plans are less common today than they were 30 years ago, workers rely on other means to provide for survivors, including life insurance, defined contribution plans, workers' compensation, and Social Security.

We also compared SBP with survivor benefit programs available to government and private-sector employees by conducting two types of analyses. First, we compared survivor benefit annuity generosity among SBP, federal civilian programs, and selected private and public defined benefit plans. We found that, measured as a percentage of FAS, SBP was more generous or in line with benefits offered by federal civilian programs and by select local public and private plans included for comparison in this study. Second, we considered detailed examples of the one-time and ongoing survivor benefits from various sources that would be available to survivors of workers who died on the job, compared with those of active-duty service members who died in the line of duty and to survivors of retired workers and military retirees.

For the line-of-duty examples, we found that SBP is at least as generous as benefits offered to a survivor of a FERS-eligible employee who dies from a service-connected death and more generous than those offered of a surviving spouse of a private-industry employee among the private-industry firms we considered. For the examples comparing survivor benefits among retirees, we found that SBP is generally in line with or more generous than FERS or private-industry survivor benefits.

We assessed SBP effectiveness by comparing the total money income and income by source of military widows with nonmilitary widows, where sources included wages, Social Security, retirement income, survivor benefits, and other income. Because results could differ by whether the widow also received Social Security (those who receive Social Security are older, on average), we did the comparisons separately for those receiving and those not receiving Social Security. We defined *military widows* as those widows for whom their main source of survivor benefits was the military, and we divided nonmilitary widows among their main source of survivor benefits: VA, company or union, federal government, state or local government, annuities, other sources, or no survivor benefits. For each category, we presented tables in Chapter Four showing the percentages receiving each type of income and the average amount of income conditional on receipt.

Overall, we found that SBP benefits were broadly comparable to survivor benefits from other sources and were a significant component of total income. For widows receiving Social Security, total income, on average, for widows whose primary source of survivor benefits was the military was comparable to total income for widows who received survivor benefits from other sources. For the military widows receiving Social Security, survivor benefits were about a third of total income, on average. For military widows not receiving Social Security, survivor benefits were just under half of total income. For these younger widows who did not receive Social Security, we also found that total income, on average, was comparable to total income for widows who received survivor benefits from company or union benefits but somewhat lower than total income of widows for whom the federal or state or local government was the main source of survivor benefits.

We considered the extent to which widows had income above and below the poverty line and found that the majority of widows, including military widows, had income that was 50 percent or more above the poverty line, especially widows who also received Social Security. That said, the percentage below the poverty line was typically lower for widows whose main source of survivor benefits was federal, state, or local government; annuities; or the "other" category than for military widows. This might not indicate a shortcoming of military survivor benefits, including SBP, but might instead be due to systematic differences in the characteristics of decedents associated with federal, state, or local government that we do not observe.

We also addressed the feasibility and advisability of having SBP provided by commercial sources. Commercially available products do not have the features of SBP, but the commercial expertise behind the many existing commercial products could be applied to develop commercial SBP. Regarding advisability, we discussed the costs of administration, of contracting, and of transition associated with commercialization, as well as the requirement that commercial providers receive a competitive return on investment and yet hold capital to protect against the possibility of bankruptcy. We also noted that DoD could consider whether it would want commercial providers to provide the same quality of service as is currently provided.

The overall conclusion from this analysis is that SBP is well structured to serve the role of providing survivor benefits to service members and military retirees, and SBP benefits generally compare well to those of public and private plans. Using commercial sources to provide survivor benefits appears feasible; however, the advisability of shifting to commercial sources requires information not currently available about internal and external cost and quality of service under different approaches to outsourcing.

Other Benefits and Sources of Support Available to Survivors of Service Members and Military Retirees

There are a number of sources of benefits and support available to the survivors of service members who die on duty or survivors of military retirees, in addition to SBP, DIC, and SSIA. This appendix describes them.

Death Gratuity

The death gratuity, paid by DoD, is a tax-free $100,000 payment to survivors of certain eligible reserve-status military personnel, as well as active-duty military members who die on duty or within 120 days of release from active duty (DoD, undated-a). Eligibility for the death gratuity does not depend on the cause of death. Service members can designate any person to receive part of or the whole benefit. Any undesignated amount is distributed in whole to the first person or in equal shares to the first living group in following hierarchy: spouse, children (or grandchildren, by representation, if the child or children are deceased), parents, executor or administrator of estate, other next of kin.

SGLI

Active and reserve component personnel are automatically enrolled in SGLI, and enrollees pay a premium for it. SGLI is available to active-duty and ready-reserve members, and they are entitled to 120 days of free coverage after separation or two years of free coverage for totally disabled veterans (VA, 2017f). The insurance payout is not subject to income tax and is available as a lump-sum payment or 36 monthly payments. The maximum insured amount is $400,000, and that is the default, although members may reduce the amount or opt out completely. SGLI is a VA program that is administered by a commercial source, the Prudential Insurance Company of America.

VGLI

Upon separation from the armed forces, former service members have one year and 120 days to enroll in VGLI, with coverage up to the amount they had in SGLI (VA, 2017f). This is also a VA program. VGLI coverage can be increased every five years, in $25,000 increments, to a maximum of $400,000. If a member applies for VGLI within 240 days of separation, there is no health review needed to obtain coverage. Unlike SGLI, VGLI premiums increase with age. The insurance payout is not subject to income tax and is available as a lump sum or 36 monthly payments.

S-DVI

Most personnel who have separated from service may apply for S-DVI if they have *any* service-connected disability rating but are otherwise in good health (VA, 2017f). S-DVI is a VA program. The deadline to apply for coverage is two years from the date someone is granted a service-connected disability rating from VA. The maximum amount of coverage is $10,000. But completely disabled veterans may be eligible for a waiver of premiums and may also receive an additional $30,000 of supplemental S-DVI. Premiums must be paid for the supplemental coverage, and the insurance payout is not subject to income tax.

Housing

If a service member is killed on active duty, DoD will pay survivors 365 days of BAH at the rate to which the service member was entitled if he or she lived off base or 365 days of free occupancy in base housing (37 U.S.C. 403[l]). This is not subject to income tax.

Just as DoD pays for a move when members separate from service, survivors are entitled to be reimbursed to move their household goods and one motor vehicle. They may elect to receive this benefit within a three-year eligibility window after the service member's death.

The VA Home Loan Guaranty program is available to eligible surviving spouses of eligible deceased veterans. Under this program, VA guarantees loans made by commercial lenders. A veteran is eligible if he or she died of service-connected causes, died of non–service-connected causes but was rated totally disabled for ten or more years prior to death or within five years of separation from active duty, or was a former prisoner of war who was rated totally service-connected-disabled for more than one year (VA, 2016, p. 32). The spouse is eligible as long as he or she does not remarry prior to age 57. The surviving spouse can use this loan guaranty one time. There is no limit on the lender regarding the borrowed amount, but VA does limit how much it may guarantee. The size of the loan that can be taken without needing to make a down payment is typically four times this maximum guarantee, and it varies by county (VA, 2016, p. 33; VA, 2017e).

VA also offers Veterans' Mortgage Life Insurance for severely disabled service members and veterans who have a mortgage and title for a home on which they spent Specially Adapted Housing money (VA, 2017f). This insurance can assist survivors in paying off the remainder of the mortgage. Coverage is the maximum of the remaining amount owed or $200,000 and is paid directly to the lender. Premiums are based on age, mortgage balance and years of payments remaining, and amount of Veterans' Mortgage Life Insurance.

Health Care

If a member is killed on active duty and had served at least 30 days at the time of death, surviving family members may continue their active-duty family member (ADFM) health care coverage and costs for three years (DoD, Defense Health Agency, 2017b, p. 1). As long as they keep their ADFM status, they also are eligible for the TRICARE dental program at no cost (DoD, Defense Health Agency, 2017b, p. 4). After the three years of coverage, the spouse is no longer considered an ADFM and is only eligible for retiree family member coverage and costs, but children keep ADFM status until they are no longer eligible for this benefit. The annual enrollment fee for an individual in TRICARE Prime is $282.60, and for a family it is $565.20 (Tricare.mil, 2016). Surviving spouses can keep this benefit until remarriage, and children can keep ADFM status until they are married, turn 21, or turn 23 (if a full-time student). If the child is incapacitated and if the injury occurred while still eligible for TRICARE, the child may be eligible for extended coverage.

Upon the death of a military retiree, the survivors can keep the same coverage and costs as they had at the time of the retiree's death, until the spouse remarries or the children lose eligibility, as above. The enrollment fees for TRICARE Prime are as above, or, if the spouse is at retirement age, he or she would be enrolled in TRICARE for Life and pay only Medicare Part B premiums, with no copays or deductibles. The 2017 Medicare Part B monthly premium ranges from $134.00 for an individual with yearly income of $85,000 or less to $428.60 for an individual with yearly income of $214,000 or more (U.S. Centers for Medicare and Medicaid Services, undated).

In either scenario, if children "age out" (21 or 23) of coverage but remain unmarried and are not covered by their own employee insurance, they may purchase TRICARE Young Adult until age 26 (DoD, Defense Health Agency, 2017a). The 2017 monthly premium is $319 for TRICARE Young Adult Prime and $216 for TRICARE Young Adult Standard (p. 4).

VA has its own program for survivors: Civilian Health and Medical Program of the Department of Veterans Affairs (CHAMPVA). This program provides eligible survivors with coverage for most medical expenses. To be eligible, the survivor cannot be eligible for TRICARE, as outlined above, and must be either the spouse or child of a service member who died on duty, the spouse or child of a service member who died from a VA-rated service-connected disability, or the spouse or child of a service member who was VA-rated as totally disabled at the time of death (VA, 2016, p. 52): "However, in most of these cases, these family members are eligible for TRICARE, not CHAMP-VA" (p. 53).

Education

VA offers the DEA program to the surviving spouse and children of service members who die of a service-connected disability or who die on active duty (VA, 2017a). DEA provides $1,024 per month directly to the beneficiary for up to 45 months for degree programs and other types of educational pursuits. Generally, a surviving spouse is eligible to use these benefits for ten years after becoming eligible, but it could be for up to 20 years for a surviving spouse of certain totally disabled veterans or service members' killed on duty. The spouse will lose benefits if the spouse remarries before age 57. If the second marriage ends, the spouse is eligible again.

Children, regardless of marital status, may receive the benefits between the ages of 18 and 26, with some exceptions.

If a service member dies in the line of duty, VA offers the Fry Scholarship to the surviving spouse and children. The scholarship pays full in-state tuition at public universities and up to $22,805.34 per year at private universities, in addition to a $1,000 annual stipend and monthly BAH paid directly to the beneficiary for up to 36 months of benefits (VA, 2017a). Generally, the BAH rate is for a local E-5 with dependents. Children, regardless of marital status, are eligible for this benefit until age 33, and spouses are eligible until remarriage or until 15 years after the service member's death.

If a survivor is eligible for the Fry Scholarship and DEA, the survivor may typically choose only one. These educational benefits may be received concurrently with DIC for a surviving spouse; however, children will not receive DIC if they elect to receive DEA (VA, 2010, p. 14).[1]

Commissary and Exchange

If a member is killed on duty or dies when retired from the military, surviving family members can continue to use the commissary, base exchange, and some Morale, Welfare and Recreation (MWR) facilities with virtually the same eligibility rules as above (DoD, 2014a, pp. 10, 54).

Child Care

If a service member dies in a combat-related incident, the surviving spouse may use military child development facilities for any children under the age of 13 (DoD, 2014b, p. 14).

Burial

Most deceased veterans and service members killed on duty are entitled to a headstone or marker and burial flag from VA and are entitled to burial at a national cemetery, with certain exceptions (VA, 2016). In addition, DoD may provide for military funeral honors on request.

For deaths on duty, DoD pays for virtually all expenses related to the remains, including identification, recovery, preparation, funeral director's services, hearse and other transportation of remains, and internment. If a survivor pays for these expenses to make private arrangements, the survivor is generally reimbursed (10 U.S.C. 1481 et seq.).

VA offers certain burial benefits to survivors of certain retirees, but these do not apply for active-duty deaths (VA, 2017d). To be eligible, survivors must have paid for the funeral or burial and not have been reimbursed by some other source. Additionally, the service member must have died of a service-related disability, died while receiving DIC, or died while in the care of VA (with some additional qualifying cases). VA pays up to $2,000 for burial expenses for service-related deaths. For non–service-related deaths, VA either provides for burial in a national cemetery or pays the survivor $749 for a plot-internment allowance. VA also provides

---

[1]   There are also various states that offer tuition assistance to survivors of service members who die on duty. For instance, someone might receive full in-state tuition in Minnesota and use DEA on top of it.

for burial and funeral expenses: up to $749 if the service member died while in a VA hospital or up to $300 in other instances.

Social Security

SSA has benefits that would provide for a family of a deceased retiree, military or otherwise. SSA provides survivor benefits to eligible individuals whose earnings were subject to Social Security taxes. To be eligible for survivor benefits, the employee had to have earnings subject to Social Security taxes for at least ten years, or at least 1.5 years in the three years preceding death if the employee had a dependent child under age 16. Survivor benefits are calculated as a percentage of the deceased basic benefit, which is also known as the primary insurance amount (PIA). The PIA is a progressive formula that is based on average indexed monthly earnings (AIME)—that is, the 35 highest years of indexed earnings divided by 12. If an individual died before age 62, then the number of years used to compute the AIME is reduced by the difference in years between the age at death and age 62 (Liou, 2016). If the deceased individual was claiming Social Security benefits, then the survivor benefits are calculated based on that amount, even if the deceased was receiving reduced benefits because of early retirement.

In general, surviving spouses without dependent children must be at least age 60 to begin claiming Social Security benefits, or at least age 50 if disabled. However, if a surviving spouse claims benefits before reaching full retirement age, those benefits will be reduced. Benefits for surviving spouses without dependent children range from 71.5 percent of the PIA at age 60 to 100 percent at the surviving spouse's full retirement age. A surviving spouse with dependent children under age 16 is eligible to claim Social Security survivor benefits equal to 75 percent of the PIA regardless of his or her own age. Children under age 18 (or 19 if in high school or at any age if disabled before age 22) are eligible for survivor benefits equal to 75 percent of the PIA. A surviving spouse with a dependent child and who is at least age 62 and received at least 50 percent of support from the deceased worker is eligible for benefits equal to 82.5 percent of the PIA if one parent was eligible at the time of the worker's death and 75 percent of the PIA for each parent if both were eligible. The total amount a family may receive from Social Security benefits is capped. This cap depends on the PIA and ranges between 150 percent and 188 percent of the PIA.

A working surviving spouse who is younger than full retirement age is subject to the Social Security earnings test. If earnings exceed the earnings test limit, then survivor benefits will be reduced. The earnings test limit was $16,920 in 2017. For each $2 of income earned above the limit, Social Security benefits are reduced by $1. Additionally, if a survivor receives a pension from certain government jobs, the survivor benefit may be reduced by the Government Pension Offset (SSA, undated-c). Surviving spouses who remarry before age 60 are not eligible for Social Security survivor benefits.

Table A.1 outlines these PIA benefits.

If a spouse is eligible for his or her own SSA benefit, the spouse can forgo the survivor benefit and receive his or her own SSA pension (SSA, undated-e). Finally, if a surviving spouse remarries before age 60, or 50 if disabled, the spouse is no longer eligible for these survivor benefits while married.

The Social Security lump-sum death payment is available to a surviving spouse or child. The lump sum is $255 and is received if the spouse or child was already receiving Social Secu-

Table A.1
Overview of PIA Benefits

Annuitant	Percentage of PIA
Spouse, full retirement age and older	100%
Spouse, age 60 (full retirement age)	71.5–100% (increasing with age)
Disabled spouse, ages 50–59	71.5%
Spouse, any age, with child under age 16	75%
Unmarried child under 18, 19 and under if in secondary school or below, or if disabled	75% (each child)
Dependent parent(s), age 62+	82.5% (1 parent), 150% (2 parents)
Combined maximum amount of family benefit	150–188%

SOURCE: Rates from SSA, undated-e.

rity benefits because of the deceased member or became eligible for benefits because of the death of the member (SSA, undated-e).

Up to 85 percent of Social Security benefits are subject to income tax. The amount of Social Security benefits subject to income tax depends on the beneficiary's combined income and filing status. Combined income is equal to 50 percent of Social Security income plus all other income, including tax-exempt interest. In 2016, if combined income was greater than $25,000 and the taxpayer filed as single, head of household, or as a qualifying widow or widower with a dependent child, then at least part of the benefits were taxable. For married couples filing jointly, the income threshold at which Social Security benefits started to be taxed was $32,000 in 2016.

Unpaid Pay and Allowances

Survivors are entitled to unpaid pay and allowances owed to the member at the time of death, including unpaid basic pay, payment for up to 60 days of accrued leave, and other unreceived amounts (DoD, Under Secretary of Defense for Personnel and Readiness, 2011, p. 909; 37 U.S.C. 501; U.S. Army Human Resources Command, 2017). This is true for both on-duty and retiree deaths. However, the benefit is smaller for retiree survivors, on average, as there is no leave accrued or possible per diem and other travel expenses that an active-duty member might have been owed at the time of death.

Tax Forgiveness

Survivors may receive a tax benefit if the service member died in a combat zone or from injuries sustained in one. In this instance, survivors do not pay an income tax, or they are refunded any income tax paid for the tax years spanning the entry into the combat zone to the time of death. An analysis of the Defense Manpower Data Center's Casualty File from 2003 to 2006 showed that the value of this benefit was $2,463, on average, in 2017 dollars (Miller, Heaton, and Loughran, 2012, p. 13).

Parents' DIC

VA offers need-based Parents' DIC to certain surviving parents of eligible veterans. Eligible veterans are those who died on duty or those who died from service-connected causes. Eligible parents include biological, adoptive, and foster parents who have an annual income below a certain threshold. As of December 1, 2016, the threshold was $14,680, or $19,733 if the surviving parent was living with a spouse (VA, 2017h). The rate varies with income, marital status, and number of parents (one or two). The maximum benefit was $622 per month per parent, and the benefit can be as small as $5 per month per parent. Parents may also receive a monthly allowance of $337 if they are entitled to Aid and Attendance (see the eligibility discussion in the DIC section in Chapter Two). This benefit is not subject to income tax.

VA Survivors Pension

VA offers the needs-based Survivors Pension, also known as the Death Pension, to certain low-income families of eligible deceased veterans. Most veterans are eligible if they had at least one day of active-duty service during a war-time period (VA, 2016, p. 57). The spouse of a surviving veteran is eligible as long as he or she remains unmarried. A child remains eligible until turning age 18, or age 23 if he or she is an eligible student. The child retains eligibility if "incapable of self-support" because of an injury that occurred prior to age 18 (VA, 2016, p. 57).

The amount of the pension is the quantity needed to bring the survivor to an income threshold, once other income (including social security) is taken into account (VA, 2016, p. 56). The threshold is higher with dependents and those eligible for VA Housebound and Aid and Attendance (see the eligibility discussion in the DIC section in Chapter Two), but the current annual income threshold without dependents or special needs is $8,656 (VA, 2017b). A child-only recipient (no parent receiving this benefit) has an annual income threshold of $2,205. This benefit is not subject to income tax.

Minimum Income Widow Annuity

The Minimum Income Widow Annuity is a part of SBP and is paid by DoD, but it has a small and diminishing group of beneficiaries. Eligible beneficiaries are all widows receiving a Spanish-American War pension or any other widow who is not eligible for SBP and DIC, is eligible for the Survivors Pension from VA, has an income below a set minimum threshold (not including income from the VA pension), and is a widow of a spouse who was entitled to military retired pay and who died on or before March 20, 1974. As of December 1, 2016, the annual income threshold was $8,656, and the maximum monthly annuity was $721.33 (DoD, Under Secretary of Defense [Comptroller], Appendix R, 2017). For Spanish-American War pension widows, the minimum income annuity is offset by the RSFPP. The annuity is subject to income tax.

ACMSS

The ACMSS is related to but not technically a part of SBP. This annuity was established in the NDAAs for FYs 1988 and 1989 (Pub. L. 100-180). The ACMSS was paid to spouses of military members who were entitled to retired pay and died before November 1, 1953. The purpose was to provide for those who could not have received benefits from the RSFPP, the precursor to SBP (DoD, Under Secretary of Defense for Personnel and Readiness, 2011, p. 739). This was then extended in the FY 1998 NDAA (Pub. L. 105-85) to provide for spouses who would not have been able to receive SBP benefits. Now, unmarried surviving spouses of active-duty retirees who retired before September 21, 1972, and died on or before March 20, 1974, are eligible to receive the ACMSS. They must have been married to the service member at the time of retirement and the time of death or married at least one year before the service member's death. The monthly annuity was $250.78 as of December 1, 2016, and is increased at the same time and the same percentage as retired pay (Air Force Retiree Services, undated). This amount is offset by the Minimum Income Widow allowance, RSFPP, SBP, and DIC.

Other Benefits

Survivors of deceased veterans may be eligible for educational and vocational counseling, financial counseling, and fiduciary services from VA, as well as civil-service preference when applying for federal jobs (FedsHireVets.gov, undated). Additionally, survivors may be eligible for military survivor benefits from state and local governments and nonprofit organizations.

Description of CSRS and FERS

CSRS

Employees covered by CSRS generally entered federal civilian service before January 1, 1984.[1] CSRS consists of a defined benefit plan in which both the federal government and the employee contribute to fund the plan. Employee contributions range from 7 to 8 percent of pay. Employees covered by CSRS do not pay into Social Security and are thus not eligible for Social Security retirement, disability, or survivor benefits. CSRS employees may make contributions to TSP, which is the federal employee defined contribution plan described in further detail below. The federal government does not make any employer contributions to TSP for CSRS employees.

The CSRS annuity is based on the high-3 average salary and years of service. The high-3 average salary is the average of the highest average basic pay earned during any three consecutive years of service. The CSRS annuity calculation is based on the following schedule:

- 1.5% × high-3 average salary × first five years
- 1.7% × high-3 average salary × next five years
- 2.0% × high-3 average salary × years greater than ten.

Eligibility for benefits varies by age and years of service, as summarized in Table B.1.

Survivor Benefits—Annuitant

Married CSRS employees are automatically enrolled in a joint and survivor annuity equal to 55 percent of their retirement annuities when they retire. This survivor annuity is paid through a reduction in annual benefits equal to the sum of the 2.5 percent of the first $3,600 and 10 percent of the annuity above $3,600. With consent of the spouse, the participant can select a less generous joint and survivor annuity. The cost of the less generous annuity is the

Table B.1
Normal and Early Retirement Ages Under CSRS

Full Retirement Age	Years of Service
62	5
60	20
55	30

---

[1] Employees covered by CSRS had the opportunity to change over to the FERS system during the 1987 and 1998 open seasons.

sum of 2.5 percent of the first $3,600 and 10 percent of the annuity above $3,600 and below the selected base that the participant chooses. Child survivors are eligible for the same benefits as those detailed in the next section.

Survivor Benefits—Current Employee

A surviving spouse of an employee with at least 18 months of service who died while subject to CSRS deductions is eligible for an annuity equal to 55 percent of the maximum of the either of following two annuity calculations. The first is the annuity calculated as if the employee had retired on the date of death. The second option is calculated as the minimum of 40 percent of the employee's high-3 average salary or the annuity calculated as if the employee had reached age 60.

Children are eligible for a survivor annuity if they are unmarried and under age 18, ages 18–22 and a full-time student, or over 18 and incapable of supporting themselves because of a disability that occurred before age 18. The amount of the survivor annuity does not depend on employee pay but is based on the number of children and the presence of a living parent. These benefits are subject to COLA. Monthly benefits reported here were effective December 1, 2016, through November 30, 2017. Children with one living parent receive the lesser of $512 per month per child and $1,537 per month divided by the total number of children. Children with no living parent receive the lesser of $614 per month per child or $1,844 per month divided by the number of children.

Survivor Benefits—Former Employee, Nonannuitant

No survivor benefits are available to survivors of a former employee who was not an annuitant.

FERS

Employees who entered federal civilian service on or after January 1, 1984, are covered under FERS.[2] FERS consists of three components (1) the Basic Benefit Plan, (2) TSP, and (3) Social Security. We describe the first two components, the Basic Benefit Plan and TSP here, and Social Security is described in Appendix A.

The Basic Benefit Plan is a defined benefit plan that provides employees with a guaranteed annuity based on the high-3 average salary and years of service. Vesting occurs after five years of service. The high-3 average salary is based on the highest average basic pay earned during any three consecutive years of service. Employees hired before 2013 contribute 0.8 percent of their pay, employees hired in 2013 contribute 3.1 percent of their pay, and employees hired in 2014 or later contribute 4.4 percent of their pay to fund the Basic Benefit Plan. The Basic Benefit Plan annuity calculation is based on the schedule depicted in Table B.2, and eligibility for full or reduced benefits varies by age and years of service, as summarized in Table B.3.

TSP is a defined contribution plan. Employees can allocate contributions using pretax dollars, after-tax dollars, or a combination of the two. There are five basic funds that employees can contribute to: a government securities investment fund, a fixed-income index investment

---

[2] FERS also includes employees (e.g., rehires, transfers, and conversions) hired after December 31, 1986, with less than five years of creditable service or who transferred to FERS during open season. Details may be found in Chapter Ten of the *CSRS and FERS Handbook for Personnel and Payroll Offices* (U.S. Office of Personnel Management, 1998).

Table B.2
FERS Annuity Benefit Calculation

Age and Years of Service	Formula
Under age 62 at separation for retirement or age 62 or older with less than 20 years of service	1% × high-3 average salary × years of service
Age 62 or older at separation with 20 or more years of service	1.1% × high-3 average salary × years of service

Table B.3
Full and Early Retirement Ages Under FERS

Age	Years of Service
Full retirement age	
62	5
60	20
Minimum retirement age	30
Early retirement age	
Minimum retirement age	10

fund, a common stock index investment fund, a small capitalization stock index investment fund, and an international stock investment index fund. TSP also offers life-cycle funds that are various combinations of the five basic funds, based on an expected year of retirement.

The federal government automatically contributes 1 percent of an employee's pay into TSP. Additionally, the federal government matches 100 percent of the first 3 percent of employee pay contributed and matches 50 percent of the next 2 percent of employee pay contributed. In total, the government contributes a maximum of 5 percent of an employee's pay to TSP. Employees hired after July 31, 2010, are automatically enrolled in TSP (but can opt out), with a contribution rate of 3 percent of pay. While individuals are immediately vested in their own contributions, government contributions are vested after three years of service. Retirees may withdraw benefits from their TSPs as a lump sum, monthly payments, annuity, or a combination of the three options. Minimum distributions are required when the participant reaches age 70.5.

Survivor Benefits—Annuitant

Married FERS-eligible employees are automatically enrolled in a joint and survivor annuity equal to 50 percent of their retirement annuities when they retire, which are paid for with a 10 percent reduction in the annuitant's retirement benefit. With consent of the spouse, the joint and survivor annuity can be reduced to 25 percent, for a cost equal to 5 percent of the retirement annuity. Child survivors are eligible for the same benefits as those detailed in the next section.

Retirees have an option to purchase an annuity with a survivor benefit option using their TSP account balances. There are two survivor benefit options: a 50 percent and a 100 percent joint and survivor annuity. Under the 50 percent option, the survivor, who may be the former federal employee *or* the joint annuitant, would receive 50 percent of the annuity paid out when both spouses are alive. Under the 100 percent option, the survivor annuity is equal to the annuity paid out when both spouses are alive, with the annuity generally being less generous than the 50 percent joint life annuity. A surviving spouse may also receive an annuity if the TSP participant opts for a single life annuity with a cash refund or "ten-year certain." Under the cash-refund option, the remaining TSP balance may be used to purchase an annuity. Under the "ten-year certain" option, if the participant dies before ten years of benefits have been paid, then the benefits get disbursed to the surviving spouse until the ten years are met. The annuity options do not have to be purchased with the entire TSP account balance.

A surviving spouse of a retired federal employee covered by FERS may also receive Social Security survivor benefits, as detailed in Appendix A.

Survivor Benefits—Current Employee

Upon the death of an employee, survivors may be eligible for up to four types of benefits: (1) Basic Employee Death Benefit, (2) dependent survivor annuity, (3) spouse survivor annuity, and (4) TSP. If the current employee had at least 18 months of creditable service and died while subject to FERS, then survivors are eligible to receive a lump-sum benefit, called the Basic Employee Death Benefit, and surviving dependent children are eligible for a dependent survivor annuity. The Basic Employee Death Benefit is equal to the greater of 50 percent of the employee's final salary or 50 percent of the average high-3 average salary plus, as of December 1, 2016, $32,423.56. The $32,423.56 is adjusted for cost of living. The survivor annuity per dependent is equal to (the total amount payable to all children under CSRS less the total amount payable to all children by Social Security) divided by the number of children. In most cases, Social Security dependent survivor benefits will offset the FERS dependent survivor annuity (U.S. Office of Personnel Management, 1998).

If the employee had at least of ten years of creditable service, then the surviving spouse is eligible for an annuity equal to 50 percent of the employee's annuity had he or she retired on the date of death.

The final benefit comes from the deceased's TSP account. A beneficiary participant account in the name of the surviving spouse will be created if the spouse's share is $200 or more. This account will invest the spouse's share into a life-cycle fund based on the year in which the surviving spouse turns 62, unless the spouse chooses to withdraw the money as a single payment, monthly payments, an annuity, or a combination of these options.

Survivor Benefits—Former Employee, Nonannuitant

For survivors to be eligible for benefits, the former employee must have had at least ten years of creditable service, five of which had to have included civilian service covered by FERS deductions. A surviving spouse gets 50 percent of the deceased former employee's basic annuity if the survivor elects to begin receiving the annuity on the date the deceased former employee would have met the age and service requirements for an unreduced annuity. The survivor annuity is reduced by a present-value conversion factor if the survivor elects to receive the annuity the day after death. Child survivors are not eligible for any of these survivor benefits.

Additional Benefits

Survivors of CSRS and FERS annuitants and current employees may be able to continue federal employee health coverage if they were enrolled at the time of death and the spouse is eligible for a survivor annuity.

Survivors may receive a life insurance payment from FEGLI if the annuitant or current employee had coverage.

If a survivor annuity is not available after death, (e.g., when years-of-service requirements are not met), then a lump sum in the amount of the employee's retirement contributions may be payable.

For work-related deaths, benefits may be payable through OWCP. Survivors must choose between these benefits and benefits offered through CSRS or FERS. OWCP provides an annuity to survivors and children, up to $800 in reimbursement for funeral expenses, up to $200 to cover expenses for terminating the deceased status as a federal employee, and a gratuity up to $100,000 if an employee was killed while working with the military in a contingency operation. The survivor annuity for a spouse with no children equals 50 percent of the employee's salary at the time of death. For spouses with children, the annuity equals the employee's final salary multiplied by the minimum of either 75 percent or 45 percent plus number of kids multiplied by 15 percent. If there were one child, for example, the percentage would be 60 percent (= 45 + 1 × 15), and with two children the percentage would be 75 percent. For three or more kids, the percentage stays at 75 percent. Child benefits end at age 18, or age 23 if in school. Child benefits continue indefinitely if the child is disabled and incapable of caring for himself or herself. The benefits are adjusted for cost of living each year and are not subject to federal income tax.

Tables B.4 and B.5, respectively, summarize the details of SBP, CSRS, FERS, Social Security, and selected public- and private-employer–sponsored defined benefit plans.

Table B.4
Military SBP, Federal Civilian Retirement Systems, and Social Security

	Military Survivor Benefit	CSRS	FERS	Social Security
Pension eligibility				
Regular	20+ years of active-duty military service (reserve service can be "converted" to active-duty service with a point system) or medical retirement	Age 62+ and 5 years of service, age 60+ and 20 years of service, or age 55+ and 30 years of service	A minimum retirement age and 30+ years of service (minimum retirement age is 55 for those born before 1948 and 57 for those born in 1970 and after), age 60+ with 20 years of service, or age 62+ with 5 years of service	At least 10 years of work and minimum retirement age Minimum retirement age based on birth year: age 65 if born in 1937 or earlier, age 65 + 2 months × (birth year – 1937) if born in 1938–1942, age 66 if born in 1943–1954, age 66 + 2 months × (birth year – 1954) if born in 1955–1959, and age 67 if born in 1960 or later
Early	TERA: at least 15 but less than 20 years of active service between 2012 and 2025	Not applicable	A minimum retirement age with 10+ years of service	At least age 62 with 10 years of work
Vesting	20 years, but there is an exception for TERA: 15 years and medical retirement	5 years	5 years	10 years
Employee contribution	Regular retirement system: none BRS: automatically enrolled into TSP, a defined contribution plan, in which the government contributes 1% of pay and, after two years of service, matches 1:1 for the first 3% of pay and at 50% for the next 2% of pay contributed by the employee	7–8% of pay	0.8% of pay if hired before 2013, 3.1% of pay if hired in 2013, or 4.4% of pay if hired in 2014 or later Employees are automatically enrolled in TSP, a defined contribution plan, in which the government contributes 1% of pay and matches 1:1 for the first 3% of pay and at 50% for the next 2% of pay contributed by the employee; employees hired after July 31, 2010, are automatically enrolled into the TSP at 3%	6.2% of pay up to the Social Security wage base ($127,200 in 2017)

Table B.4—Continued

	Military Survivor Benefit	CSRS	FERS	Social Security
Pension amount				
Regular	Entered service before September 8,1980: 2.5% × years of service × final basic pay. Entered service after September 7, 1980: 2.5% × years of service × high-36. Entered service after July 31, 1986, and selected CSB/REDUX: (3.5% × years of service − 30) × high-36 until age 62, and then at and above age 62, pay is 2.5% × years of service × high-3. If fewer than 12 years of total service as of December 31, 2017, may opt into BRS: 2% × years of service × high-3	First 5 years: 1.5% of high-3. Second 5 years: 1.75% of high-3. All years over 10: 2% of high-3	Age 62 or older at separation with 20 or more years of service = 1.1% × high-3 average salary × years of service. Under age 62 at separation for retirement or age 62 or older with less than 20 years of service = 1% × high-3 average salary × years of service. High-3 average salary is the highest average basic pay earned in any 3-year consecutive period.	Based on a 3-tiered calculation known as PIA and based on AIME for the highest-earning 35 years. In 2017, 90% × first $885 of AIME + 32% of AIME above $885 and through $5,336 + 15% × AIME above $5,336. Benefits are capped, with the cap varying by age at retirement and year.
Early	2.5% × years of service × TERA reduction factor × high-36	Not applicable	Reduction of 5% per year for each year of payment below age 62	Between age 62 and the minimum retirement age based on birth year. Benefit is reduced 5/9 of 1% for each month before normal retirement age, up to 36 months. If the number of months exceeds 36, then the benefit is further reduced by 5/12 of 1% per month.

Table B.4—Continued

	Military Survivor Benefit	CSRS	FERS	Social Security
Other	Disability retired pay: Member chooses either (years of service) × 2.5% × (high-36) OR (disability %, not more than 75) × (high-36). If member joined prior to September 8, 1980, use basic pay instead of high-36 SBP coverage and pension for CSB/REDUX are computed as if the service member had not selected CSB/REDUX, except the CPI adjustment for the annuity is penalized by 1%; only members who entered after July 31, 1986, are eligible for CSB/REDUX. BRS participants can receive TSP benefits as a lump sum, monthly payments (fixed monthly amounts paid until balance is exhausted), annuity, or some combination of the three. Minimum distributions are required at age 70.5. Tax-free contributions (e.g., from earnings in combat zones) are tax-exempt when distributed; withdrawals are proportionally taxed and nontaxed.		Participants can receive TSP benefits as a lump sum, monthly payments (fixed monthly amounts paid until balance is exhausted), annuity, or some combination of the 3; minimum distributions are required at age 70.5. Certain individuals who retire before age 62 may be eligible for a special retirement supplement that approximates the Social Security benefit earned while in federal service (see U.S. Office of Personnel Management, 1998).	

Table B.4—Continued

	Military Survivor Benefit	CSRS	FERS	Social Security
Survivor annuity— retirement	Default annuity is 55% of retirement pension. Otherwise, it is 55% of base amount, where base amount can be a minimum of $300 to a maximum of the full pension. Spousal coverage cost is 6.5% of base amount. Base amount can be up to 55% of retired pay. NIP cost is 10% of base amount + 5% for every 5-year difference in age (max of 40%). Child coverage is determined actuarially. Can reach paid-up status if member has made 360 months of payments and is 70 years of age or older. Then service member does not need to pay for coverage.	Default is a joint and survivor annuity equal to 55% of the worker's full annuity before reductions. With spousal consent, the joint and survivor annuity may be reduced to 55% of a chosen amount of reduced annuity. To pay for the survivor benefit, the annual retiree annuity is reduced by 2.5% of the first $3,600 and 10% of the annuity above that amount, up to the full retiree annuity amount (or reduced annuity if a partial survivor annuity is selected). Full survivor annuity = 55% of worker's full annuity before reductions; partial survivor annuity = 55% of chosen amount of reduced annuity	Default is 50% joint and survivor annuity, in which the annual retiree annuity is reduced by 10%. With spousal consent, the joint and survivor annuity may be reduced to 25% of the full retiree annuity amount with an annual retiree annuity reduction of 5%. Can purchase TSP joint and survivor annuity at 50% or 100% if spouse is not more than 10 years younger than participant. The 50% joint and survivor annuity applies when either the spouse or participant dies. Surviving spouses also get benefits if participants requesting a single life annuity name the spouse as the beneficiary and opt for a cash refund (where the remaining TSP account balance used to purchase the annuity gets paid to the beneficiary) or a "10-year certain" (if participant dies before receiving annuity payments for 10 years, then monthly annuity payments continue to the surviving spouse until the 10 years are met). The participant does not need use all of the TSP account balance to purchase an annuity.	Deceased worker must have at least 10 years of work. For surviving widows with dependent children, the service member must have worked at least 1.5 years in the 3 years prior to death. Percentage of deceased spouse's Social Security benefits with percentage varying by surviving widow's age, disability status, and presence of dependents. Spouse age 60 to minimum retirement age: 71.5–100% Disabled spouse ages 50–59: 71.5% Spouse any age with child under age 16: 75% Not eligible for survivor benefits if spouse remarries before age 60. One-time lump-sum payment of $255 can be made to the qualifying surviving spouse or child; survivors must apply for this payment within two years of the death.

Health insurance: surviving spouse and children can continue coverage if service member was enrolled at death and if spouse is eligible for a survivor annuity.

Option to continue FEGLI coverage upon retirement with options to continue coverage at current levels, 50% reduced, and 75% reduced, with premium costs decreasing with the level of coverage. Eligible to continue coverage if entitled to an immediate CSRS or FERS annuity, was insured for 5 years of service immediately prior to annuity start date or insured for the full employment period that an employee was eligible to be insured if employed for less than 5 years, was enrolled in FEGLI on date of retirement, and had not converted to an individual policy.

Table B.4—Continued

	Military Survivor Benefit	CSRS	FERS	Social Security
Survivor annuity— current employee	If service members die on duty, they receive 41.25% of high-36 earnings. If they die on duty while not in the line of duty but have served more than 20 years, their survivors are (generally) eligible for 55% of the retired pay to which the deceased members would have been entitled at the time of deaths. For those with TSP accounts: TSP creates a beneficiary participant account in the name of the surviving spouse if the spouse's share is $200 or more. TSP will invest the spouse's share into a life-cycle fund based on the year in which the surviving spouse turns 62, unless the spouse chooses to withdraw the money as a single payment, monthly payments, an annuity, or a combination of these options.	Employee had 18 months of service and died while subject to CSRS deductions; 55% of maximum of either (1) the annuity calculated as if employee retired on date of death or (2) the minimum of 40% of employee's high-3 salary or the annuity calculated by increasing employee's length of service until he or she would have reached age 60.	Survivor annuity: Employee had at least 10 years of creditable service and died while employed. 50% of the employee's basic annuity calculated as if employee retired on date of death. TSP: TSP creates a beneficiary participant account in the name of the surviving spouse if the spouse's share is $200 or more. TSP will invest the spouse's share into a life-cycle fund based on the year in which the surviving spouse turns 62, unless the spouse chooses to withdraw the money as a single payment, monthly payments, an annuity, or a combination of these options. Basic employee death benefit: Employee had at least 18 months of creditable service and died while subject to FERS deductions. A lump sum plus the greater of (1) 50% of employee's final salary or (2) 50% of average of highest three years' salary upon death. Lump sum is equal to $15,000 increased by CSRS COLA beginning December 1, 1987. For deaths after December 12016, the lump sum is $32,423.56. Benefit can be paid out as a lump sum or in 36 monthly installments. Spouse may also be eligible for a spousal annuity supplement if the surviving spouse is entitled to a spouse survivor annuity, is under 60, is entitled to Social Security survivor benefits, and is not eligible for Social Security disability benefits or benefits for caring for a child (see U.S. Office of Personnel Management, 1998).	Same as the survivor annuity for retired service members

Table B.4—Continued

	Military Survivor Benefit	CSRS	FERS	Social Security
Survivor annuity— current employee		Health insurance: Surviving spouse and children can continue coverage if employee had at least 18 months of service, was enrolled for coverage at time of death, and at least one family member is due a survivor annuity. Basic FEGL coverage pays out the greater of (1) annual salary rounded up to the next even $1,000, plus $2,000 or (2) $10,000. Employees under age 45 get an "extra benefit" at no additional cost that doubles the basic benefit; it is reduced 10% for each year above age 35 until age 45. Employee pays 2/3 of cost, and government pays 1/3 of cost; employees can opt out of coverage or purchase greater coverage.		
Additional benefits for service-connected deaths	For active-duty deaths, regardless of cause, or deaths within 120 days of separation from active duty when the deaths are service-connected, spouses also receive a nontaxable death gratuity of $100,000. If no spouse, the gratuity goes to children or other next of kin. Survivors can also receive a lump-sum death payment of $255 (SSA), the Fry Scholarship (VA) or DEA (VA), DIC (VA), housing benefits (DoD, VA), SGLI (VA), TRICARE (DoD), child care (DoD), burial allowances for service-connected retiree deaths, and other benefits.	Benefits provided by OWCP: Spouse, no children: monthly annuity = 50% of employee's salary at time of death. Spouse, yes children: monthly annuity = Minimum (75%, 45% + # kids × 15%) of employee's salary at time of death. Spouse's annuity continues for life unless he or she remarries before age 55. If spouse remarries before age 55, then annuity ends and he or she gets one final lump-sum payment equal to 24 months of benefits. Child benefits end at age 18, but at 23 if child is in school or indefinitely if child is disabled and incapable of caring for self. OWCP annuities are adjusted for cost of living each year and are not subject to federal income taxes. OWCP provides up to $800 in funeral costs and for full cost to ship body to employee's home and up to $200 to cover expenses of terminating deceased status as a federal employee. OWCP provides a gratuity of up to $100,000 if an employee is killed while working with the military in a contingency operation. Survivors must choose between receiving OWCP benefits and CSRS/FERS survivor benefits. Social Security survivor benefits offset the OWCP annuities dollar for dollar.		

Table B.4—Continued

	Military Survivor Benefit	CSRS	FERS	Social Security
Survivor annuity— former employee, nonannuitant	Regular retirement system: none BRS: TSP survivor benefits are the same as that for current employees	None	Employee had 10 years of service, of which at least 5 years were as a civilian covered by FERS deductions. Note that benefits for survivors of employees who had reached the minimum retirement age plus at least 10 years of service, but had not begun to receive retirement benefits, are calculated as if they were an annuitant. Benefit is 50% of deceased former employee's basic annuity if the survivor elects to begin receiving annuity on date the deceased former employee would have met the age and service requirements for an unreduced annuity. Amount of survivor annuity is reduced if the survivor elects to receive annuity the day after death by a present-value conversion factor TSP survivor benefits are the same as that for current employees.	Same as survivor annuity for retired service members

Table B.4—Continued

	Military Survivor Benefit	CSRS	FERS	Social Security
Dependent annuity	Default annuity is 55% of retirement pension. Otherwise, the annuity 55% of base amount, where base amount can be a minimum of $300 to a maximum of the full pension. Annuity is divided among all children. Children receive the pension only if the surviving spouse is unable to receive it (under "spouse and children" coverage) because of death or early remarriage. However, members can elect to have coverage only for dependents. Children must be under 18, or under 22 and a full-time unmarried student, to be eligible. Once they are no longer eligible, premiums cease. If the children are incapacitated, they are eligible forever, and members can also elect to deposit the annuity in an SNT.	Dependents get a COLA monthly annuity based on the presence of a living parent and number of total children. Amounts effective December 1, 2016, through November 30, 2017, are reported. One living parent: lesser of (1) $512 per month per child or (2) $1,537 per month divided by number of children No living parent: lesser of (1) $614 per month per child or (2) $1,844 per month divided by number of children Child must be unmarried and under 18, ages 18–22 and full-time student, or over 18 and incapable of self-support because of a disability that occurred before age 18.	Applicable to current and retired employees Benefits equal the total amount payable to all children under CSRS less total amount payable to all children by Social Security, divided by number of children. In general, Social Security survivor dependent benefits will completely offset the FERS survivor dependent annuity (see U.S. Office of Personnel Management, 1998).	Eligible for 75% of deceased Social Security benefits if surviving children are under age 18 and unmarried (under 19 if attending secondary school or below) or eligible at any age if disabled (and disability occurred before age 22) Dependent parents age 62 or older are also eligible for survivor benefits: one surviving parent gets 82%, and two surviving parents get 75% each.
Other		If monthly survivor annuity is not available, then lump sum in the amount of employee's retirement contributions may be payable upon death.	If monthly survivor annuity is not available, then lump sum in the amount of employee's retirement contributions may be payable upon death.	
Size	As of September 30, 2016: 1,085,769 retirees and 321,476 annuitants (on average)	As of September 30, 2014: 1,469,000 retirees and 511,000 survivors	As of September 30, 2014: 590,000 retirees and 54,000 survivors	As of December 31, 2016: 44,266,144 retirees and dependents and 6,031,093 survivors (see SSA, undated-d)

Table B.4—Continued

	Military Survivor Benefit	CSRS	FERS	Social Security
Notes	Benefits and cost are adjusted for any changes in retired pay. The premiums are nontaxable income, but the annuity itself is taxable. SBP is very inflexible in that coverage is nearly impossible to change after retirement.	Covered employees pay no OASDI (old age, survivors, and disability insurance) tax but must pay the Medicare tax (1.45%). Not eligible for Social Security Surviving spouses who remarry before age 55 are not eligible for a spousal survivor annuity. High-3 average salary is the highest average basic pay earned in any 3-year consecutive period.	Pay Social Security and Medicare taxes Eligible for Social Security Surviving spouses who remarry before age 55 are not eligible for a spouse survivor annuity. High-3 average salary is the highest average basic pay earned in any 3-year consecutive period.	Maximum family benefit cap is imposed on both retirement and survivor benefits. The caps generally equal to about 150 to 180% of the PIA. Surviving spouses who remarry before age 60 are not eligible for a spousal survivor annuity.

Table B.5
Selected Public- and Private-Employer–Sponsored Defined Benefit Plans

	Los Angeles Fire and Police Pension	Chicago Public Schools	Washington State Employees	Kaiser Permanente Employee Pension Plan	Ford Motor Company United Auto Workers Retirement Plan	Exxon Mobil Pension Plan
Pension eligibility						
Regular	At least 50 years of age and 20 years of service	At least age 67 with 10 years of service	At least age 65	At least age 65	At least age 65	At least age 65 as a terminee or at least age 60 as a retiree
Early	Below age 50 and at least 20 years of service	At least age 62 with 10 years of service	At least 55 with 20 years of service	At least age 55 with at least 10 years of service	At least 30 years of service or age 55 with 10 years of service	At least age 55 with at least 15 years of service
Vested	Only own contributions are refundable	10 years	5 years	5 years	5 years	5 years or age 65, whichever happens first
Employee contribution	11% of pay until 25 years of service, then 9% of pay until 33 years of service	9% of pay (7.5% for retirement pension, 1% for spouse's pension, and 0.5% for automatic increases in retirement pension); Board of Education pays for 7% of the required contributions	7.38% employee as of June 1, 2017 (Washington State Department of Retirement Systems, 2017a)	Varies; 1 to 10% of pay	None	None after December 31, 1999

Table B.5—Continued

	Los Angeles Fire and Police Pension	Chicago Public Schools	Washington State Employees	Kaiser Permanente Employee Pension Plan	Ford Motor Company United Auto Workers Retirement Plan	Exxon Mobil Pension Plan
Pension amount						
Regular	Years of service percentage × FAS FAS is based on 24 months of average monthly pay at employee's permanent rank over any 24-month consecutive period of employee's choosing Years of service percentage starts at 40% for 20 years, increases 3 percentage points per year until 25 years, increases 4 percentage points per year until 30 years, and increases 5 percentage points until 90% at 33 years	2.2% × FAS × years of service FAS is based on average of 8 highest years in the 10 years preceding retirement; capped at $111,571.63 in 2015, increases by 3% or 50% of increase in CPI for preceding year, whichever is less	2% × FAS × years of service FAS is the average of the 60 consecutive highest-paid service credit months	1.45% × FAS × years of service FAS is the average compensation for the highest 60 consecutive months in the last 120 months of employment	Annuity ranges from $53.55 to $54.30 × years of service, depending on employee class; benefit rates apply to retirement after October 1, 2010	(1.6% × FAS × years of service) – Social Security offset FAS is the average for the highest 36 months in the last 10 years of employment Social Security offset is 1.5% of estimated Social Security benefit multiplied by pension service up to a max of 33.33 years

Table B.5—Continued

	Los Angeles Fire and Police Pension	Chicago Public Schools	Washington State Employees	Kaiser Permanente Employee Pension Plan	Ford Motor Company United Auto Workers Retirement Plan	Exxon Mobil Pension Plan
Early	Called *deferred pension* FAS × years of service percentage Years of service percentage = 2% per year of service up to 20 years of service + 3% for each year up to 30 years of service, capped at 70% at 30 years	Reduction of 0.5 to 1% for each month that the age of the member is below age 67	Reduction of 5% per year under age 65 for those with at least 30 years of service. Larger reductions based on state actuary tables for those with less than 30 years of service	Accrued normal retirement benefit earned until termination date, reduced 5% per year for each year the benefit starting date precedes age 65	Percentage of normal retirement benefit ranging from 0.210 at age 42 to 1.0 at age 62.	Reduction of 5% per year below age 60 to 75% at age 55. Those under age 62 get a pre–Social Security pension that is equal to the greater of the amount of the Social Security benefit offset taken into account in calculating retirement income or $150 if age 60 or 61 (reduced $5 for each year prior to age 60 to $125 at age 55)
Survivor annuity— retired	Default survivor annuity is equal to 70% of service pension Can purchase up to 100% of service pension; reduction in service pension to fund greater joint and survivor pension is based on age of retiree and spouse and current actuarial assumptions of the pension board	Default survivor annuity is equal to 66.67% of the service pension One-time payment of the lesser of $10,000 and most recent salary earned for 6-month period less 20% of the death benefit for each year that the member has been on pension, to a minimum of $5,000	Default is no survivor annuity—survivor gets remaining contributions plus interest as a lump sum; option to purchase a joint and survivor annuity at 50%, 66.67%, or 100%	Default survivor annuity is equal to 50% of the service pension; option to purchase a joint and survivor annuity is equal to 66.67%, 75%, or 100%. The 100% option comes with a 15-year guaranteed period (if both spouses die before 15 years of payment, then the beneficiary gets paid the same amount until 15 years is reached) and pop-up (if joint annuitant dies before participant, then the monthly annuity increases for the rest of the participant's life)	Default survivor annuity is equal to 65% of the life income benefit based on the later of the participant's age at retirement or 62; participant annuity is reduced by 5% with additional adjustment for age difference between spouses Option to choose 50%, 75%, or 100% joint and survivor annuity	Joint and survivor income, reduced actuarially from amount for unmarried employee, with 50% of reduced income payable to the survivor spouse for life. Default option does not guarantee payment for 5 years. Employees can purchase joint and survivor annuity at 1%, 25%, 50%, or 100% and with 5, 10, 15, or 20 years of guaranteed benefits.

112 An Assessment of the Military Survivor Benefit Plan

Table B.5—Continued

	Los Angeles Fire and Police Pension	Chicago Public Schools	Washington State Employees	Kaiser Permanente Employee Pension Plan	Ford Motor Company United Auto Workers Retirement Plan	Exxon Mobil Pension Plan
Survivor annuity—current employee	Service-connected death: 80% of FAS Non–service-connected death with less than 5 years of service: refund of pension contributions; if at least one year of service, then survivors are entitled to a 12-month annuity equal to 50% of FAS × years of service Non–service-connected death with at least 5 years of service: 50% of FAS	Employee had at least 1.5 years of service Default survivor annuity is equal to 66.67% of the pension the member had earned at date of death Refund of total contributions less contributions for survivor pension is payable One-time payment of less of $10,000 and salary earned for most recent 6 months	Survivor gets accumulated contributions plus interest if less than 10 years of service. If at least 10 years of service, survivor can choose to receive a lump sum or monthly benefit, where monthly benefit is calculated as if participant had retired and chosen a 100% joint and survivor annuity.	Default for benefits beginning on or after January 1, 2010, is equal to 50% of the pension, which is the actuarial equivalent of a 100% joint and survivor annuity with the 15-year guaranteed period and pop-up, payable at participant's normal retirement date. Starting earlier results in a 5% reduction per year for each year the benefit starting date precedes age 65.	Employee had at least 5 years of service (10 such years if no service was accrued after 1988); 50% of life income benefit	Less than 5 years of service: nothing Between 5 and 15 years of service: survivor gets 50% of the amount payable under the 50% default joint and survivor annuity option, with benefits beginning between when the participant would have reached age 50 or age 65 (earlier payments result in reductions in benefits) Greater than 15 years of service: Survivor gets a lump-sum benefit calculated as if participant had retired on date of death and elected a lump-sum payment option to be paid at age 50, or at actual age if older at time of death. The lump-sum payment is the actuarial value of the annuity at the date of death. If participant was under age 50, the benefit is the present value of the age-50 lump sum. For those with more than 15 years of service, they also get the pre–Social Security pension as a single payment.

Table B.5—Continued

	Los Angeles Fire and Police Pension	Chicago Public Schools	Washington State Employees	Kaiser Permanente Employee Pension Plan	Ford Motor Company United Auto Workers Retirement Plan	Exxon Mobil Pension Plan
Survivor annuity—former employee, nonannuitant	No annuity—refund of contributions plus interest	Employee had at least 10 years of service Default survivor annuity is equal to 66.67% of the pension the member had earned at date of death; refund of total contributions less contributions for survivor pension is payable; there is a one-time payment of the lesser of $10,000 and salary earned for most recent 6 months	Survivor gets accumulated contributions plus interest if there are less than 10 years of service; if there are at least 10 years of service, survivor can choose to receive a lump sum or monthly benefit, where monthly benefit is calculated as if participant had retired and chosen a 100% joint and survivor annuity	Same as current employee	Employee had at least 5 years of service (10 such years if no service was accrued after 1988) Before early retirement: 50% of life benefit that would have been payable to participant at date of death, with reductions for early commencement and adjustment for age difference between spouses After early retirement: 65% of life benefit that would have been payable to participant, with appropriate reduction for early retirement, assuming that retirement would have occurred at the later of age 62 or age of death (5% reduction plus adjustment for age difference between spouses)	No information available

Table B.5—Continued

	Los Angeles Fire and Police Pension	Chicago Public Schools	Washington State Employees	Kaiser Permanente Employee Pension Plan	Ford Motor Company United Auto Workers Retirement Plan	Exxon Mobil Pension Plan
Dependent annuity	25% of survivor benefits for one dependent 40% of survivor benefit for two dependents 50% of survivor benefit for three or more dependents Total survivor benefits capped at 100% of members' FAS or 100% of the retired member's salary adjusted for cost of living	Benefits divided equally among all survivors Retirees: 66.67% of the member's pension Current employees: pension based on 60% of total average salary at time of death ($600 maximum) or 50% of the retirement pension earned by the member, whichever is greater	If no surviving spouse exists, then children get the benefit from 100% joint and survivor annuity if there were at least 10 years of service	Monthly benefit for 120 months determined as if the participant had retired the day before death and elected a life annuity for 120 months	No information available	No information available
Notes	Based on "tier 6" employees, hired on or after July 1, 2011 Benefits are adjusted for cost of living Plan description as of July 2016 See Los Angeles Fire and Police Pensions, 2016	Based on "tier 2" employees, hired on or after January 1, 2011 Benefit calculations include automatic annual increase of retirement annuity of 3% or 50% of increase in CPI from preceding year, whichever is less See Chicago Teachers' Pension Fund, undated	Based on "PERS Plan 2" Some specifics apply only to employees hired on or after May 1, 2013 Benefits are adjusted for cost of living See Washington State Department of Retirement Systems, 2017b	Description applies to unionized employees Plan information based on 2015 Form 5500	Plan description based on 2015 Form 5500, except for current employee benefits, which are based on 2007 information from United Auto Workers Local 387, 2007.	Plan information based on 2015 Form 5500 and the Exxon Mobil Family website (http:// exxonmobilfamily.com)

NOTES: Descriptions are based on our interpretation of plan descriptions and are simplified for illustrative purposes. Form 5500 was developed by the IRS, Department of Labor, and Pension Benefit Guaranty Corporation for employee benefits to meet annual reporting requirements under ERISA and the Internal Revenue Code.

Descriptions of Detailed Examples in Chapter Three

This appendix describes the assumptions and estimated survivor benefits used in the section "Comparing SBP with Other Programs: Detailed Examples," in Chapter Three. Appendix D contains three additional detailed examples.

Current Employee Death Examples

Enlisted

For the enlisted example, we assume that an individual is born on January 1, 1994, and enters the military at age 20 on January 1, 2014. After three years of service, the enlisted member, an E-4, is killed in action, on January 1, 2017, at the age of 23. The salary history is assumed to be the estimated pay profile for an enlisted member based on the 2007 Greenbook and is inflation-adjusted to 2017 dollars (DoD, Directorate of Compensation, 2007).[1] Using this salary history, we calculate an SBP benefit equal to 41.25 percent of the high-36 pay, or 55 percent of 75 percent of the high-36 pay. This is estimated to be $8,647 per year.

Because the death occurred on duty, the spouse would be eligible for DIC from VA, which currently has a base rate of $15,095 per year for spouses. As a result, in this example, DIC offsets the SBP amount completely, and the spouse would receive $15,095 of DIC, plus $3,720 of SSIA per year to compensate for the offset. The spouse would also receive an additional DIC allowance of $3,740 per year per dependent child under age 18 and a flat-rate DIC transition allowance of $3,240 each year for two years if the spouse has one or more dependents.

For example, for a surviving spouse with one dependent, the total DIC annuity would be $25,795 for the first two years and $22,555 thereafter until the child turns 18. This is tax-free except for the SSIA component.

If there are dependents, the spouse is also eligible for an annuity from SSA based on the number and age of the children. Each child under age 18 would receive $9,696 per year. While at least one child is under age 16, the spouse would also receive $9,696 per year. The maximum family benefit is $19,411 per year. When the children are 16 or older, the spouse no longer receives SSA benefits until full retirement age (or the spouse can take a reduced amount starting at age 60, or 50 if disabled).

After factoring in SSA with the DIC annuity, the total annuity the first year is $18,815 with no dependents, $45,187 with one child who is under age 16, $35,491 with one child who

---

[1] The 2007 enlisted pay profile was used to maintain comparability with the corresponding civilian pay profile, which is based on median earnings in 2007 of male, year-round full-time workers holding an associate's degree from the U.S. Census Bureau (DeNavas-Walt, Proctor, and Smith, 2008). Both pay profiles are inflation-adjusted to 2017 dollars for our analysis.

is age 16 or 17, $48,946 for two children who are under age 16, and $48,927 for two children who are ages 16–17.

The survivor would also receive a lump-sum death benefit of $255 from SSA, with the same tax-exempt rules as the SSA annuity. Because the death was on duty, the spouse would receive a death gratuity from DoD of $100,000 and a lump-sum payment of one year of BAH, which, for an E-4 with dependents at Ft. Bragg, North Carolina, is $14,148. Assuming that the service member carried full SGLI coverage, the spouse would also receive $400,000. The death gratuity, BAH, and SGLI benefits are not subject to income tax. Finally, the spouse would receive any unpaid pay and allowances, which would not be subject to income tax, since the death was in a combat zone, and would also have tax forgiveness for the income earned by the service member spanning the tax years when the member was in the combat zone, including the tax year in which the member was killed. Assuming that the service member had half of a month of combined unpaid days and unused leave, the unpaid pay and allowances would be $1,900, based on the pay profile used. As mentioned in Appendix A, an analysis of the Defense Manpower Data Center's Casualty File from 2003 to 2006 showed that the value of the tax-forgiveness benefit was $2,463, on average, in 2017 dollars (Miller, Heaton, and Loughran, 2012, p. 13). In total, we estimate a lump-sum benefit of $518,775 for the surviving spouse.

There are other benefits that survivors are eligible for that are not included in the comparison. Because the death occurred on duty, the survivors would be reimbursed by DoD for any burial costs incurred. The spouse and children would also be eligible to receive the Fry Scholarship or DEA, both offered by VA. They could choose only one, not both. The Fry Scholarship pays full in-state tuition at public universities or up to $22,805.34 per year at private universities, in addition to a $1,000 annual stipend and monthly BAH paid directly to the beneficiary for up to 36 months of benefits. DEA provides $1,024 per month directly to the beneficiary for up to 45 months for degree programs and other types of educational pursuits.

The spouse and children would also be eligible for health care and dental care through TRICARE. The spouse and children would receive this at no cost for three years, and then the spouse would pay annual enrollment fees (currently $282.60 for TRICARE Prime), but children would remain in TRICARE at no cost until they marry, turn 18, or turn 23 (if a full-time student). Surviving spouses may keep TRICARE until they remarry. If the child is incapacitated and the injury occurred during eligibility for TRICARE, he or she may be eligible for extended coverage. In either scenario, if children age out of ADFM status but remain unmarried and are not covered by their own employee insurance, they may purchase TRICARE Young Adult until they are age 26. The 2017 monthly premium is $319 for TRICARE Young Adult Prime and $216 for TRICARE Young Adult Standard.

The survivors may receive life insurance, either VGLI, up to $400,000, or S-DVI, up to $40,000. Either option would have required the service member to opt in and pay premiums.

There are many other benefits that the survivors could receive. The family is entitled to one move at government expense, if they leave their housing within three years of the service member's death. The spouse could utilize military child-development facilities for all dependents under age 13. Survivors could also continue to use commissary, base exchange, and some MWR services with the same age-out rules as TRICARE. The spouse would receive ten points for derived preference on civil-service exams, since the death occurred on duty during a war period. The spouse is eligible for the VA Home Loan Guaranty, since the service member died on duty. The surviving spouse can use this loan guaranty only one time. There is no limit on the amount that a lender can take, but VA does have limits on how much it will guarantee.

The size of the loan that can be taken without needing to make a down payment is typically four times this maximum guarantee, and it varies by county. There are additional counseling services that the spouse could receive from VA, as well as numerous state and local benefits.

The deceased member would be entitled to a headstone or marker and burial flag from VA and burial at a national cemetery.

Federal Civilian Employee Under FERS, Enlisted Equivalent

For this example, we assume that a federal civilian employee is born on January 1, 1987, and enters federal civilian service at age 20 on January 1, 2007. After ten years of service, the employee dies from a service-connected death at age 30, on January 1, 2017. The salary history during the ten years of service is assumed to be the estimated civilian equivalent for an enlisted member.[2] We assume that a surviving spouse chooses to receive survivor benefits through the OWCP, as opposed to FERS survivor benefits, because OWCP benefits tend to be more generous. In the examples with dependent children, we assume that the children would be eligible for OWCP dependent survivor benefits until they turn age 18. Survivors would receive the deceased employee's FERS employee contributions as a refund, which is estimated to be $12,774.[3] Additionally, we assume that the service-connected death was related to work with the military in a contingency operation, which entitles the survivor to receive up to a $100,000 death gratuity. Other lump-sum benefits offered by OWCP and Social Security are estimated to be $1,255.[4] Furthermore, we assume that the employee had basic FEGLI, which entitles survivors of employees to receive two times the sum of the annual salary rounded up to the next even $1,000 plus $2,000.[5] The final salary of the employee is estimated to be $52,897, yielding a life insurance payment of $110,000. While the Social Security lump-sum payment is subject to income tax, OWCP benefits and life insurance benefits are not subject to income tax. Total estimated cash lump-sum benefits are $224,029.

We assume that during the service tenure, the employee contributed 5 percent of his or her salary to TSP, making the total employer and employee contribution equal to 10 percent of the employee's salary after accounting for employer-matching contributions. We also assume that the TSP account balance had an annual rate of return of 5 percent. We assume that the survivors would cash out the balance of TSP, which is estimated to be $50,513 on the date of death. This lump-sum distribution would be subject to income tax.

Survivors are predicted to receive the greater of estimated Social Security survivor benefits and OWCP survivor annuity payments, since Social Security offsets OWCP annuity

---

[2] The civilian equivalent pay profile for an enlisted member used was the median income for an associate's degree holder (DeNavas-Walt, Proctor, and Smith, 2008).

[3] The FERS contribution rate is assumed to be 3.1 percent, which is the current rate that would be withheld from newly hired FERS-eligible employees. We do not include interest earned in this calculation of the refund. In practice, the portion of the refund equal to FERS contributions made is not subject to income tax, while the portion of the refund because of interest earned on contributions is subject to income tax.

[4] OWCP lump-sum benefits include up to $800 for funeral expenses and up to $200 to cover expenses for terminating the deceased's status as a federal employee. The Social Security lump sum is equal to $255.

[5] The basic life insurance amount is the sum of an employee's annual salary rounded up to the next even $1,000 plus $2,000 under FEGLI. This program provides an extra benefit to employees under age 45 for free. The extra benefit is equal to the basic life insurance amount for employees age 35 or younger and is reduced 10 percent per year above age 36 until age 45, when the extra benefit is phased out completely.

payments. The estimated annual cash annuity from OWCP and Social Security ranges from $26,449 to $40,838, depending on the presence and age of the surviving children.

We also note that survivors of federal employees may be eligible to continue federal employee health benefit insurance coverage. This benefit is not included in the comparison.

Private-Industry Employee, Enlisted Equivalent

For this example, we assume that the private-industry employee is born on January 1, 1987, and begins working at the age of 20 on January 1, 2007. After ten years of service, the employee dies from a work-related death at age 30, on January 1, 2017. We assume that the individual participates in an employer-sponsored defined contribution plan and an employer-sponsored life insurance plan and is covered by Social Security and CA workers' comp.

For this example, we assume that the private-industry employee participates in a defined contribution plan instead of a defined benefit plan, since participation in defined benefit plans has decreased over time, and private-industry workers are more likely to participate in a defined contribution plan than in a defined benefit plan. For the defined contribution plan, we assume that the deceased contributed 4.3 percent of his or her salary pretax each year and that the employer matched 70 percent of those contributions, for an employer contribution of 3 percent of salary per year.[6] As a result, total employee and employer contributions to the defined contribution plan equaled 7.3 percent of pay for each year employed. The defined contribution account balance is estimated to be $33,879 on the date of death, and we assume that the surviving spouse would choose to liquidate the account by taking a lump sum payout in the year of death. This lump sum payout would be subject to income tax.

We assume that the individual participated in employer-sponsored life insurance and chose to be insured for $250,000, which is the median maximum for private-industry employees with access to a fixed multiple of earnings life insurance benefit plan, as reported by BLS (Perez and Groshen, 2016).

We assume that the private-industry employee is covered by CA workers' comp and is eligible for the lump-sum payment and a burial expense reimbursement of up to $10,000. When the surviving spouse has no dependent children, he or she is eligible for a lump-sum payment of $250,000, which is paid out in installments at the same rate as temporary disability benefits, which is two-thirds of the final salary. The final salary is estimated to be $45,690, making the annual installment payment $30,460 per year until the eighth year after death, when $250,000 is paid off. For a surviving spouse with dependent children, we assume that the annual installment payment of $30,460 continues until the youngest child reaches age 18.

Social Security survivor benefits range from $16,980 to $40,838, depending on the age and presence of children. We assume that the surviving spouse without dependent children does not claim Social Security survivor benefits until reaching full retirement age. As a result, those benefits are not included in the discussion below comparing survivor benefits paid out

---

[6] Published tabulations from the BLS NCS for 2015 (Perez and Groshen, 2016) show that the median maximum potential employer contribution was 3 percent among private-industry employees participating in savings and thrift plans that specify matching contributions. The maximum potential employer contribution is the maximum employee contribution subject to matching multiplied by the employer matching percentage. The median employer matching percent was 70 percent among those in savings and thrift plans that specify a matching percentage. While plans may offer employer matching without specifying a matching percentage, we divide the 3 percent median maximum potential employer contribution by 70 percent to get a predicted employee contribution rate of 4.3 percent. See Tables 59 and 62 for details in Perez and Groshen (2016) for details.

20 years after death because we assume that the spouse would not have reached full retirement age.

Annuitant Death Examples

Officer Annuitant Under Regular Retirement Plus Federal Civilian Service Under FERS

For this example, we assume that an individual is born on January 1, 1947; enters commissioned military service at the age of 23 on January 1, 1970; retires from the military after 20 years of service; begins federal civilian service on January 1, 1990; and retires from federal civilian service after 20 years. The salary history is equal to the estimated earnings profile for a commissioned officer during the first 20 years of employment and equal to the earnings profile for the civilian equivalent to an officer during the past 20 years.[7] We assume that the individual dies at age 70, on January 1, 2017.

A surviving spouse is predicted to receive an annual survivor annuity from SBP ($24,847), FERS ($14,400), and Social Security ($30,960) for a total annual annuity equal to $70,206.

Cash lump-sum benefits consist of the $255 payment from Social Security, a life insurance payment from FEGLI, and a refund of unpaid DoD retired pay. FERS-eligible employees may continue to be covered by FEGLI when they retire if they meet certain criteria.[8] We assume that the FERS annuitant in our example is eligible to continue coverage and chooses the cheapest option, in which the basic coverage amount,[9] which is estimated to be $125,000, is reduced 2 percent per month over age 65 until 25 percent of coverage, or $31,250, remains. Survivors receive a refund of unpaid DoD retired pay, which we estimate as the expected value of half a pay period, or $1,882. The total cash lump sum is estimated to be $31,505.

We assume that, during the employee's federal civilian service tenure, the employee had contributed 5 percent of his or her salary to the TSP, making the total employer and employee contribution equal to 10 percent of his or her salary after accounting for employer-matching contributions. We assume that the TSP account balance had an annual rate of return of 5 percent, yielding an estimated balance of $440,880 on the date of death. We assume that the surviving spouse is age 70.5 on the date of death and would receive required minimum distributions from the TSP beginning in the year of death.[10]

Officer Annuitant Under BRS Plus Federal Civilian Service Under FERS

This example has the same assumptions and benefits as those listed under the "Officer Annuitant Under Regular Retirement Plus Federal Civilian Service" section, with the following

---

[7] The federal earnings pay profile assumes that an individual begins working at age 25 and has a bachelor's degree or higher. For our example, we assume the individual would begin working at age 23 to maintain comparability with the example of the commissioned officer retiree. See DeNavas-Walt, Proctor, and Smith, 2008.

[8] To continue FEGLI coverage when retiring, the retiree must be entitled to retire on an immediate annuity under FERS, be insured for five years of service immediately prior to starting the FERS annuity (or the entire period of service during which an employee was eligible for coverage if less than five years), be enrolled in FEGLI on date of retirement, and have not converted to an individual policy.

[9] Basic coverage equals the FAS rounded up to the next even $1,000 plus $2,000.

[10] Required minimum distributions are estimated using Schwab's online individual retirement account calculator; see Schwab, undated.

exceptions: The annual survivor annuity from SBP is reduced by 20 percent, from $24,847 to $19,877, and the refund of unpaid DoD retired pay is reduced by 20 percent, from $1,882 to $1,506. In addition, we assume that the employee had contributed 5 percent of his or her salary to the TSP during his or her military and federal civilian service career, making the total employer and employee contribution equal to 10 percent of the salary after accounting for employer-matching contributions. The estimated TSP account balance on the date of death is $693,818.

FERS Annuitant, Officer Equivalent

For this example, we assume that a federal civilian employee is born on January 1, 1947; enters federal civilian service at the age of 23 on January 1, 1970; and works for 40 years before retiring. The salary history during the 40 years of service is assumed to be the estimated federal earnings profile for an individual with a bachelor's degree or higher.[11] We assume that the federal civilian employee dies at age 70, on January 1, 2017.

We assume that the married couple has a 50 percent FERS survivor annuity that is estimated to be $19,220 per year. Estimated Social Security survivor benefits for the spouse are $30,108 per year. As a result, total annual cash annuity payments from survivor benefits are $49,328.

Cash lump-sum benefits consist of the $255 payment from Social Security and a life insurance payment from FEGLI. FERS-eligible employees may continue to be covered by FEGLI when they retire if they meet certain criteria. We assume that the FERS annuitant in our example is eligible to continue coverage and chooses the cheapest option, in which the basic coverage amount, estimated to be $84,000 in our example, is reduced 2 percent per month after age 65 until 25 percent of coverage, or $21,000, remains. The total cash lump-sum payments from Social Security and FEGLI are estimated to be $21,255.

We assume that, during this service tenure, the employee had contributed 5 percent of his or her salary to the TSP, making the total employer and employee contribution equal to 10 percent of the salary after accounting for employer-matching contributions. We assume that the TSP account balance had an annual rate of return of 5 percent, yielding an estimated balance of $574,816 at the date of death. We assume that the surviving spouse is age 70.5 on the date of death and would receive required minimum distributions from the TSP beginning in the year of death.

Private-Industry Annuitant, Officer Equivalent

For this example, we assume that an individual is born on January 1, 1947; enters a private-industry job at the age of 23 on January 1, 1970; and works for 40 years before retiring. The salary history during the 40 years of service is assumed to be the pay profile for an estimated civilian equivalent to an officer.[12] We assume that the private-industry retiree dies at age 70, on January 1, 2017.

We assume that the surviving retiree has two sources of income support: the deceased spouse's defined contribution plan and Social Security. For the defined contribution plan, we

---

[11] The federal earnings pay profile assumes that an individual begins working at age 25. For our example, we assume the individual would begin working at age 23 to maintain comparability with the example of the commissioned officer retiree. See DeNavas-Walt, Proctor, and Smith, 2008.

[12] This pay profile is equal to the 80th percentile of income for master's degree holders in management occupations.

assume that the deceased contributed 4.3 percent of his or her salary each year and that the employer matched 70 percent of those contributions, for an employer contribution of 3 percent of salary per year. As a result, total employee and employer contributions to the defined contribution plan equal 7.3 percent of pay each year employed. The estimated total defined contribution account balance available on the date of death is $613,445. We assume that the surviving spouse is age 70.5 on the date of death and would receive required minimum distributions from the TSP beginning in the year of death.

Social Security survivor benefits would provide the surviving spouse with a $255 lump-sum payment and an annual survivor annuity of $31,332.

Enlisted Annuitant Under Regular Retirement Plus Federal Civilian Service Under FERS

This example assumes that an individual is born on January 1, 1947; enters military service at the age of 20 on January 1, 1967; retires from the military after 20 years of service; begins federal civilian service on January 1, 1987; and retires from federal civilian service after 20 years. The salary history is equal to the estimated earnings profile for an enlisted service member during the first 20 years of employment and equal to the earnings profile for a civilian enlisted equivalent for the last 20 years.[13] We assume that the individual dies at age 70, on January 1, 2017.

A surviving spouse is predicted to receive an annual survivor annuity from SBP ($12,923), FERS ($6,799), and Social Security ($24,828), for a total annual annuity equal to $44,550.

Cash lump-sum benefits consist of the $255 payment from Social Security, a life insurance payment from FEGLI, and refund of unpaid DoD retired pay. FERS-eligible employees may continue to be covered by FEGLI when they retire if they meet certain criteria. We assume that the FERS annuitant in our example is eligible to continue coverage and chooses the cheapest option, in which basic coverage equals the FAS rounded up to the next even $1,000 plus $2,000. The basic coverage amount, which is estimated to be $58,000 in our example, is reduced 2 percent per month after age 65 until 25 percent of coverage, $14,500, remains. Survivors receive a refund of unpaid DoD retired pay, which we estimate as the expected value of half a pay period, $979. The total cash lump sum is estimated to be $14,755.

We assume that, during the employee's federal civilian service tenure, the employee had contributed 5 percent of his or her salary to the TSP, making the total employer and employee contribution equal to 10 percent of the salary after accounting for employer-matching contributions. We assume that the TSP account balance had an annual rate of return of 5 percent, yielding an estimated balance of $221,287 on the date of death. We assume that the surviving spouse is age 70.5 on the date of death and would receive required minimum distributions from the TSP beginning in the year of death.[14]

Enlisted Annuitant Under BRS Plus Federal Civilian Service Under FERS

This example has the same assumptions and benefits as those listed under the "Enlisted Annuitant Under Regular Retirement Plus Federal Civilian Service Under FERS" section,

---

[13] The earnings profile for the enlisted service member is based on the 2007 Greenbook (DoD, Directorate of Compensation, 2007), and the federal earnings profile is based on the 2007 median civilian income for associate's degree holders (DeNavas-Walt, Proctor, and Smith, 2008).

[14] Required minimum distributions are estimated using Schwab's online individual retirement account calculator; see Schwab, undated.

except for the following: The annual survivor annuity from SBP is reduced by 20 percent, from $12,923 to $10,338, and the refund of unpaid DoD retired pay is reduced by 20 percent from $979 to $783. In addition, we assume that the employee had contributed 5 percent of his or her salary to the TSP while in the military and federal civilian service, making the total employer and employee contribution equal to 10 percent of the salary, after accounting for employer-matching contributions. The estimated TSP account balance on the date of death is $349,059.

FERS Annuitant, Enlisted Equivalent

For this example, we assume that a federal civilian employee is born on January 1, 1947; enters federal civilian service at the age of 20 on January 1, 1967; and works for 40 years before retiring. The salary history during the 40 years of service is assumed to be the estimated civilian equivalent for an enlisted member, which is the 2007 median civilian income for associate's degree holders (DeNavas-Walt, Proctor, and Smith, 2008). We assume that the federal civilian employee dies at age 70, on January 1, 2017.

We assume that the married couple has a 50 percent FERS survivor annuity, which is estimated to be $13,598 per year. Estimated Social Security survivor benefits for the spouse are $26,052 per year. As a result, total annual cash annuity payments from survivor benefits are $39,650.

Cash lump-sum benefits consist of the $255 payment from Social Security and a life insurance payment from FEGLI. FERS-eligible employees may continue to be covered by FEGLI when they retire, if they meet certain criteria.[15] We assume that the FERS annuitant in our example is eligible to continue coverage and chooses the cheapest option, in which basic coverage equals the FAS rounded up to the next even $1,000 plus $2,000. The basic coverage amount, which is estimated to be $58,000 in our example, is reduced 2 percent per month after age 65 until 25 percent of coverage, or $14,500, remains. The total cash lump-sum payments from Social Security and FEGLI are estimated to be $14,755.

We assume that, during service tenure, the employee contributed 5 percent of his or her salary to the TSP, making the total employer and employee contribution equal to 10 percent of the salary after accounting for employer-matching contributions. We assume that the TSP account balance had an annual rate of return of 5 percent, yielding an estimated balance of $405,234 at the date of death. We assume that the surviving spouse is age 70.5 on the date of death and would receive required minimum distributions from the TSP beginning in the year of death.

Private-Industry Annuitant, Enlisted Equivalent

For this example, we assume that an individual is born on January 1, 1947; enters a private-industry job at the age of 20 on January 1, 1967; and works for 40 years before retiring. The salary history during the 40 years of service is assumed to be the estimated civilian equivalent for an enlisted member, which is the 2007 median civilian income for associate's degree holders

---

[15] To continue FEGLI coverage when retiring, the retiree must be entitled to retire on an immediate annuity under FERS, be insured for five years of service immediately prior to starting the FERS annuity (or the entire period of service during which an employee was eligible for coverage if less than five years), be enrolled in FEGLI on date of retirement, and have not converted to an individual policy.

(DeNavas-Walt, Proctor, and Smith, 2008). We assume that the private-industry retiree dies at age 70 on January 1, 2017.

The surviving retiree has two sources of income support: the deceased spouse's defined contribution plan and Social Security. For the defined contribution plan, we assume that the deceased contributed 4.3 percent of his or her salary each year and that the employer matched 70 percent of those contributions, for an employer contribution of 3 percent of salary per year.[16] As a result, total employee and employer contributions to the defined contribution plan equal 7.3 percent of pay for each year employed. The estimated total defined contribution account balance available on the date of death is $295,821. We assume that the surviving spouse is age 70.5 on the date of death and would receive required minimum distributions from the TSP beginning in the year of death.

Social Security survivor benefits would provide the surviving spouse with a $255 lump-sum payment and an annual survivor annuity of $26,052.

---

[16] See discussion under the section "Private-Industry Annuitant, Officer Equivalent."

Additional Detailed Examples

Los Angeles Police Officer Killed in the Line of Duty

To provide a comparison between military SBP and benefits offered to an employee with an inherently dangerous job, we created an example that compares the benefits for survivors of an enlisted member killed in action with those for survivors of a Los Angeles police officer. For this comparison, the hypothetical enlisted member killed in action has the same characteristics, and survivors have the same benefits as those discussed for the death of the current enlisted employee in Appendix C.

For this example, we assume that the Los Angeles police officer is born on January 1, 1987, and enters the Los Angeles Police Department at the age of 20 on January 1, 2007. After ten years of service, the employee is killed in the line of duty at age 30, on January 1, 2017. Los Angeles police officers who are killed in the line of duty may receive benefits from LAFPPF and CA workers' comp.[1] Salaries for Los Angeles police officers range from $60,907 to $93,973. For our example, we assume that the FAS for the Los Angeles Police Department survivor annuity calculation and the final salary for the CA workers' comp calculation is the midpoint of the salary range for Los Angeles police officers—$77,440. Los Angeles police officers do not contribute to Social Security and are therefore not eligible for Social Security benefits. Similar to the enlisted example, we construct two cases, one in which the Los Angeles police officer has a surviving spouse only and one in which the surviving spouse has two surviving children (one age 1 and one age 3 on the date of the service member's death).

LAFPPF provides a spouse annuity equal to 80 percent of the FAS. The LAFPPF dependent annuity is a percentage of the spouse annuity (25 percent for one dependent, 40 percent for two dependents, and 50 percent for three or more dependents). The sum of the spouse and dependent annuities are capped at 100 percent of the police officer's FAS. Dependent annuities are assumed to end when children turn 18.

CA workers' comp includes a lump-sum payment and a burial expense allocation of up to $10,000. The lump-sum payments are $250,000 for one dependent, $290,000 for two dependents, and $320,000 for three dependents. The lump-sum payment is paid out in weekly installments equal to two-thirds of the final average weekly wage, up to the maximum for temporary disability payments ($1,172.57 in 2017). A surviving spouse cannot receive both the lump-sum payment and the LAFPPF spouse annuity, but the child dependents may receive

---

[1] For additional information, see Los Angeles Fire and Police Pensions (2016) and California Department of Industrial Relations (2017).

both types of benefits.[2] For this example, we assume that the spouse waives the lump-sum payment and opts for the LAFPPF spouse annuity because the LAFPPF spouse annuity is generally more generous than that provided by CA workers' comp. When we examine cases in which the surviving spouse has children, we assume that the CA workers' comp lump-sum payment would be $40,000 when there is one child and $70,000 when there are two children. Once the CA workers' comp lump-sum payment is paid out, surviving children continue to receive a weekly benefit that is paid out at the same rate as temporary disability payments until they turn 18.

We include two other survivor benefits in our example. First, we include the lump-sum payment, equal to $343,589 as of October 1, 2016 (U.S. Department of Justice, undated), which is provided to survivors of public-safety officers killed in the line of duty by the U.S. Department of Justice Public Safety Officers benefit program.[3] Second, we include the City of Los Angeles Basic Life Insurance payout of $10,000. We note that police officers may join various unions to obtain more-generous life insurance policies, but we decided to include the least-generous option in our calculation.

Altogether, survivors would receive a one-time lump-sum cash payout totaling $363,589. A surviving spouse with no children would receive an annual annuity of $61,952 from the LAFPPF. The total LAFPPF annual annuity for a surviving spouse with children is estimated to be $77,440 per year when there are two surviving children. When there are surviving children, we assume that the estimated CA workers' comp dependent benefits are equal to $51,627 each year until the youngest child reaches age 18.[4]

Benefits received as a result of a death of a public-safety officer killed in the line of duty are not subject to income tax. This includes benefits paid from the U.S. Department of Justice Public Safety Officers benefit program and survivor benefits provided from a government plan.[5]

Table D.1 summarizes the assumptions and types of survivor benefits available in the hypothetical examples for an enlisted member killed in action and a Los Angeles police officer killed in the line of duty.

Figure D.1 compares the one-time payments and total present discounted cumulative benefits paid 30 years after the death. Although the one-time payment is larger for survivors of the enlisted member (about $0.5 million) than for the survivors of the Los Angeles police officer (about $0.4 million), total cumulative benefits are more than 1.5 times greater for survivors of the Los Angeles police officer than those for survivors of the enlisted member.

Figure D.2 presents cash annuity payments in 2017 dollars to the surviving spouse when there are two surviving children. The cash annuity for survivors of the Los Angeles police

---

[2] If a surviving spouse receives OWCP benefits, then the LAFPPF spouse annuity will be reduced by 25 percent each month until the OWCP benefits are completely paid back to the state of California.

[3] *Public-safety officers* are defined under 42 U.S.C. 3796b(4). This definition includes individuals serving in a public agency in an official capacity as a law enforcement officer or firefighter. The U.S. Department of Justice Public Safety Officers benefit program also includes higher-education financial assistance equal to $1,024 per month of full-time attendance for maximum of 45 months. The spouse of a deceased public-safety officer is eligible for education assistance that can be used at any point in time, while children are eligible up until their 27th birthdays. Our example excludes these benefits.

[4] Surviving children continue to receive CA workers' comp benefits even after the lump-sum payment is paid out. Benefits are paid at the same rate as temporary disability benefits, which are equal to two-thirds of the final salary.

[5] See IRS Publication 559, "Survivors, Executors and Administrators," for details.

Table D.1
Current Employee Death Summary of Assumptions and Benefits, Enlisted Versus Los Angeles Police Officer

	Enlisted	Los Angeles Police Officer
Date of birth	1/1/1994	1/1/1987
Date entered employment	1/1/2014	1/1/2007
Years of service	3	10
Date of death	1/1/2017	1/1/2017
Cash annuity	DIC, SSIA, Social Security	LAFPP, CA workers' comp
Cash lump sum	BAH, death gratuity, SGLI, unpaid pay or allowances, tax forgiveness, Social Security	CA workers' comp, City of Los Angeles Basic Life Insurance, U.S. Department of Justice Public Safety Officers Benefit
Other resources	*Fry Scholarship or DEA, burial, childcare, TRICARE, and other minor benefits*	*U.S. Department of Justice Public Safety Officers Benefit education benefits*

NOTE: Italicized benefits are not included in the figures.

Figure D.1
Current Employee Death Comparison of Survivor Benefits 30 Years After Death, Enlisted Versus Los Angeles Police Officer

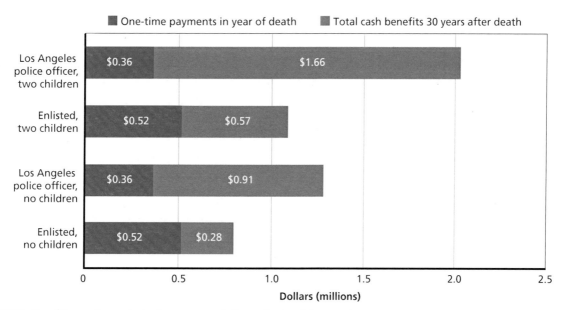

NOTE: Benefits are discounted using an annual discount rate of 6 percent.
RAND RR2236-D.1

Figure D.2
Current Employee Cash Annuity Comparison, Enlisted Versus Los Angeles Police Officer, Two Children (2017 Dollars)

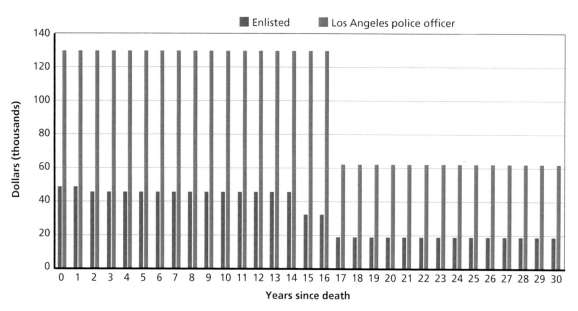

officer is much greater than that offered by SBP, which leads to cumulative benefits over a 30-year horizon that are greater than those provided by SBP. This is a result of the relative high generosity of the survivor annuity, which provides an annuity equal to 80–100 percent of the deceased's final salary. In addition, survivors with dependents receive two-thirds of the deceased's final salary through CA workers' comp until the youngest dependent reaches age 18. Note that the generosity of workers' compensation programs varies by state, and the generosity of survivor benefits among police officers varies across localities and states. As a result, this large difference in survivor benefits between survivors of the Los Angeles police officer and of an enlisted member is not necessarily true for law-enforcement officers in other states.

Officer Annuitant—SBP- and DIC-Optimization Examples

These examples demonstrate when retired service members, officers, would benefit from choosing DIC over SBP for themselves and their spouses and selecting the SBP benefit only for their children. The examples are, respectively, for families with one child and two children.

We assume that an individual is born on January 1, 1970, and commissions as a military officer at age 23 on January 1, 1993. The officer is married to a spouse who was also born on January 1, 1970. After 20 years of service, the officer retires and does not seek additional work. The retired officer dies seven years later, on January 1, 2017, at age 47, because of a service-related illness. The salary history is assumed to be the estimated pay profile for an officer based on the 2007 Greenbook (DoD, Directorate of Compensation, 2007). Using this salary history, we calculate an SBP benefit of 55 percent of the retirement benefit for a retiree, which, in this case, is 50 percent of high-36 pay, for a total of $24,272 per year. We assume, initially, that the service member has spouse and child SBP coverage.

If the service member chooses SBP for the spouse and any children, the surviving spouse's SBP benefits are subject to a DIC offset. Since the service member died of a service-connected illness, the surviving spouse is entitled to DIC from VA, which is currently equal to $15,095 per year for spouses. In this example, DIC partially offsets the SBP amount, and the spouse would receive $15,095 of DIC and $9,177 of SBP, plus $3,720 of SSIA per year to compensate for the offset. The spouse would also receive an additional DIC allowance of $3,740 per year per dependent child under age 18 and a flat-rate DIC transition allowance of $3,240 each year for two years if the spouse has one or more dependents; either of these allowances would offset the remaining SBP balance. The DIC benefit and allowances are not subject to income tax, but SSIA and SBP are included as taxable income.

If there are dependents, the spouse is also eligible for an annuity from SSA based on the number and age of the children. While at least one child is under age 16, the spouse would receive $20,700 per year. Each child under age 18 would also receive $20,700 per year. The maximum family benefit is $48,325 per year. When the children are age 16 or older, the spouse no longer receives SSA benefits until full retirement age (or the spouse can take a reduced amount starting at age 60, or 50 if disabled). At a minimum, 15 percent of this benefit is tax-exempt, depending on the surviving spouse's income.

Factoring in SSA with the DIC and SBP annuities, the total annuity the first year is $27,992 with no dependents, $69,392 with one child under age 16, $35,491 with one child age 16 or 17, $48,946 for two children under age 16, and $48,927 for two children ages 16–17.

The survivor would also receive a lump-sum death benefit of $255 from SSA, with the same tax-exempt rules as the SSA annuity and any unpaid retired pay due. Assuming that the retiree died halfway through a pay period, this would be $1,838 of taxable income based on the pay profile used. Assuming that the death was due to a service-related disability and that the family paid for funeral expenses out of pocket, VA would reimburse up to $2,000 for burial expenses and up to $300 for burial and funeral expenses. VA would also provide a headstone or marker and burial flag, and the deceased member would be entitled to burial at a national cemetery.

If the officer opts for SBP coverage for the children only, the children (assumed to be under age 16 on the date of the retired officer's death) would receive SBP and SSA benefits, while the spouse would receive DIC and SSA benefits. Since the spouse is not receiving SBP, none of the SBP is offset by DIC. In this case, the annuity total for the first two years is $87,747 for a spouse and one dependent and $98,412 for a spouse and two dependents.

Figures D.3 and D.4 depict annual benefits under the SBP option for a spouse and a child or children versus the SBP for children only. Figure D.3 shows that, during the first 20 years after the date of death, annual benefits are greater under the child-only option than under the full-SBP option when the child is a one-year-old on the date of death. If the child is instead a ten-year-old on the date of death, then the child-only SBP option is greater than the full SBP option for the first five years after the date of death. A similar pattern is shown in Figure D.4 when we compare benefits for a survivor with two young children versus two older children. These figures demonstrate that, once the children become too old to receive benefits, the remaining benefit for the spouse declines significantly. Consequently, the older the children are when the service member dies, the option to choose SBP for children only becomes less attractive.

Figure D.3
Full SBP Versus Child-Only SBP, Annual Benefits, One Child (2017 Dollars)

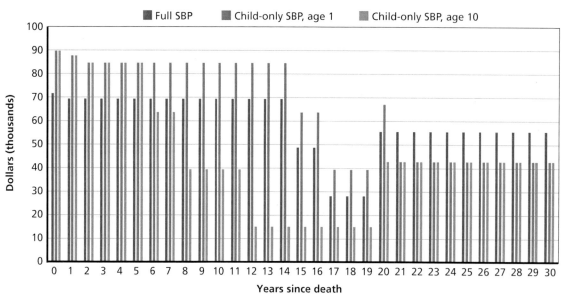

RAND RR2236-D.3

Figure D.4
Full SBP Versus Child-Only SBP, Annual Benefits, Two Children (2017 Dollars)

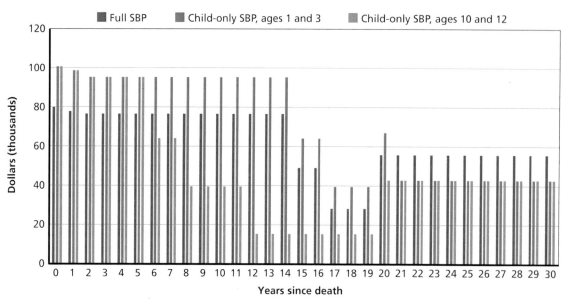

RAND RR2236-D.4

Figure D.5 shows the present discounted sum of the benefits over 30 years and depicts how the difference in total benefits varies between the SBP option for all and SBP option for children only by the surviving children's ages. As seen in these examples, it is only beneficial to choose the SBP option for children only when the children are young on the retired officer's date of death and not when the children are older.

By implication, it is optimal to select child-only SBP option if members know that they will die when their children are very young. Otherwise, the spouses will receive significantly less income over their lifetimes if there are no dependent children or if the dependent children are older when the member dies.

Regardless of the SBP beneficiary designation, the survivors are eligible for the DEA program, offered by VA. DEA provides $1,024 per month directly to the beneficiary for up to 45 months for degree programs and other types of educational pursuits.

The spouse and children are also eligible for health care and dental care through TRICARE at the same costs and coverage that they had at the time of the retiree's death. For TRICARE Prime, this would be a $565.20 annual enrollment fee for the entire family or $282.60 for the spouse only. The spouse can keep coverage until remarriage, and the children would remain in TRICARE until they marry, turn 18, or turn age 23 if they are full-time students. If a child is incapacitated and the injury occurred while still eligible for TRICARE, the child may be eligible for extended coverage. In either scenario, if children age out but remain unmarried and are not covered by their own employee insurance, they may purchase TRICARE Young Adult until they are age 26. The 2017 monthly premium is $319 for TRICARE Young Adult Prime and $216 for TRICARE Young Adult Standard.

Figure D.5
Full SBP Versus Child-Only SBP, Comparison of Cumulative Survivor Benefits 30 Years After Death

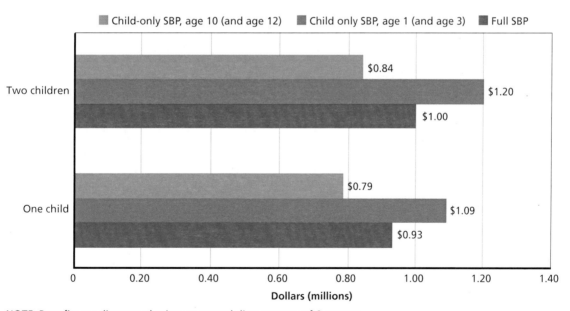

NOTE: Benefits are discounted using an annual discount rate of 6 percent.
RAND RR2236-3.5

There are other benefits that the survivors may receive. Survivors can continue to use commissary, base exchange, and some MWR services with the same age-out rules as TRICARE. The spouse can receive ten points for derived preference on civil-service exams, since the veteran served during a war period. The spouse is also eligible for the VA Home Loan Guaranty, since the service member died from a service-connected causes. The surviving spouse can use this loan guaranty one time. There is no limit on the amount that a lender can take, but VA limits how much it guarantees. The size of the loan that can be taken without needing to make a down payment is typically four times this maximum guarantee, and it varies by county. There are additional counseling services that the spouse could receive from VA, as well as numerous state and local benefits.

Adjustment for Differences in Widows' Characteristics Using an IPW Approach

Method Overview

As discussed in Chapter Four, we want to compare the financial status of widows receiving survivor benefits from the military with widows with similar characteristics who either do not receive survivor benefits or receive them from other sources. Thus, we need to control for differences in observed characteristics among these groups. For example, Table 4.1 and Table 4.2 indicate that widows who receive survivor benefits from the military are less likely to be black and Hispanic than widows who do not receive survivor benefits. Another difference is educational attainment. Widows receiving survivor benefits from the military are more educated than those who do not receive survivor benefits or who receive them from VA. For widows with Social Security income (Table 4.2), those receiving survivor benefits from the military are also more educated than widows receiving survivor benefits from companies or unions or from other sources. Also, among widows without Social Security income, a larger percentage receiving survivor benefits from the military (and from VA) reported having a disability that prevents them from working, in comparison with other group of widows.

To control for differences in these observed characteristics, we use an IPW approach, as proposed by Rosenbaum and Rubin (1983). This approach generates weights that allow us to create comparison groups that are similar, on average, based on observed characteristics (such as race or education), to widows receiving survivor benefits from the military. This allows muting the role of these observed characteristics and directly comparing outcomes, such as total income or poverty rates, between these (weighted) comparison groups and widows receiving benefits from the military.[1]

To implement the IPW approach, we created weights separately for each group of widows who could serve as a comparison to widows receiving survivor benefits from the military. As discussed, when these weights are applied to the comparison group, they make that group appear similar, based on average characteristics, to widows receiving survivor benefits from the military.

---

[1] We chose to apply IPW methods instead of regression methods because IPW methods do not make assumptions about the functional form of the outcome of interest—for instance, total income. In comparison, regression methods include such assumptions as linearity and separability of the effects of demographics and other observed characteristics. In addition, the IPW method allows us to easily maintain the original mean values for the population of interest (widows receiving survivor benefits from the military) but to adjust the mean values for other widows, according to the distribution in their observed characteristics. This is harder to accomplish with a regression method. Nevertheless, both methods rely on the assumption that there are not unmodeled factors that affect the outcome and whether the widow receives survivor benefits, as well as the source of benefits.

In defining the comparison groups, we also distinguish by whether the widow receives Social Security income. Thus, for widows who receive survivor benefits (mainly) from the military and have no Social Security income, we have seven potential comparison groups:

1. widows with no survivor benefits and no Social Security income
2. widows with survivor benefits mainly from VA and no Social Security income
3. widows with survivor benefits mainly from companies or unions and no Social Security income
4. widows with survivor benefits mainly from federal employers and no Social Security income
5. widows with survivor benefits mainly from state or local government employers and no Social Security income
6. widows with survivor benefits mainly from regular payments from annuities or paid-up life insurance and no Social Security income
7. widows with survivor benefits mainly from other sources and no Social Security income.[2]

Similarly, for widows who receive survivor benefits (mainly) from the military and have Social Security income, we have the following seven potential comparison groups:

1. widows with Social Security income and no survivor benefits
2. widows with Social Security income and survivor benefits mainly from VA
3. widows with Social Security income and survivor benefits mainly from companies or unions
4. widows with Social Security income and survivor benefits mainly from federal employers
5. widows with Social Security income and survivor benefits mainly from state or local government employers
6. widows with Social Security income and survivor benefits mainly from regular payments from annuities or paid-up life insurance
7. widows with Social Security income and survivor benefits mainly from other sources.

To create the weights that we apply to each of these 14 comparison groups, we run 14 separate logistic regressions. In each regression, we include only widows receiving survivor benefits (mainly) from the military and widows from the corresponding comparison group. Then, we model the probability that an observation (i.e., a widow) belongs to the group receiving survivor benefits (mainly) from the military, based on the widow's observed characteristics, as shown in the equation:

$$ln\left(\frac{\Pr\left[\text{Benefits from the military}\right]}{1-\Pr\left[\text{Benefits from the military}\right]}\right)=\beta X.$$

The variable X denotes the characteristics we include in the model, which are the characteristics we are interested in balancing between the potential comparison group and widows receiving their benefits (mainly) from the military. Those characteristics are age (in age catego-

---

[2]   Other sources include U.S. railroad retirement survivor pension, workers' compensation pension, black-lung survivor pension, regular payments from estates or trusts, and other unspecified sources.

ries), race, Hispanic origin, education, household size, and having a work disability. Each logistic regression is estimated using the person-level sampling weight provided in the CPS ASEC, which we denote by w_i^{CPS}.

After running the logistic regression, we construct a probability measuring how likely it is that a widow in the comparison group would belong to the group receiving survivor benefits (mainly) from the military. We denote that probability as p_i. In other words,

$$p_i = \frac{e^{\hat{\beta}\chi}}{1+e^{\hat{\beta}\chi}}.$$

Finally, the IPW entails that when we construct the weighted mean value of a variable—for example, total income—we weight observations of widows receiving survivor benefits from the military using their original sampling weight (w_i^{CPS}), but we weight observations of widows in the comparison group by the modified weight

$$w_i^{cps} \times \frac{p_i}{1-p_i}.$$

The key of the IPW approach is that an additional factor,

$$\frac{p_i}{1-p_i},$$

gives more weight to widows in the comparison group who are more similar (based on observed characteristics) to women receiving survivor benefits (mainly) from the military and give lower weight to widows in the comparison group who appear more different.

We apply bootstrap methods to test whether the mean value of a variable for widows receiving survivor benefits (mainly) from the military is statistically different from the mean value for widows in a comparison group, using the weights described above.[3] Our inference tests are based on 300 bootstrap replications.

Estimation Results

Table E.1 presents the estimated coefficients for the first seven logistic regressions (i.e., including widows who do not have Social Security income), while Table E.2 presents the coefficients for the next seven regressions (i.e., including widows who have Social Security income). A positive and statistically significant coefficient indicates that a widow with that characteristic is more likely to be receiving survivor benefits (mainly) from the military than to be in the comparison group. A negative statistically significant coefficient indicates that a widow with that characteristic is less likely to be receiving survivor benefits (mainly) from the military than to be in the comparison group. For example, in Table E.1 when comparing, among widows without Social Security income, those who receive military survivor benefits with those without any survivor benefits, we find that Hispanic widows are more common in the second group, while disabled widows are more common in the first group.

---

[3] See, for example, Cameron and Trivedi (2005, pp. 363–364).

Table E.1
Logistic Regressions: Widows Without Social Security Income

Characteristic	No Survivor Benefits	Main Source of Survivor Benefits					
		VA	Company or Union	Federal Government	State and Local Government	Annuities[a]	Other Sources[b]
Age (omitted category: 40–44 years)							
45–49 years	0.761	0.692	0.659	0.331	0.819	0.138	0.497
	(0.559)	(0.806)	(0.664)	(0.802)	(0.772)	(0.793)	(0.673)
50–54 years	0.211	−0.198	−0.052	−0.548	−0.098	−0.260	−0.096
	(0.547)	(0.774)	(0.634)	(0.759)	(0.676)	(0.748)	(0.643)
55–59 years	0.720	0.189	−0.206	−0.252	−0.050	0.331	0.237
	(0.518)	(0.745)	(0.602)	(0.732)	(0.647)	(0.729)	(0.606)
60–64 years	0.384	0.087	−0.408	−0.965	−0.670	0.577	−0.262
	(0.530)	(0.770)	(0.615)	(0.745)	(0.658)	(0.743)	(0.619)
65–69 years	−0.182	−0.344	−0.626	−1.159	−0.266	−0.381	−1.148
	(0.616)	(0.853)	(0.722)	(0.835)	(0.795)	(0.877)	(0.731)
70–74 years	0.124	−0.022	−0.090	−1.639**	−0.289	2.159*	−0.656
	(0.624)	(0.854)	(0.733)	(0.824)	(0.779)	(1.268)	(0.711)
75–79 years	−0.371	0.137	−0.624	−2.037**	−0.758	0.145	−1.355*
	(0.610)	(0.856)	(0.701)	(0.818)	(0.793)	(0.948)	(0.695)
80–84 years	0.714	0.867	0.400	−1.267	0.709	1.423	−0.356
	(0.587)	(0.835)	(0.698)	(0.810)	(0.805)	(0.944)	(0.667)
85–89 years	0.624	0.667	0.132	−1.424*	0.958	0.500	−0.696
	(0.588)	(0.849)	(0.693)	(0.805)	(0.894)	(0.939)	(0.670)
Race (omitted category: white)							
Black	−0.528*	−0.328	−0.007	−0.256	0.243	0.188	0.671**
	(0.278)	(0.331)	(0.314)	(0.337)	(0.365)	(0.446)	(0.331)
Asian only	−0.195	1.506**	1.109**	1.014**	0.532	0.679	1.507***
	(0.454)	(0.607)	(0.533)	(0.501)	(0.615)	(0.802)	(0.578)
Other race	−0.328	−0.224	0.345	−0.637	0.249	0.301	0.897*
	(0.417)	(0.517)	(0.503)	(0.588)	(0.603)	(1.074)	(0.538)
Hispanic origin	−1.335***	−0.799	−0.734	−0.600	−0.429	−0.498	−0.432
	(0.440)	(0.515)	(0.452)	(0.568)	(0.524)	(0.735)	(0.503)

Table E.1—Continued

Characteristic	No Survivor Benefits	Main Source of Survivor Benefits					
		VA	Company or Union	Federal Government	State and Local Government	Annunities[a]	Other Sources[b]
Household size							
# members	−0.316***	−0.187*	−0.130	−0.051	0.058	0.045	−0.127
	(0.100)	(0.104)	(0.093)	(0.120)	(0.129)	(0.149)	(0.096)
# members age 5 or younger	0.216	0.289	−0.072	0.453	−0.098	0.179	−0.024
	(0.290)	(0.432)	(0.415)	(0.637)	(0.498)	(0.813)	(0.502)
Education (omitted category: bachelor's degree or more)							
Less than high school	−0.515*	−1.404***	−0.177	0.542	0.434	0.194	−0.624*
	(0.287)	(0.335)	(0.308)	(0.340)	(0.399)	(0.460)	(0.324)
High school	−0.281	−0.579*	−0.388	0.233	0.051	−0.183	−0.529*
	(0.238)	(0.313)	(0.267)	(0.295)	(0.307)	(0.356)	(0.287)
Some college	0.211	0.195	0.061	0.143	0.384	0.097	0.108
	(0.256)	(0.359)	(0.293)	(0.318)	(0.335)	(0.390)	(0.332)
Associate's degree	−0.076	−0.353	−0.188	0.250	0.071	−0.329	−0.367
	(0.341)	(0.435)	(0.379)	(0.442)	(0.417)	(0.514)	(0.420)
Work disability	0.812***	0.132	0.779***	0.454*	0.421	0.653**	0.376*
	(0.185)	(0.228)	(0.221)	(0.240)	(0.285)	(0.330)	(0.222)
Constant	−4.243***	−0.123	−1.366**	−0.073	−0.765	−0.243	−0.517
	(0.494)	(0.771)	(0.574)	(0.781)	(0.682)	(0.778)	(0.634)
Observations	18,701	654	1,237	667	508	373	801

SOURCE: Data from CPS ASEC, 1996–2015 (see Flood et al., 2017).

NOTES: The outcome is 1 if widow receives survivor benefits (mainly) from the military and 0 if widow belongs to the comparison group (each column is a separate regression). Sample includes widows age 40 and older without Social Security income. All estimations are weighted using person-level weights for the analysis of the CPS ASEC. Estimations are done using Stata software. The table reports the estimated coefficients from logistic models.

*** $p < 0.01$; ** $p < 0.05$; * $p < 0.1$.

[a] Main survivor pension is from regular payments from annuities or paid-up life insurance.

[b] Main survivor pension is from the combination of other sources: U.S. railroad retirement survivor pension, workers' compensation pension, black-lung survivor pension, regular payments from estates or trusts, and other unspecified sources.

Table E.2
Logistic Regressions: Widows with Social Security Income

Characteristic	No Survivor Benefits	Main Source of Survivor Benefits					
		VA	Company or Union	Federal Government	State and Local Government	Annuities[a]	Other Sources[b]
Age (omitted category: 40–44 years)							
45–49 years	1.496	2.642**	0.135	0.659	1.679	1.505	1.381
	(1.149)	(1.306)	(1.221)	(1.996)	(1.369)	(1.239)	(1.232)
50–54 years	1.785	2.273*	0.489	1.777	0.974	2.656**	1.917
	(1.107)	(1.206)	(1.184)	(2.050)	(1.274)	(1.246)	(1.179)
55–59 years	1.751	2.027*	0.622	1.100	1.761	2.534**	2.391**
	(1.081)	(1.165)	(1.164)	(1.942)	(1.266)	(1.225)	(1.163)
60–64 years	2.208**	2.142**	0.577	0.991	1.401	3.209***	2.414**
	(1.018)	(1.082)	(1.083)	(1.891)	(1.135)	(1.083)	(1.059)
65–69 years	2.089**	2.334**	0.613	0.844	1.444	3.047***	2.416**
	(1.010)	(1.072)	(1.075)	(1.883)	(1.123)	(1.069)	(1.049)
70–74 years	2.196**	2.514**	0.741	0.954	1.759	2.889***	2.594**
	(1.009)	(1.070)	(1.073)	(1.881)	(1.121)	(1.064)	(1.046)
75–79 years	2.202**	2.495**	0.762	1.017	2.022*	2.840***	2.711***
	(1.008)	(1.070)	(1.073)	(1.881)	(1.120)	(1.064)	(1.046)
80–84 years	2.106**	2.523**	0.698	0.935	1.789	3.009***	2.415**
	(1.009)	(1.071)	(1.073)	(1.881)	(1.120)	(1.064)	(1.046)
85–89 years	1.968*	2.430**	0.749	0.898	1.806	2.716**	2.057**
	(1.009)	(1.071)	(1.074)	(1.883)	(1.121)	(1.065)	(1.046)
Race (omitted category: white)							
Black	−0.642***	−0.730***	0.125	−0.538**	0.269	0.480	−0.156
	(0.179)	(0.207)	(0.189)	(0.217)	(0.247)	(0.292)	(0.237)
Asian only	1.007***	0.997***	1.521***	1.022***	1.727***	2.247***	1.799***
	(0.215)	(0.310)	(0.269)	(0.371)	(0.405)	(0.653)	(0.467)
Other race	0.698***	0.715**	1.612***	0.366	1.568***	1.291***	0.860**
	(0.241)	(0.317)	(0.292)	(0.356)	(0.364)	(0.459)	(0.371)
Hispanic origin	−0.936***.	−0.399	−0.303	−0.766**	−0.343	−0.241	−0.077
	(0.250)	(0.316)	(0.266)	(0.328)	(0.332)	(0.388)	(0.343)

Table E.2—Continued

| Characteristic | No Survivor Benefits | Main Source of Survivor Benefits | | | | | |
		VA	Company or Union	Federal Government	State and Local Government	Annarities[a]	Other Sources[b]
Household size							
# members	−0.068	0.032	0.086*	0.058	0.083	0.213**	0.188***
	(0.043)	(0.058)	(0.044)	(0.058)	(0.061)	(0.083)	(0.065)
# members age 5 or younger	−0.038	−0.030	0.099	0.399	−0.297	−0.393	−0.793*
	(0.207)	(0.333)	(0.279)	(0.390)	(0.380)	(0.521)	(0.445)
Education (omitted category: bachelor's degree or more)							
Less than high school	−0.933***	−0.845***	−0.702***	−0.003	−0.141	0.215	−0.417**
	(0.131)	(0.163)	(0.140)	(0.172)	(0.180)	(0.213)	(0.171)
High school	−0.552***	−0.278*	−0.635***	−0.330**	−0.208	0.058	−0.158
	(0.116)	(0.150)	(0.124)	(0.148)	(0.154)	(0.169)	(0.154)
Some college	−0.043	−0.093	−0.125	0.046	−0.032	0.129	0.114
	(0.129)	(0.171)	(0.140)	(0.169)	(0.176)	(0.191)	(0.176)
Associate's degree	0.199	−0.111	0.153	0.268	0.401*	0.301	0.189
	(0.180)	(0.221)	(0.193)	(0.229)	(0.241)	(0.252)	(0.253)
Work disability	0.092	−0.372***	0.039	0.043	−0.060	−0.016	−0.186*
	(0.086)	(0.105)	(0.092)	(0.110)	(0.115)	(0.130)	(0.112)
Constant	−5.785***	−2.561**	−2.494**	−1.283	−1.985*	−3.156***	−2.807***
	(1.010)	(1.079)	(1.075)	(1.890)	(1.128)	(1.063)	(1.048)
Observations	67,793	2,653	7,835	2,437	2,136	1,735	2,282

SOURCE: Data from CPS ASEC, 1996–2015 (see Flood et al., 2017).

NOTES: The outcome is 1 if widow receives survivor benefits (mainly) from the military and 0 if widow belongs to the comparison group (each column is a separate regression). Sample includes widows age 40 and older without Social Security income. All estimations are weighted using person-level weights for the analysis of the CPS ASEC. Estimations are done using Stata software. The table reports the estimated coefficients from logistic models. Each column represents a separate estimation.

*** $p < 0.01$; ** $p < 0.05$; * $p < 0.1$.

[a] Main survivor pension is from regular payments from annuities or paid-up life insurance.

[b] Main survivor pension is from the combination of other sources: U.S. railroad retirement survivor pension, workers' compensation pension, black-lung survivor pension, regular payments from estates or trusts, and other unspecified sources.

Adjusted Comparison of Characteristics

Table E.3 and Table E.4 present the mean values for the widows' characteristics that were previously shown in Table 4.1 and Table 4.2, but now observations are weighted using the updated weights discussed earlier. We see that the new weighted means of the demographic characteristics across all columns are no longer statistically different from the values reported in the column on military survivor benefits. The only exceptions are total income and employment status (the latter variable was not included in the logistic models because it can be endogenous to the receipt of survivor benefits). Therefore, the new weights are ensuring that when we compare the financial status of widows in different groups, we are comparing widows who are, on average, similar based on observed characteristics. We used these new weights in our comparison of income and participation in government programs in Chapter Four.

Table E.3
Adjusted Comparison of Widows' Characteristics by Main Source of Survivor Benefits, Conditional on Not Receiving Social Security Payments

| Characteristic | No Survivor Benefits | Main Source of Military or VA Survivor Benefits | | Other Main Source of Survivor Benefits | | | | |
		Military	VA	Company or Union	Federal Government	State and Local Government	Annuities[a]	Other Sources[b]
Percentage of all widows	17.1%	0.2%	0.4%	1.0%	0.4%	0.3%	0.2%	0.6%
Total money income (pretax)	30,747*	41,708	35,510	42,300	49,573*	47,774	49,617	47,752
Age	61.6	61.7	61.3	61.5	61.8	62.0	61.1	61.6
Race								
White	85.4%	85.4%	84.9%	85.0%	85.9%	85.4%	82.2%	86.6%
Black	9.9%	9.9%	10.5%	10.1%	9.7%	10.3%	11.4%	9.4%
Asian only	2.4%	2.4%	2.2%	2.4%	1.9%	2.1%	2.1%	1.8%
Other race	2.3%	2.3%	2.4%	2.4%	2.4%	2.1%	4.2%	2.2%
Hispanic origin	2.1%	2.1%	2.0%	2.0%	2.0%	1.8%	3.2%	2.1%
Education								
Less than high school	15.3%	15.3%	14.7%	14.5%	13.4%	16.1%	13.3%	14.2%
High school	31.0%	31.0%	31.2%	30.7%	32.3%	30.7%	36.5%	30.9%
Some college	22.5%	22.4%	23.8%	23.5%	22.5%	25.0%	20.1%	22.8%
Associate's degree	8.3%	8.3%	7.9%	8.4%	7.9%	6.9%	9.2%	8.8%
Bachelor's degree or more	22.9%	23.0%	22.4%	22.8%	23.8%	21.4%	20.9%	23.3%

Table E.3—Continued

Characteristic	No Survivor Benefits	Main Source of Military or VA Survivor Benefits		Other Main Source of Survivor Benefits				
		Military	VA	Company or Union	Federal Government	State and Local Government	Annuities[a]	Other Sources[b]
Household size								
# members	1.61	1.61	1.60	1.64	1.67	1.65	1.56	1.62
# members age 5 or younger	0.03	0.03	0.03	0.03	0.04	0.03	0.02	0.04
Employment status								
Not in labor force	45.6%*	58.8%	60.5%	50.5%*	54.1%	57.4%	56.8%	54.9%
Unemployed	2.6%	3.4%	1.6%	2.7%	0.9%	1.7%	2.6%	2.4%
Self-employed	4.9%*	1.9%	4.8%	3.2%	3.4%	2.0%	4.3%	5.0%*
Wage or salary worker[c]	37.2%*	23.9%	22.6%	31.2%	23.6%	25.1%	26.7%	28.1%
Government employee[d]	9.8%	12.0%	10.5%	12.4%	17.9%	13.8%	9.7%	9.6%
Work disability	30.3%	30.3%	29.2%	30.4%	29.8%	31.4%	28.2%	28.5%

SOURCE: Data from CPS ASEC, 1996–2015 (see Flood et al., 2017).
NOTES: Sample includes widows age 40 and older who are not receiving income from Social Security. All calculations are weighted using person-level weights for the analysis of the CPS ASEC, adjusted for differences in observed characteristics with the IPW methodology.

* $p < 0.05$ (there is a statistical significant difference at the 95% confidence level in comparison to the value in the military survivor benefits column, based on 300 bootstrap replications).

[a] Main survivor pension is from regular payments from annuities or paid-up life insurance.

[b] Main survivor pension is from the combination of other sources: U.S. railroad retirement survivor pension, workers' compensation pension, black-lung survivor pension, regular payments from estates or trusts, and other unspecified sources.

[c] Includes family workers.

[d] Includes armed forces, federal employment, state employment, and local government employment.

Table E.4
Adjusted Comparison of Widows' Characteristics by Main Source of Survivor Benefits, Conditional on Receiving Social Security Payments

| Characteristic | No Survivor Benefits | Military or VA Survivor Benefits | | Other Sources of Survivor Benefits | | | | |
| | | Main Source | | Main Source | | | | |
		Military	VA	Company or Union	Federal Government	State and Local Government	Annuities[a]	Other Sources[b]
Percentage of all widows	65.3%	1.0%	1.7%	7.3%	1.4%	1.2%	0.8%	1.3%
Total money income (pretax)	24,443*	39,781	34,028*	35,180*	40,444	41,134	40,288	47,238*
Age	76.5	76.4	76.5	76.5	76.5	76.6	76.5	76.5
Race								
White	90.9%	90.9%	90.6%	90.5%	90.7%	90.4%	91.0%	89.5%
Black	3.9%	3.9%	3.9%	3.9%	4.0%	4.1%	3.7%	4.1%
Asian only	2.9%	2.8%	2.8%	3.0%	3.0%	2.9%	2.7%	3.7%
Other race	2.3%	2.3%	2.6%	2.5%	2.2%	2.7%	2.7%	2.7%
Hispanic origin	1.4%	1.4%	1.5%	1.4%	1.5%	1.5%	1.3%	1.3%
Education								
Less than high school	18.0%	18.0%	17.8%	17.9%	17.6%	17.9%	17.4%	17.2%
High school	35.5%	35.5%	35.6%	35.3%	35.6%	35.2%	34.8%	35.6%
Some college	19.9%	19.9%	20.1%	20.0%	20.2%	19.9%	21.3%	20.0%
Associate's degree	9.6%	9.6%	9.6%	9.6%	9.7%	9.5%	9.8%	10.0%
Bachelor's degree or more	17.0%	17.0%	17.0%	17.2%	16.9%	17.4%	16.8%	17.2%
Household size								
# members	1.43	1.43	1.43	1.44	1.43	1.45	1.46	1.45
# members age 5 or younger	0.01	0.01	0.01	0.01	0.01	0.02	0.02	0.01
Employment status								
Not in labor force	90.3%	90.4%	94.8%*	91.9%	90.0%	92.3%	93.1%	94.1%*
Unemployed	0.5%	0.4%	0.3%	0.3%	0.6%	0.5%	0%*	0.3%
Self-employed	1.6%	1.7%	1.5%	1.5%	2.4%	1.5%	1.6%	2.0%

Table E.4—Continued

| Characteristic | No Survivor Benefits | Military or VA Survivor Benefits Main Source | | Other Sources of Survivor Benefits Main Source | | | | |
		Military	VA	Company or Union	Federal Government	State and Local Government	Annuities[a]	Other Sources[b]
Wage or salary worker[c]	6.1%	5.8%	2.9%*	5.1%	5.2%	4.2%	4.1%	3.2%*
Government employee[d]	1.4%	1.6%	0.5%*	1.2%	1.8%	1.6%	1.2%	0.4%*
Work disability	29.1%	29.1%	29.2%	29.0%	29.3%	29.1%	28.6%	28.3%

SOURCE: Data from CPS ASEC, 1996–2015 (see Flood et al., 2017).

NOTES: Sample includes widows age 40 and older who are not receiving income from Social Security. All calculations are weighted using person-level weights for the analysis of the CPS ASEC, adjusted for differences in observed characteristics with the IPW methodology.

* $p < 0.05$ (there is a statistical significant difference at the 95% confidence level in comparison to the value in the military survivor benefits column, based on 300 bootstrap replications).

a Main survivor pension is from regular payments from annuities or paid-up life insurance.

b Main survivor pension is from the combination of other sources: U.S. railroad retirement survivor pension, workers' compensation pension, black-lung survivor pension, regular payments from estates or trusts, and other unspecified sources.

c Includes family workers.

d Includes armed forces, federal employment, state employment, and local government employment.

Example Illustrating DoD's Subsidy to SBP

In this appendix, we present an example indicating that a subsidy is needed to cover the SBP liability of retired service members—not only the liability of those who die on duty.

We use the SBP NCP for full-time personnel, and the example illustrates DoD's subsidy to SBP. Recall from Chapter Two that DoD's Office of the Actuary (2017b) estimates DoD's SBP subsidy at 44.6 percent for the FY 2016 cohort of retirees. A thorough estimation of cost-sharing requires the DoD's Office of the Actuary data and models, and it accounts for member and spouse mortality rates, designation of beneficiaries, beneficiary eligibility,[1] benefits paid to the survivors of service members who died on duty, and factors related to the performance of the military retirement fund. Moreover, DoD's cost also includes the personnel and facilities now used in the SBP program. This is not counted as part of the 44.6 percent subsidy, but it is a cost that would presumably be shifted, in large part, to commercial firms if they provided SBP. The example does not account for all of these factors, but it is sufficient to indicate that DoD cost-sharing is sizable and helps cover SBP benefits not only for survivors of service members who die on duty but also for survivors of retirees.

In the example, an enlisted member enters service at age 20 and retires as an E-7 at age 40 after 20 years of service, having been promoted from E-6 two years earlier. Basic pay for the high-36 is used in computing the member's retired pay. The member elects to cover full retired pay and pays an SBP premium of 6.5 percent. The member designates his or her spouse as beneficiary, and there is no divorce. The member dies at age 73. The spouse begins receiving SBP in the next year and dies at 85 after 12 years of SBP at 55 percent of the member's retired pay. The example uses assumptions from DoD's Office of the Actuary for FY 2015 for real (inflation adjusted) basic pay growth of 0.5 percent per year, retirement fund growth of 2.5 percent per year (DoD, Office of the Actuary, 2017a, Table D-1) and assumes the COLA to retired pay holds constant its real value as of the time of retirement.

In Table F.1, retired pay is $28,083 per year, and the SBP premium is 6.5 percent of this ($1,825). The member has paid 30 years of SBP premiums by age 70; no further premiums are paid after age 70 or when premiums have been paid for at least 360 months (30 years). The compounded value of the premiums at age 73 when the retiree dies is $88,458. The surviving spouse receives 55 percent of retired pay, $15,445 per year. This amount is constant from year to year because it is fully adjusted for cost-of-living increases. The survivor lives to age 85 and receives 12 years of the SBP survivor annuity benefit. At age 73, the amount needed to fund

---

[1] For instance, a child designated as beneficiary might be too old to be eligible for SBP benefits when the retiree dies. A spouse designated as beneficiary might divorce and remarry before age 55, in which case the benefit would be suspended but would be reinstated if that marriage ended by divorce or the spouse's death.

Table F.1
Example of DoD Cost-Sharing in SBP

Item	Amount
Retired pay ($/year)	$28,083
SBP premium ($/year)	$1,825
Number of years premium paid	31
Value of premiums plus interest at death at age 73	$88,458
SBP benefit ($/year)	$15,445
Amount needed at death to fund SBP benefit for 12 years	$158,436
Number of years SBP benefit paid	12
DoD subsidy in this case	$69,978
DoD subsidy as percentage of needed amount	44%

these payments is $158,436. This amount, with an annual payment of $15,445 and the remainder invested at a real rate of 2.5 percent per year, would be just enough to cover the spouse's SBP benefits. To ensure that full amount of $158,436 is available, DoD in effect contributes $69,978 in addition to the retiree's contributions of $88,458. This is DoD's subsidy to SBP in this particular example. It is 44 percent of the amount needed at age 73 to fund the surviving spouse's SBP benefits.[2] The example illustrates the point that support from DoD is necessary to fund the SBP benefits that will be paid to the survivor of a military retiree. By implication, DoD's subsidy to SBP is not limited to funding the SBP benefits for the survivors of service members who die on duty.

A second part of the example considers the SBP accrual charges paid by the entering cohort of enlisted personnel. This, too, is a simplification because a more general example would include officer accrual charges. Our example assumes an SBP NCP of 1.2 percent, typical progression through the enlisted ranks, and an average year-to-year continuation rate of 90 percent. At this continuation rate, 12 percent of entrants complete 20 or more years of service. The SBP accrual charges are paid throughout the careers of the cohort and continue through 30 years of service. The charges earn interest and have an accumulated real value of $99,539 per member completing 20 years of service. This point is chosen because those completing 20 years of service constitute the major at-risk population for participating in SBP. Note that the accrual charge is applied to the basic pay bill at each year of service, yet not all members will reach retirement, not all who reach retirement will participate in SBP, and not all who participate will elect to cover 100 percent of retired pay.

The value of the accumulated accrual charges, plus interest, is $99,539 per member of the cohort completing 20 years of service. Thus, after allowing for the subsidy of $69,978 in the example, there is a positive remainder of $29,561. DoD has come out ahead in this case.

---

[2]   It is coincidental that this percentage is close to the DoD's Office of the Actuary estimate of 44.6 percent. The percentage in the example would change if we changed the death ages of the retiree and the surviving spouse.

References

Air Force Retiree Services, "Annuity for 'Forgotten Widows,'" fact sheet, undated. As of December 13, 2014:
http://www.retirees.af.mil/Portals/53/documents/SBP/
Annuity%20for%20Forgotten%20Widows.pdf?ver=2016-10-07-113750-100

Asch, Beth J., James Hosek, and Michael G. Mattock, *Toward Meaningful Compensation Reform: Research in Support of DoD's Review of Military Compensation*, Santa Monica, Calif.: RAND Corporation, RR-501-OSD, 2014. As of November 30, 2017:
https://www.rand.org/pubs/research_reports/RR501.html

Baldwin, Marjorie L., and Christopher F. McLaren, *Workers' Compensation: Benefits, Coverage, and Costs (2014 Data)*, Washington, D.C.: National Academy of Social Insurance, October 2016. As of September 1, 2017:
https://www.nasi.org/sites/default/files/research/NASI_Workers_Comp_Report_2016.pdf

Bee, Adam, and Joshua Mitchell, *Do Older Americans Have More Income Than We Think?* Suitland, Md.: U.S. Census Bureau, SESHD Working Paper 2017-39, 2017.

Better Business Bureau, "Office of Servicemembers' Group Life Insurance," webpage, undated. As of December 13, 2017:
https://www.bbb.org/new-jersey/business-reviews/insurance-companies/
office-of-servicemembers-group-life-insurance-in-roseland-nj-24002628

BLS—*See* Bureau of Labor Statistics.

Bureau of Labor Statistics, *National Compensation Survey: Retirement Plan Provisions in State and Local Government in the United States, 2016*, Washington, D.C.: U.S. Department of Labor, Bulletin 2786, April 2017.

California Department of Industrial Relations, "Workers' Compensation Benefits," webpage, December 2017. As of October 1, 2017:
https://www.dir.ca.gov/dwc/workerscompensationbenefits.htm

Callan, Patrick M., Christopher M. Schmid, and Michael Voogd, *Analysis of Servicemembers' Group Life Insurance (SGLI) Program: History, Current Issues and Future Implications*, Monterey, Calif.: Naval Postgraduate School, June 2011. As of December 18, 2017:
http://www.dtic.mil/dtic/tr/fulltext/u2/a547799.pdf

Cameron, Adrian Colin, and Pravin K. Trivedi, *Microeconometrics: Methods and Applications*, Cambridge, UK: Cambridge University Press, 2005.

Charles Schwab, "RMD Calculator," webpage, undated. As of December 12, 2017:
http://www.schwab.com/public/schwab/investing/retirement_and_planning/understanding_iras/
ira_calculators/rmd

Chicago Teachers' Pension Fund, "Retirement Benefits," webpage, undated. As of December 15, 2017:
http://www.ctpf.org/active_members/serviceretirement.htm

DeNavas-Walt, Carmen, Bernadette D. Proctor, and Jessica C. Smith, *Income, Poverty, and Health Insurance Coverage in the United States: 2007*, Washington, D.C.: U.S. Census Bureau, P60-235, August 2008.

DFAS—*See* U.S. Department of Defense, Defense Finance and Accounting Service.

DoD—*See* U.S. Department of Defense.

FedsHireVets.gov, "Family Member Preference (Derived Preference)," webpage, U.S. Office of Personnel Management, undated. As of December 14, 2017:
https://fedshirevets.gov/job/familypref/index.aspx

Flood, Sarah, Miriam King, Steven Ruggles, and J. Robert Warren, "Integrated Public Use Microdata Series, Current Population Survey: Version 5.0," data set, Minneapolis: University of Minnesota, 2017.

Gustman, Alan, Thomas L. Steinmeier, and Nahid Tabatabai, "Updated Pension Wealth Data File in the HRS Panel: 1992 to 2010 Part III," researcher-contributed data set, Ann Arbor, Mich.: Health and Retirement Study, 2014.

Health and Retirement Study, 1992–2010 HRS Core Fat Files public-use data set, produced and distributed by the University of Michigan with funding from the National Institute of Aging grant number NIA U01AG009740), Ann Arbor, Mich., 2017.

HRS—See Health and Retirement Study.

IRS, "Retirement Topics—Qualified Joint and Survivor Annuity," webpage, last updated August 26, 2017. As of December 7, 2017:
https://www.irs.gov/retirement-plans/plan-participant-employee/
retirement-topics-qualified-joint-and-survivor-annuity

Kamarck, Kristy N., Don J. Jansen, Lawrence Kapp, R. Chuck Mason, and Barbara Salazar Torreon, *FY2017 National Defense Authorization Act: Selected Military Personnel Issues*, Washington, D.C.: Congressional Research Service, R44577, January 23, 2017.

Knapp, David, Kristine Brown, James Hosek, Michael G. Mattock and Beth J. Asch, *Retirement Benefits and Teacher Retention: A Structural Modeling Approach*, Santa Monica, Calif.: RAND Corporation, RR-1448-RC, 2016. As of December 1, 2017:
https://www.rand.org/pubs/research_reports/RR1448.html

Liou, Wayne, *How Social Security Benefits Are Computed: In Brief*, Washington, D.C.: Congressional Research Service, 2016.

Los Angeles Fire and Police Pensions, *Tier 6 Summary Plan Description*, Los Angeles, July 2016. As of December 15, 2017:
https://www.lafpp.com/sites/default/files/files/tier-6-spd-july-2016-final-web-rev-9-13-16.pdf

Mattock, Michael G., James Hosek, and Beth J. Asch, *Reserve Participation and Cost Under a New Approach to Reserve Compensation*, Santa Monica, Calif.: RAND Corporation, MG-1153-OSD, 2012. As of December 1, 2017:
https://www.rand.org/pubs/monographs/MG1153.html

Military Benefit Association, "Level Term Life Insurance," webpage, undated. As of December 13, 2017:
https://www.militarybenefit.org/insurance-plans/level-term/

Miller, Amalia R., Paul Heaton, and David S. Loughran, *Analysis of Financial Support to the Surviving Spouses and Children of Casualties in the Iraq and Afghanistan Wars*, Santa Monica, Calif.: RAND Corporation, TR-1281-OSD, 2012. As of December 1, 2017:
https://www.rand.org/pubs/technical_reports/TR1281.html

National Military Family Association, "Benefits for Survivors of Active Duty Deaths," Arlington, Va., April 2008. As of December 15, 2017:
http://support.militaryfamily.org/site/DocServer/Survivor_Benefits_Fact_sheet_4-08.pdf?docID=12501.

Perez, Thomas A., and Erica L. Groshen, *National Compensation Survey: Employee Benefits in the United States, March 2015*, Washington, D.C.: Bureau of Labor Statistics, U.S. Department of Labor, Bulletin 2782, September 2015.

———, *National Compensation Survey: Employee Benefits in the United States, March 2016*, Washington, D.C.: Bureau of Labor Statistics, U.S. Department of Labor, Bulletin 2785, September 2016.

RAND Corporation, RAND HRS Data, Version P, produced by the RAND Center for the Study of Aging, with funding from the National Institute on Aging and the Social Security Administration, Santa Monica, Calif., August 2016.

Rosenbaum, Paul, and Donald B. Rubin, "The Central Role of the Propensity Score in Observational Studies for Causal Effects," *Biometrika*, Vol. 70, No. 1, 1983, pp. 41–55.

Rothbaum, Jonathan L., and Income Statistics Branch, *Comparing Income Aggregates: How Do the CPS and ACS Match the National Income and Product Accounts, 2007–2012*, Suitland, Md.: U.S. Census Bureau, SEHSD Working Paper 2015-1, January 14, 2015.

Solis, Hilda L., and Keith Hall, *National Compensation Survey: Employee Benefits in the United States, March 2009*, Washington, D.C.: Bureau of Labor Statistics, U.S. Department of Labor, Bulletin 2731, September 2009.

Special Subcommittee on Survivor Benefits, House Armed Services Committee, *Inquiry into Survivor Benefits*, Washington, D.C.: U.S. Government Printing Office, 1970.

SSA—*See* U.S. Social Security Administration.

Tricare.mil, "Prime Enrollment Fees," webpage, Defense Health Agency, U.S. Department of Defense, last updated June 2, 2016. As of August 2017:
https://tricare.mil/Costs/HealthPlanCosts/PrimeOptions/EnrollmentFees

United Auto Workers Local 387, *Benefits Book*, Flat Rock, Mich., 2007.

United States Code, Title 10, Subchapter II, Survivor Benefit Plan, Sections 1447–1455, January 7, 2011.

United States Code, Title 10, Section 1481, Recovery, Care, and Disposition of Remains: Decedents Covered, January 3, 2012.

United States Code, Title 29, Section 1055, Requirement of Joint and Survivor Annuity and Preretirement Survivor Annuity, January 3, 2012.

United States Code, Title 37, Section 403, Basic Allowance for Housing, January 3, 2012.

United States Code, Title 37, Section 501, Payments for Unused Accrued Leave, January 7, 2011.

United States Code, Title 38, Section 1313, Dependency and Indemnity Compensation to Children, January 3, 2012.

United States Code, Title 42, Section 3796b, Definitions, January 7, 2011.

U.S. Army Human Resources Command, "Unpaid Pay and Allowance UPPA," webpage, last updated August 9, 2017. As of December 19, 2017:
https://www.hrc.army.mil/content/Unpaid%20Pay%20and%20Allowances%20UPPA

U.S. Centers for Medicare and Medicaid Services, "Part B Costs," webpage, Medicare.gov, undated. As of September 15, 2017:
https://www.medicare.gov/your-medicare-costs/part-b-costs/part-b-costs.html

U.S. Department of Defense, "Death Gratuity," webpage, *Military Compensation*, undated-a. As of July 18, 2017:
http://militarypay.defense.gov/Benefits/Death-Gratuity/

———, "Retirement," webpage, *Military Compensation*, undated-b. As of September 15, 2017:
http://militarypay.defense.gov/Pay/Retirement/

———, "The Uniformed Services Blended Retirement System," webpage, *Military Compensation*, undated-c. As of September 15, 2017:
http://militarypay.defense.gov/BlendedRetirement/

U.S. Department of Defense, Defense Finance and Accounting Service, "Concurrent Retirement and Disability Pay (CRDP)," webpage, last updated October 9, 2013. As of December 5, 2017:
https://www.dfas.mil/retiredmilitary/disability/crdp.html

———, *DoD Commissary Program*, Washington, D.C., Department of Defense Instruction 1330.17, June 18, 2014a.

———, *Child Development Programs (CDPs)*, Washington, D.C., Department of Defense Instruction 6060.02, August 5, 2014b.

————, "Cost," webpage, last updated March 20, 2015a. As of December 5, 2017:
https://www.dfas.mil/retiredmilitary/provide/sbp/cost.html

————, "Eligible Beneficiaries," webpage, last updated November 20, 2015b. As of December 5, 2017:|
https://www.dfas.mil/retiredmilitary/provide/sbp/coverage.html

————, "Changing or Stopping Your Coverage," webpage, last updated March 23, 2016a. As of December 5, 2017:
https://www.dfas.mil/retiredmilitary/provide/sbp/change.html

————, "Special Needs Trust," webpage, last updated July 20, 2016b. As of December 5, 2017:
https://www.dfas.mil/retiredmilitary/provide/sbp/special-needs-trust.html

————, "Advantages & Disadvantages," webpage, last updated March 15, 2017a. As of December 5, 2017:
https://www.dfas.mil/retiredmilitary/provide/sbp/advantages.html

————, "2012–2025 Temporary Early Retirement Authority," webpage, May 15, 2017b. As of December 5, 2017:
https://www.dfas.mil/retiredmilitary/plan/retirement-types/2012-18tera.html

————, "Paying for SBP," webpage, last updated November 29, 2017c. As of December 5, 2017:
https://www.dfas.mil/retiredmilitary/provide/sbp/payment.html

U.S. Department of Defense, Defense Health Agency, "TRICARE Young Adult Program," Washington, D.C., fact sheet, January 2017a.

————, "TRICARE Survivor Benefits," Washington, D.C., fact sheet, May 2017b.

U.S. Department of Defense, Directorate of Compensation, *Selected Military Compensation Tables*, Washington, D.C., April 1, 2007. As of July 30, 2017:
http://militarypay.defense.gov/Portals/3/Documents/Reports/GreenBook_APRIL_40YOS_2007_Dist.pdf

U.S. Department of Defense, Office of the Actuary, *Valuation of the Military Retirement System: September 30, 2007*, Washington, D.C., December 2008. As of July 1, 2017:
http://actuary.defense.gov/Portals/15/Documents/valbook2007.pdf?ver=2012-06-01-144013-840

————, *Valuation of the Military Retirement System: September 30, 2015*, Washington, D.C., April 2017a. As of July 2017:
http://actuary.defense.gov/Portals/15/Documents/
MRF%20ValRpt%202015%20Final%20v10.pdf?ver=2017-04-13-123844-423

————, "2016 SBP Subsidy Estimate," email from Richard Allen to Felix Knutson, June 8, 2017b.

————, *Statistical Report on the Military Retirement System: Fiscal Year 2016*, Washington, D.C., July 2017c. As of August 2017:
http://actuary.defense.gov/Portals/15/Documents/
MRS_StatRpt_2016%20v4%20FINAL.pdf?ver=2017-07-31-104724-430

U.S. Department of Defense, Under Secretary of Defense (Comptroller), *Financial Management Regulation*, Vol. 7B: *Military Pay Policy and Procedures—Retired Pay*, Washington, D.C., DoD 7000.14-R, April 2017. As of July 30, 2017:
http://comptroller.defense.gov/Portals/45/documents/fmr/Volume_07b.pdf

U.S. Department of Defense, Under Secretary of Defense for Personnel and Readiness, *Military Compensation Background Papers: Compensation Elements and Related Manpower Cost Items, Their Purposes and Legislative Backgrounds*, 7th ed., Washington, D.C., November 2011.

U.S. Department of Justice, Bureau of Justice Assistance, "Benefits by Year," webpage, undated. As of September 1, 2017:
https://psob.bja.ojp.gov/knowledge-base/benefits-by-year/

U.S. Department of the Treasury, *Annual Report on the Insurance Industry*, Washington, D.C., September 2017.

U.S. Department of Veterans Affairs, "Dependents' Educational Assistance Program (DEA)," Washington, D.C., April 2010. As of August 2017:
http://www.benefits.va.gov/gibill/docs/pamphlets/ch35_pamphlet_2.pdf

———, *2012 VA Performance and Accountability Report*, Washington, D.C., 2012.

———, "Pension: Aid and Attendance and Housebound," webpage, last updated December 8, 2015. As of September 30, 2017:
https://www.benefits.va.gov/pension/aid_attendance_housebound.asp

———, *Federal Benefits for Veterans, Dependents, and Survivors, Office of Public and Intergovernmental Affairs*, Washington, D.C., 2016. As of August 30, 2017:
https://www.va.gov/opa/publications/benefits_book/2016_Federal_Benefits_for_Veterans.pdf

———, "Education and Training: Survivors and Dependents Assistance," webpage, last updated March 9, 2017a. As of August 30, 2017:
http://www.benefits.va.gov/gibill/survivor_dependent_assistance.asp

———, "Pension: Survivors Pension," webpage, last updated June 16, 2017b. As of September 15, 2017:
https://www.benefits.va.gov/pension/spousepen.asp

———, "Compensation: Benefits Description," webpage, last updated August 28, 2017c. As of December 6, 2017:
https://www.benefits.va.gov/compensation/

———, "Compensation: Burial Benefits," webpage, last updated October 23, 2017d. As of December 1, 2017:
http://www.benefits.va.gov/compensation/claims-special-burial.asp

———, "VA Home Loans: Loan Limits," webpage, last updated November 30, 2017e. As of December 6, 2017:
https://www.benefits.va.gov/homeloans/purchaseco_loan_limits.asp

———, "Life Insurance," webpage, last updated October 26, 2017f. As of December 1, 2017:
http://www.benefits.va.gov/insurance/index.asp

———, "Compensation: Dependency and Indemnity Compensation—Effective 12/1/17," webpage, last updated November 16, 2017g. As of December 1, 2017:
http://benefits.va.gov/Compensation/current_rates_dic.asp

———, "Pension: Parents Dependency and Indemnity Compensation—Effective 12/1/16," webpage, last updated November 16, 2017h. As of December 1, 2017:
https://benefits.va.gov/Pension/current_rates_Parents_DIC_pen.asp

U.S. Office of Personnel Management, *CSRS and FERS Handbook for Personnel and Payroll Offices*, Washington, D.C., April 1998. As of August 1, 2017:
https://www.opm.gov/retirement-services/publications-forms/csrsfers-handbook/

———, *Civil Service Retirement and Disability Fund: Annual Report Fiscal Year Ended September 30, 2015*, Washington, D.C., January 2016. As of December 18, 2017:
https://www.opm.gov/about-us/budget-performance/other-reports/
2015-civil-service-retirement-and-disability-fund-annual-report.pdf

U.S. Social Security Administration, "Annual Benefits Paid from the OASI Trust Fund, by Type of Benefit, Calendar Years 1937–2016," webpage, undated-a. As of September 18, 2017:
https://www.ssa.gov/oact/STATS/table4a5.html

———, "Number of Survivors Receiving Benefits on December 31, 1970–2016," webpage, undated-b. As of September 18, 2017:
https://www.ssa.gov/oact/STATS/SRVbenies.html

———, "Retirement Planner: Government Pension Offset (GPO)," webpage, undated-c. As of July 30, 2017:
https://www.ssa.gov/planners/retire/gpo.html

———, "Social Security Beneficiary Statistics," webpage, undated-d. As of December 15, 2017:
https://www.ssa.gov/oact/STATS/OASDIbenies.html

———, "Survivors Planner: How Much Would Your Benefit Be?" webpage, undated-e. As of July 30, 2017:
https://www.ssa.gov/planners/survivors/ifyou5.html

———, "Online Calculator," webpage, last updated April 2017. As of December 10, 2017:
https://www.ssa.gov/planners/retire/AnypiaApplet.html

VA—*See* U.S. Department of Veterans Affairs.

Washington State Department of Retirement Systems, *Employer Handbook*, Olympia, Wash., 2016. As of December 10, 2017:
http://www.drs.wa.gov/employer/handbook/

———, "DRS Email 17-009 Contribution Rates for LEOFF, PERS, PSERS and WSPRS," webpage, June 1, 2017a. As of December 15, 2017:
http://www.drs.wa.gov/employer/DRSN/drs-email-17-009-new-contribution-rates-2017

———, *PERS Plan 2 Handbook: Public Employees' Retirement System*, Olympia, Wash., November 2017b. As of December 15, 2017:
http://www.drs.wa.gov/member/handbooks/pers/plan-2/pers2hbk.pdf